DATE DUE

Elizabethan Grotesque

Neil Rhodes

Elizabethan Grotesque

Routledge & Kegan Paul

LONDON, BOSTON
AND HENLEY

First published in 1980
by Routledge & Kegan Paul Ltd
39 Store Street,
London WC1E 7DD,
9 Park Street,
Boston, Mass. 02108, USA and
Broadway House, Newtown Road,
Henley-on-Thames, Oxon RG9 1EN

Set in 10/12 Linotron Sabon by
Input Typesetting Ltd
London
and printed in Great Britain by
Lowe & Brydone Ltd
Thetford, Norfolk

British Library Cataloguing in Publication Data
Rhodes, Neil
  Elizabethan grotesque.
  1. Grotesque in literature
  2. English literature – Early modern, 1500–1700 –
  History and criticism
  I. Title
  820'.9'3   PR429.G/   80 40875

ISBN 0 7100 0599 7

For Carol Clark

Contents

Preface

Elizabethan Grotesque is a title which begs a good many questions, so I had better begin by explaining the scope of this book. It stems originally from an interest in Nashe and from the belief that his writing deserves rather more critical discussion than it has so far received; in particular I felt that his peculiar achievement could be properly assessed only in a much wider context than G. R. Hibbard provided in *Thomas Nashe: A Critical Introduction* (Routledge & Kegan Paul, 1962). Hibbard's book is still the only available introduction to Nashe, and as such it remains valuable, but his 'life and works' approach is too limited to deal with a writer as haphazardly experimental as Nashe. A clearer view of his work requires the perspective not only of earlier sixteenth-century prose, but also that of the English comic drama which followed, and was influenced by, Nashe's literary experiments in the 1590s. Consequently, this is not so much a book about Nashe as about the origins and development of the comic grotesque in Elizabethan prose and drama, in which Nashe played a major role.

I have divided the book into two parts. The first part deals initially with the nature of the grotesque and attempts to provide a working definition of the term within the context of late sixteenth-century culture. (A universal definition does not seem to me feasible; every age produces its own version of the grotesque and these versions have too little in common to be susceptible of useful generalisation.) Chapters 2, 3 and 4 discuss the comic prose of the 1590s in this light and are concerned largely with Nashe and Nashe's literary ambience. Chapter 5 is a linking section between the first and second parts of the book; it deals with the relationship between non-dramatic prose and the satirical drama written at the very end of the century. In Part II I turn to a more specific discussion of five plays – three by Shakespeare, two by Jonson. Here the

topics introduced earlier are used, I hope, to illuminate the central
concerns of these major achievements and to explain both their
novelty and their comic power.

Finally, a word on 'influence'. Parts of this book fall into the
somewhat discredited category of the influence study. The discredit,
I suppose, is due to the feeling that such an approach tells us little
of interest about the literary work itself, but also to the fact that
in the Renaissance period direct verbal borrowings are very hard
to prove, anyway. No part of the argument of this book depends
upon such evidence alone, though in the case of Nashe and Shakespeare especially such evidence is adduced. I believe we need to be
less conservative in our attitudes to literary influence and to realise
that direct influence may comprise the borrowing of stylistic patterns and techniques (e.g. Aretino and Nashe) as well as specific
locutions. To the first objection I would say merely that the way
in which writers learn from one another, and the way in which
literary works are shaped by the presence of another, must always
remain a subject of critical interest. The book that follows is based
on that assumption, but also on the assumption that the cultural
history of a period – one aspect of it, at any rate – can be viewed
through the medium of its use of language.

Acknowledgments

I should first like to thank Emrys Jones and Glenn Black for their constant help and encouragement during the progress of this book. Carol Clark has also read successive drafts and offered valuable advice on the French and Italian material, while Rotraut Spiegel assisted me with two German studies on the subject. Sarah Carpenter read the work in its later stages and suggested many improvements. Without this extensive help I could not have completed the work, and I am grateful to each of them; the faults that remain are entirely my own. I am grateful, too, to the Department of English Studies at Strathclyde University for both the time and the financial assistance which has enabled me to finish the book. My longest standing debt of gratitude is to Rory Stuart, with whom I first read Shakespeare.

Elizabethan comic prose and drama: a chronology

The following chronology lists most of the works discussed in the text, and is designed to help the reader rather than to satisfy the scholar. Many dates are necessarily conjectural, and some contentious; my principal authorities are McKerrow's *Nashe*, the New Arden *Shakespeare* and Harbage's *Annals of English Drama* (revised by Schoenbaum).

1583 Stubbes, *The Anatomie of Abuses*.
1584 Aretino, *Ragionamenti*, first and second parts (first London eds, publ. John Wolfe).
1588 Aretino, *Quattro Comedie*.
 'Martin Marprelate', *The Epistle* (October); *The Epitome* (November).
1589 Aretino, *Ragionamenti*, third part.
 'Martin Marprelate', *Hay any Worke for Cooper* (March); *Martin Junior* (July); *Martin Senior* (July); *The Protestatyon* (September).
 Anti-Marprelate tracts, *A Countercuffe given to Martin Junior* (August); *The Returne of Pasquill* (October); *Pappe with an Hatchet* (October, by Lyly?); *Martins Months Minde*.
1590 *An Almond for a Parrat* (winter 1589–90, by Nashe?); *The Firste Part of Pasquils Apologie* (July).
1591 Shakespeare, *2 Henry VI* (winter 1590–1?).
1592 Theophrastus, *Characters*, ed. Casaubon.
 Greene, *A Quip for an Upstart Courtier* (August).
 Nashe, *Pierce Penilesse* (September); *Summers Last Will and Testament* (October); *Strange Newes* (December).
 Harvey, *Foure Letters* (late September).
1593 Eliot, *Ortho-Epia Gallica* (containing passages, with translations, from Rabelais).

Nashe, *Christs Teares over Jerusalem* (September).

Harvey, *Pierces Supererogation* (October); *A New Letter of Notable Contents* (October).

Shakespeare, *Love's Labour's Lost* (orig. composition winter 1593–4, rev. 1595–6?).

1594 Nashe, *The Unfortunate Traveller* (March; orig. composition June 1593); *The Terrors of the Night* (November; orig. composition February 1593).

1595 Shakespeare, *The Taming of the Shrew* (1594–5?).

1596 Lodge, *Wits Miserie.*

Nashe, *Have With You to Saffron-Walden* (Autumn?, but circulated in ms. before publication).

1597 Shakespeare, *1 Henry IV* (winter 1596–7); *2 Henry IV*; *The Merry Wives of Windsor* (April).

Nashe and Jonson, *The Isle of Dogs* (summer; lost).

'Richard Lichfield', *The Trimming of Thomas Nashe.*

1598 Jonson, *Every Man In his Humour.*

1599 Anon., *The Pilgrimage to Parnassus* (winter 1598–9).

Nashe, *Lenten Stuffe* (spring?).

Dekker, *The Shoemaker's Holiday* (July).

Jonson, *Every Man Out of his Humour* (late autumn).

1600 Anon., *The Returne from Parnassus*, part I (winter 1599–1600).

1602 Anon., *The Returne from Parnassus*, part II (winter 1601–2).

Middleton, *Blurt, Master Constable*; *The Family of Love* (dates and authorship uncertain).

1603 Montaigne, *The Essays*, trans. Florio.

Dekker, *The Wonderfull Yeare.*

1604 Middleton, *The Blacke Booke*; *Father Hubburd's Tales.*

Dekker, *The Honest Whore*, part I; *Westward Ho* (with Webster).

1605 Middleton, *Your Five Gallants.*

Dekker, *The Honest Whore*, part II; *Northward Ho* (with Webster).

1606 Dekker, *Newes from Hell*; *The Seven Deadly Sinnes.*

1613 Middleton, *A Chaste Maid in Cheapside.*

1614 Jonson, *Bartholomew Fair.*

1653 Rabelais, *Gargantua and Pantagruel*, trans. Urquhart.

Part I

· 1 ·
Literary grotesque:
a sixteenth-century background

This book is concerned with the comic and satirical writing of the late Elizabethan and early Jacobean period. More specifically, it examines the nature of the grotesque in the new styles of comic prose which developed during the 1590s, and which by the end of the decade had made a considerable impact upon the drama. It is easy to talk glibly of 'periods of transition' in the life of a culture, but the 1590s were such a period, and their transitional quality is of sharp relevance to the present study. The educational expansion of the sixteenth century had produced, by its close, a superfluity of highly articulate young men who lacked the money and social connections to support themselves; some were Londoners, while others, such as Marlowe, Nashe and Shakespeare, migrated to the metropolis in the hope of earning a living through the press and the theatre. In these circumstances the first generation of professional writers in England was formed. So much is well known, but the period is culturally transitional in other respects. The influx into the city of young, penniless intellectuals, and the simultaneous arrival of the prodigal offspring of country gentlemen created among writers like Nashe a vivid sense of the city as a new subject for literature. In a time of post-war penury, of plague, famine and inflation, the foolish ostentation of the young rich, and their exploitation by ruthless opportunists, stimulated a vision of the new urban society which was both horrible and fascinating.[1] The beginnings of satirical journalism were suddenly generated, but it was unclear what form such writing should take. The prototype for secular onslaughts on social vice was the sermon, while the forms and images of festive ritual still held powerful meanings for any Elizabethan venturing into the field of primitive sociology. The tone, too, of the early satirical journalism vacillated wildly between the strident invective of the pulpit orator and the flippant, verbal

3

tumbling tricks of the clown, the lord of misrule and similar rep-
resentatives of the folk culture of late medieval England. So the
comic prose of the 1590s, which attempts a radical move towards
topical, journalistic satire, is nevertheless the product of an uneasy
relationship between sermon and festive comedy, priest and clown.
It is this uncertainty of tone (and, in pamphlet literature, of authorial persona) which creates a grotesque vision of the physical life
of the community. The Elizabethan grotesque derives from the
unstable coalescence of contrary images of the flesh: indulged,
abused, purged and damned.

Antecedents of this kind of grotesque can perhaps be found in
the poetry of Langland and Skelton. However, it is unclear to what
extent their work was known in late Elizabethan England, and still
less clear that it could have prompted the rise of satirical journalism
during the 1590s.[2] A more immediate starting point for the development of comic prose at that time is the Marprelate controversy.
Martin Marprelate was the pseudonym of a Puritan writer, or
writers, who published during 1588–9 a series of pamphlets at-
tacking the episcopacy.[3] The success of these attacks – the bishops
were clearly very worried – was due entirely to the novelty of tone
and style, which was a mixture of evangelism and buffoonery, rude
colloquialism and caustic personal satire. Clerical counterblasts
were unlikely to have the same literary appeal: before the appearance of Martin, Dr John Bridges, Dean of Sarum, had lumbered to
the rescue of the establishment with a work of such turgidity[4] that
it could serve only as fuel for Martin's rejoinders. The bishops felt
obliged to call in professionals, and a number of young writers
(among them, almost certainly, Nashe and Lyly) were employed to
deal with Martin in his own terms. Stimulated by Martin's belligerent style, and with the security of the establishment behind
them, the anti-Marprelate pamphleteers produced a number of
quite venomous satires. Martin, the clowning preacher, was ridiculed as a May-game scapegoat and figuratively purged with the
apparatus of medical and judicial torture. The performance is a
model of one kind of Elizabethan grotesque.

In the years following the controversy, the 'low' style of comic
prose which it released was exploited chiefly by Nashe. His restless
experimentation with topical satire and the picaresque novel in-
formed his treatment of the more traditional modes of sermon and
festive comedy, and the extraordinarily physical vivacity of his

style rapidly provoked emulation. For writers such as Lodge, Dekker and the young Middleton (the 'T. M.' of *The Blacke Booke* and *Father Hubburd's Tales*) Nashe's grotesque manner seemed the appropriate instrument to describe the common and appalling spectacles of human dereliction which the city afforded. At the same time his satirical pungency, vividly demonstrated in his demolition of the Cambridge don, Gabriel Harvey, set the tone for much professional writing in the last years of the century.

This sudden vogue for satire, while clearly the product of social and economic factors, was accelerated by the publication in the 1580s of Aretino's comedies and dialogues,[5] and it was Aretino who provided another immediate stimulus to Nashe's writing. Urban and sophisticated, Aretino's satire invested the sordid realities of everyday life with a grotesque, physical energy which was to become typical of Elizabethan satirical journalism and satirical drama. Although his notorious reputation among the Elizabethans, like that of Machiavelli, is generally supposed to be founded on nothing but hearsay, the availability of his work and its stylistic similarity to the comic writing of the 1590s would suggest that this is not entirely true. In the case of Nashe, at least, there seems to be a specific debt to Aretino, as I hope to demonstrate later.

Towards the end of the decade these developments were beginning to have some impact on the drama, and satirical comedies began to oust the history play and the romantic comedy from theatrical repertoires. The two parts of *Henry IV*, with their combination of saturnalia and satire, are among the first plays to show the influence of Nasheian grotesque, while Dekker and Middleton, Shakespeare and Jonson, each exploit, in different ways, the comic prose techniques with which Nashe had experimented. This change in dramatic trends which occurred at the end of the 1590s can be traced to the popularity of the comic prose pamphlet, and I believe that the subject as a whole can best be discussed through the theme of the grotesque. First, then, we must decide what – in terms of late sixteenth-century culture – the 'grotesque' means.

The only full-length study of the grotesque in Elizabethan literature is Willard Farnham's *The Shakespearean Grotesque* (Oxford, 1971). The faults of this book are plain. An unusual critical term is appropriated from art history; an opening chapter discusses the early pictorial grotesque (medieval manuscript illumination and the like); then follows a general book about Shakespeare, in which this still undefined term is gratuitously larded on to anything in the drama approximate to the image of man as both rational and animal, and hence, we are asked to believe, grotesque. He does not explain what medieval manuscript illumination has to do with Shakespearean drama, nor does he consider whether the grotesque can be used in a non-pictorial sense, anyway. And because the only real connection between the first chapter and the rest of the book is the theme of mingled 'high' and 'low' elements in art, the grotesque is unhelpfully confused with the burlesque, the theme of *le monde renversé*, comic abuses of rhetoric (in the Falstaff plays), and so on. Finally, he does not discuss Nashe, whose influence on the grotesque of *Henry IV* – to which Farnham devotes nearly a third of his book – is unmistakable, and central to the novelty of the play in English drama.

The few modern analysts of this term have been aware of a penumbra of associated concepts around that of the grotesque, which has made definition elusive. Indeed, Philip Thomson manages to zig-zag around eight 'related terms and modes' while producing his own definition.[6] Of these, the term most necessary to disentangle from the grotesque before approaching sixteenth-century writing is the burlesque. Perhaps the earliest attempt to do so was by the German scholar, Heinrich Schneegans.[7] The gist of his argument is that the burlesque is a degrading mode, in which the comedy derives from the demeaning of a lofty subject by an inappropriately lowly style, while the grotesque is an exaggeration of the inappropriate to monstrous dimensions. The burlesque is 'that flippant mode which, without reason, drags the sublime in the dust',[8] whereas the grotesque, being 'an impossibly exaggerated caricature of something which should not exist in reality',[9] has a moral and satirical impact which the burlesque lacks. This is a fundamentally sensible discrimination, and it does not deserve the ridicule loaded upon it by Bakhtin in his otherwise excellent book on Rabelais. Having rejumbled Schneegans's careful distinctions, Bakhtin concludes with breath-taking self-assurance, 'such is the true objective content of the examples given by Schneegans'.[10] The core of his objection is that Schneegans's narrowly satirical definition of the grotesque fails to account for the positive and exuberant aspects of Rabelais, on whom he bases a large part of his book. This is certainly true, but where both writers go wrong is in

assuming that there is an absolute rift between satire and saturnalia, and that the grotesque must operate within one or other
of these modes. One of the aims of the present study is to show
that this is not the case: in the sixteenth and early seventeenth
centuries satire, saturnalia, and, indeed, the sermon were forms
which frequently interlocked, and it is from the uneasiness of their
mutual relationships that the Elizabethan grotesque is generated.

What Schneegans says about the burlesque, however, is important to us. Travesties of the heroic in the manner of Lucian, or of
formal rhetoric in the manner of Rabelais, form the substance of
much in Nashe, and travesties of the prognostication or the cour-
tesy book are a staple of Dekker's pamphlets. But these are not
grotesques; indeed, we cannot reasonably refer to a literary work
as 'a grotesque', because the grotesque, being properly a word
applied to the visual arts, does not correspond to a literary style.
Given Schneegans's definition of the burlesque, we may well find
grotesque elements within that mode, but these elements will be
essentially visual and cannot characterise the mode itself. This is
not to say that the burlesque is non-visual. Gabriel Harvey, pillo-
rying Nashe with rather more expertise than usual, writes (*à propos*
of Nashe's notoriety) in *Pierces Supererogation* (1593): 'S. Fame
is disposed to make it a Hallyday. She hath already put-on her
wispen garland over her powting Cros-cloth: and behold with what
an Imperiall Maiestie she commeth riding in the ducking-chariot
of her Triumphe.'[11] The image of the 'ducking-chariot' is a burlesque in microcosm, a fusion of the coarse and the stately in order
to ridicule. The burlesque is, in fact, wide-ranging in the forms it
takes, but its effects are limited and specific; the grotesque, on the
other hand, occurs only in a visual form, but its effects are complex.

This complexity derives from the essential heterogeneity of the
grotesque; it is a hybrid creature, and to talk of 'pure grotesque'
is virtually a contradiction in terms. The word appears in Europe
after the discovery in Rome during the early sixteenth century of
ancient apartments decorated with bizarre animal and plant formations. As these rooms were, by this time, all underground, they
were called caves or 'grottoes' and their decoration, grotesque.
Vasari comments:[12]

> Le grottesche sono una spezie di pittura licenziosa e ridicola
> molto, fatte da gl'antichi per ornamenti di vani, dove in alcuni

luoghi non stava bene altro che cose in aria; per il che face-
vano in quelle tutte sconciature di monstri per strattezza della
natura e per gricciolo e ghiribizzo degli artefici i quali fanno
in quelle cose senza alcuna regola, apiccando a un sottilissimo
filo un peso che non si può regerre, a un cavallo le gambe di
foglie, a un uomo le gambe di gru et infiniti sciarpelloni e
passerotti; e chi piú stranamente se gli immaginava, quello
era tenuto piú valente.
[Grotesques are an irregular and highly ridiculous sort of
painting, done by the ancients to adorn vacant spaces, where
in certain places only things set up high were suitable. For
this purpose they created all kinds of absurd monsters,
formed by a freak of nature or by the whims and fancies of
the workmen, who in this kind of picture are subject to no
rule, but paint a heavy weight attached to the finest thread
which could not possibly bear it, a horse with legs of leaves,
a man with crane's legs, and any number of bumble-bees and
sparrows; so that the one who was able to dream up the
strangest things was held to be the most able.]

These fantastic hybrids – unimaginable creations composed from
incompatible elements – were immediately imitated by Raphael in
the curling plant formations, hung with rats and snakes, with
which he decorated the pillars of the Papal loggias (c.1515), and
Veneziano in his ornamental engravings of semi-human creatures.
Throughout the sixteenth century, when the term 'grotesque' is
used, it refers to this sort of thing. Montaigne commissioned murals
of this kind and reflected that his own essays were executed in the
same manner: 'il [the painter] le remplit de crotesques, qui sont
peintures fantasques, n'ayant grâce qu'en la variété et estrangeté.
Que sont-ce icy aussi, à la verité, que crotesques. . .'[13] ['he fills it
with grotesques, which are fantastic paintings, whose only beauty
is in their variety and strangeness. What am I writing here, in fact,
but grotesques. . .']. Montaigne's observation is probably the first
occasion on which the term is used of literature, and the parallel
he sees is one of form and structure. He is not, I think, suggesting
that there is anything sinister or revolting in the language and
imagery of his writing, which could be called 'grotesque'; his analogy is based on a pictorial style and its equivalent in literary form.
The style in question lacks the power to shock and disturb, which

is an essential feature of the literary grotesque I shall be discussing.[14]

There is, however, a different kind of sixteenth-century grotesque, which is not merely 'licenziosa e ridicola molto'. This is the painting of Bruegel. It is clear that his fascination with weird and monstrous imagery derives from a study of Bosch, not the Roman grottoes.[15] It is also clear that in Bruegel we are presented with a physical and substantial world, albeit 'fantastic', and not merely decorative *jeux d'esprit*.[16] The decorative and playful aspects of the grotesque, which devolve into the late eighteenth-century taste for the exotic and improbable – rococo and chinoiserie – are peripheral to the literary grotesque of the late sixteenth century, which is grossly physical and which often does have (*pace* Bakhtin) a satirical or moral purpose. The pictorial analogues here are Bruegel's designs for the seven deadly sins (1556–7) or the bizarre portraiture of Stimmer and Arcimboldi. Tobie Stimmer's 'Gorgoneum Caput' (1571), for instance, is a profile head of the Pope constructed from various emblematical objects; for the Catholics Arcimboldi produced a picture of Calvin in which the nose is a frog, the mouth a fish's head, and the beard its tail.[17] These grotesque descriptive techniques arrive in English literature with Nashe's *Pierce Penilesse* (1592):[18]

> On the other side, Dame Niggardize, his wife, in a sedge rug kirtle, that had beene a mat time out of minde . . . an apron made of Almanackes out of date (such as stand upon Screens, or on the backside of a dore in a Chandlers shop), and an old wives pudding pan on her head . . .

and in Dekker's *Newes from Hell* (1606) where Charon's boat[19]

> is made of nothing but the wormeaten ribs of coffins, nayl'd together, with the splinters of fleshlesse shin-bones, dig'd out of graves, being broken in pieces. The sculls that hee rowes with, are made of Sextons spades, which had bene hung up at the end of some great Plague.

These are grotesque images in the original sense of heterogeneous composition – Dame Niggardize is a person constructed out of objects; Charon's boat is an object made from bits of people. But in a limited way they point also to the two poles between which the grotesque oscillates, to the frivolity implied by Vasari's description, and to the macabre spirit of Bruegel. A similar kind of composition can produce quite distinct effects, and it is this sort of complexity which points to the central problems of the grotesque.

This complexity occurs when an image evokes two kinds of response which are mutually incompatible, and a tension is set up in the image itself between the elements which create one sort of effect and those which create another. How do we respond, for example, to Autolycus's description of the dire penalties which the shepherd's son may expect for his father's temerity in wedding Perdita to a prince?[20]

> He has a son – who shall be flay'd alive; then 'nointed over with honey, set on the head of wasp's nest; then stand till he be three quarters and a dram dead; then recover'd again with aqua-vitae or some other hot infusion; then . . .

and so he continues. What is funny, apart from the dramatic situation, is the casual elaboration of these atrocities, the jocular 'three quarters and a dram dead'; yet the punishments themselves, considered for what they are, are unthinkably horrifying. This unsettling technique, which drags the reader's feelings in opposite directions at once, is the most conspicuous effect of the grotesque.

As I have suggested, frivolity and the macabre, or, more generally, laughter and revulsion, are the twin polarities of the grotesque. The word is, however, used loosely in a slightly different context. It might, for instance, be applied to the passage in Lodge's *Robert of Normandy* (1591) in which Robert cuts off the breasts of a nun, after raping her, at the end of one paragraph, and in the first sentence of the next we read: 'no sooner did the mornings roseate coatch beawtifie the East with vermelion rednesse, and the faire breathing Steeds of the Sunne mount above the bosome of OCEANUS . . .'.[21] Incompatible responses are certainly being demanded, but of a different kind. The combination of horror and beauty, or the aestheticising of pain, and the physically repellent, is a characteristic not of the grotesque, but of 'decadent' imagery. Comedy, not beauty, mingles with the repulsive or macabre elements of the grotesque.

What such writing does force us to consider, however, is the question of taste. Nashe's *Christs Teares over Jerusalem* (1593), where grotesque physical imagery is deployed in a series of graphic warnings to the dissolute, is described by G. R. Hibbard as 'a monument of bad taste'.[22] Perhaps he was thinking of a passage such as the following preview of infernal torment:[23]

> For thy flaring frounzed Periwigs lowe dangled downe with love-locks, shalt thou have thy head side dangled downe with more snakes than ever it had hayres. In the moulde of thy braine shall they claspe theyr mouthes, and gnawing through every parte of thy scull, ensnarle their teeth amongst thy braines, as an Angler ensnarleth his hooke amongst weedes.

Lurid it is, but the peaceful, rustic image of fishing which Nashe finally evokes demands a more complex response than that of 'bad taste'. Our own notions of taste are inlaid with those of moral sensitivity; both the Shakespeare and the Lodge passages are offensive to that. But it is difficult to know to what extent we are justified in applying a criterion of taste which carries that sort of association to Renaissance literature. A consciousness of sin was considered more worthwhile than sympathy for earthly sufferings, and objections to jokes about the plague were based on the belief that it was God's punishment on a wicked society, not on the fact that people were dying wretchedly.

If we are going to talk about 'taste' at all, then, with reference to grotesque physical imagery, it seems wiser to refer the concept to the Elizabethan notion of decorum. This is a more purely aesthetic criterion of literary judgment, which demands a homogeneous style appropriate to the subject matter. Puttenham describes decorum as 'decencie', and continues:[24]

> But that cannot be if they discover any illfavourednesse or disproportion to the partes apprehensive, as for example ... the shape of a membred body without his due measures and simmetry, and the like of every other sence in his proper function. These excesses or defectes or confusions and disorders in the sensible objectes are deformities and unseemely to the sence.

And Bacon called the Marprelate writings 'deformed' not because he found their grotesque physical violence tasteless in a moral sense, but because they offended against decorum.[25] It was not fitting that religion be treated as a subject for low humour.

But while the objections to literary grotesque were made on grounds of decorum by the Elizabethans themselves, the Puttenham

passage does draw attention to the fact that sixteenth-century grotesque derives from the world of the body. The image Puttenham
uses for indecorous writing points to the central quality of that
writing: its fascination with the various organs of the body, their
strange functions, and their absurd resemblance to other kinds of
gross physical matter. Nor is it surprising that Puttenham should
choose such an image. It would be difficult to overemphasise the
importance of medical belief, and the physiological imagery associated with it, in sixteenth-century culture; it is ubiquitous. What
is more, medical terminology was not a specialised jargon, and the
many serious works on surgery and anatomy published at this time
(by men such as Vicary, Gale and Clowes) share the vocabulary
and general assumptions of the popular plague remedies or quasi-
medical character sketches. It is probably true that in no other
century has the imagery of medicine and the human body been so
pervasive an element in all aspects of cultural activity. Furthermore,
it is the tendency of the Elizabethan mind to analogise that accounts
for the pervasiveness of such imagery. Comments on 'the little
world of man' in those two monuments of English Renaissance
prose, Hooker's *Of the Laws of Ecclesiastical Polity* and Ralegh's
History of the World, enable us to see why the imagery of the
microcosm could enter so many aspects of life outside the merely
physical.

The existence of a commonly held body of medical and physiological belief, and thus the lack of an esoteric medical terminology,
inevitably blurs distinctions between the purely technical and the
purely entertaining works which use what seems to be medical
imagery and vocabulary. I shall take four examples and try to
illustrate how the imagery which I am defining as grotesque in
popular writing takes its colour from rather more technical trea-
tises. In Thomas Vicary's *The Anatomie of the Bodie of Man*
(1548), which is nothing if not solemnly informative, we nevertheless find this engaging description of the human reproductive process: 'as the Renet and mylke make the cheese, so doth the sparme
of man and woman make the generation of Embreon, of the which
springeth, by the vertue of kindly heate, a certayne skinne or
caule'.[26] A slightly less technical work, *The Examination of Mens
Wits*, translated from the Spanish of John Huarte in 1594, gives us
an equally vivid picture of the inside of a fat man's head: 'I avouch
that if his having a great head, proceedeth from abundance of

matter ... it is an evill token ... as it befals in very big orenges, which opened, are found scarce of juice, and hard of rinde.'[27] More popular again, but with a substantial physiological basis, is Tomaso Garzoni's *The Hospitall of Incurable Fooles* (1600), where we learn of a man 'with turbulent conceptions, wavering and inconstant motions, broken sleep, a sick braine, & an emptie soacked head, like a withered cucumber'.[28] Last, in Nashe's fantasia on dreaming, *The Terrors of the Night* (1594), we are told of a troupe of devils with 'faces far blacker than anie ball of Tobacco, great glaring eyes that had whole shelves of Kentish oysters in them, and terrible wyde mouthes'.[29] All of these writers are forced to draw their analogies from comically mundane sources, notably the grocer's shop, but the degree of aptness in the image chosen diminishes, perhaps, as we approach the popular end of the scale and Nashe's absurd 'oysters'. The comic grotesque begins where the literal credibility of such analogies falters, and the deliberately bizarre takes over.[30]

Rooting Elizabethan literary grotesque in the world of the body re-emphasises my earlier distinction between the decorative, and the more grossly physical, pictorial styles. The mingling of diverse strands of animal and vegetable growth into pleasing patterns does not contain the element of shock – comic, or disgusting, or both – which Bruegel's unsettling reminiscences of familiar bodily forms provoke. It is these kinds of resemblance that Elizabethan prose relishes. Arcimboldi's cephaloid landscapes,[31] for instance, are paralleled by Dekker's description in *The Guls Horn-Booke* (1609) of the world with [32]

> All the wrinckles, crackes, crevices and flawes that (like the Mole on *Hattens* cheek, being *os amoris*,) stuck upon it at the first creation, and made it looke most lovely; but now those furrowes are filled up with Ceruses, and Vermilion ... the breath of it stinks like the mouthes of Chambermaides by feeding on so many sweat meats.

Similarly, his comparing the parts of a human head with the parts of a house in the same work[33] echoes Brueghel's strangely anthropomorphic buildings.[34] Admittedly, Dekker's images are hardly shocking in a sinister way, but the principle is the same: the painter and the writer are both exploring a syndrome of imagery to make what Gombrich calls, in this context, 'a fresh act of classification';[35]

the grotesque relies upon images which have a physical similarity, but which normal experience classifies quite separately.

These classes may be quite general, such as animate and inanimate objects, as in Nashe's Dame Niggardize. More specifically, they could be food and the consumers of food (bits of the latter, at any rate), as in the examples I have given from Vicary and others. They may be horrific and 'homely', like the snakes of hell and the angler's hook in *Christs Teares*. They may also be – and this brings me to my last point about the physicality of the grotesque – concrete and abstract classes of experience. The most typical form this takes in the sixteenth century is the presentation of sin in graphic, physical terms. The Spanish priest, Jose de Siguenza, writing on Bosch in 1605, argued that this kind of painting was not frivolous (as Vasari would have it) but an attempt to externalise the inner, moral deformity of man:[36]

> In my opinion, the difference between the paintings of this man and those of the others is that the others try as often as possible to paint man as he looks from the outside, while this man has the courage to paint him as he is inwardly.

And Nashe in *Christs Teares* remarks:[37]

> Well did *Aristotle*, in the second of Phisickes, call sinnes Monsters of nature for as there is no Monster ordinarily reputed, but is a swelling or excesse of forme, so is there no sinne but is a swelling or rebelling against God.

This makes explicit the moral implication of physical deformity, and the prevalent idea at this time that physical and moral deformity are interdependent comes from the need felt by preachers and moralists of all sorts to give sin a physical reality. Likewise, the punishment for sin; Philip Stubbes reminded his readers that sermons on hell were not 'metaphoricall speaches', but that 'there is a hell, a materiall place of punishment.'[38] (It is also important to note that the word 'monstrous' derives from the Latin *monere*, and that in the sixteenth century it still retained its association of terrible warning or portent.) This desire to give body to what is abstract produces the images which cluster around that other, macabre and repulsive pole of the grotesque. The monstrous births, the tortured criminal, and the plague- or famine-stricken city are all objectifications of moral deformity and spiritual illness, and the analogy between the classes of experience which we would term physical and those which we would term moral or spiritual explains, I think, much of the more 'tasteless' side of Elizabethan grotesque.

The importance of physical imagery to sixteenth-century grotesque brings me to the central figure of Rabelais. No other great writer has so consistently viewed the external world in terms of the grotesque world of the body, and I would now like to consider briefly how the tone of such writing is determined by particular social phenomena. In the case of Rabelais these are popular festivities in a rural setting.

Rabelais exemplifies the elements of the grotesque which Wolfgang Kayser, in his influential book on the subject, specifically rejects. He writes, 'The grotesque instills fear of life, rather than fear of death',[39] and, by concentrating on its Romantic and post-Romantic manifestations, stresses its diseased and sinister elements. Degenerating from public spectacle to private fantasy, the grotesque loses its characteristics of exuberance and celebration which Bakhtin so excitingly explores in Rabelais. Gargantua's birth has all the qualities of comedy, repulsiveness and bodily distortion which I have defined as the elements of the grotesque, but the tone of the passage is celebratory, not disgusted:[40]

> Soubdain vindrent à tas saiges femmes de tous coustéz, et, la tastant par le bas, trouvèrent quelques pellauderies assez de maulvais goust, et pensoient que ce feust l'enfant; mais c'estoit le fondement qui luy escappoit, à la mollification du droict intestine (lequel vous appelez le boyau cullier) par trop avoir mangé des tripes.
> [Then suddenly there appeared from all directions a crowd of midwives, and feeling her below, they found various unsavoury pieces of skin which they thought were the child appearing; but it was her fundament escaping, from the softening of the straight intestine (which you call the bumgut), which came about through eating too much tripe.]

Gargantua then emerges, in an upward rather than a downward movement, from his mother's ear. Taken out of context, such a description may appal, but the occasion in question is a Shrovetide tripe-feast and this fact alone turns the sordid into the exuberant. The exuberance derives from a feeling for the gross plenitude of physical activity in a cycle of eating, excreting, and giving birth; it comes also from the very public nature of the birth – at a picnic. The grotesque in Rabelais celebrates the community of physical experience; it is a leveller.

Rabelais's fascination with the substances of physical life, and their metamorphoses, is, as Bakhtin has shown, intimately connected with his use of popular festive forms and the world of carnival. But whereas in Nashe and his imitators we frequently find this kind of ebullient recreation of the gross absurdities of the human body, the festive forms which establish that sense of the community of physical experience appear in a rather different light. Rabelais's grotesque *fête-champêtre* takes on new meaning in the context of the city, and it is the expanding metropolis of Elizabethan London which provides much of the material for the grotesque imagery of Nashe. Saturnalia drifts towards satire, and the festive violence which is so typical of Rabelais is charged with the purgatorial spirit of contemporary didactic literature. Nevertheless, the rituals of holiday were not entirely destroyed by urban culture. While festivities such as the May-game, the Charivari and the Shrovetide battles between Carnival and Lent are much less well documented in England than they are on the continent,[41] we can still find, as late as 1617, John Taylor writing of the preparations for a Shrovetide riot:[42]

> Then Tim Tatters ... with an Ensigne made of a piece of Bakers Mawkin fixt upon a Broome-staffe, he displayes his dreadfull colours, and calling the ragged Regiment together, makes an illiterate Oration, stuft with the most plentifull want of discretion: the conclusion whereof is, that somwhat they will doe, but what they know not.

But he adds that 'these have been his humours in former times, but I have some better hope of reformation in him heereafter'. Whether or not the rituals themselves continued to be enacted, their motifs are an important feature of comic drama well into the seventeenth century;[43] and one of the crucial differences between the tone of the grotesque in pamphlet literature and grotesque in the drama depends upon the festive sanction given to certain kinds of baiting, beating and vilification. In pamphlet literature, which lacks the obvious connections that drama has with festive ritual, the shadow of the sermon falls more directly upon its images of violence and physical mutation.

As the late medieval world of holiday withered, its bogies and religious obsessions – sin, hell and death – erupted into new meaning with the Londoners' experience of the plague in 1592–3, 1603–4, and for a number of years thereafter. Increasing tension about the succession, the growing number of plots, and the fear of civil war[44] simultaneously fuelled latent hysteria about social destruction. Surely the plague was God's retribution on a dissolute and unstable society, physical sickness and deformity reciprocating moral and social sickness?[45] These are the contexts of a work such as Nashe's *Christs Teares over Jerusalem*, and the swift change in tone from the elated, physical comedy of *Pierce Penilesse* to the hysteria of *Christs Teares* is not simply a result of Nashe's volatile sensibility. Mock prognostications by sophisticated writers may have ridiculed the sensational stories of monstrous births, tempests, epidemics, and what they might imply,[46] but the same kind of writer could easily be terrified by the idea of hell, a sense of which such imagery was intended to instil. Greene, for instance, writes that[47]

> sodainly taking the booke of *Resolution* in my hand, I light upon a chapter therein, which discovered unto mee the miserable state of the reprobate, what Hell was . . . such a terrour stroke into my conscience, that for very anguish of minde my teeth did beate in my head.

And if we consider the effect of warnings about eternal torture in hell upon a people accustomed to such spectacles as the public execution, or mass graves for plague-ridden corpses; if we consider, too, that their culture depended heavily upon analogy, it becomes easier to understand the vacillating tone of grotesque imagery in Elizabethan prose. As it swings from the comic to the revolting, so the tone changes from the exuberant to the admonitory.

· 2 ·

The low style in Elizabethan comic prose

1   THE LOW STYLE AND THE GROTESQUE

In the previous chapter I argued that no literary work is 'a grotesque', but that its visual elements – the imagery it uses – may be. I want now to discuss the kinds of structure and style which accommodate the grotesque and how these are conducive to the proliferation of grotesque imagery. In the second part of the chapter I shall consider in detail the possibility of Nashe's debt to Aretino, and in doing so I hope to isolate the salient stylistic features of Elizabethan grotesque in its more satirical forms.

The structure of most late sixteenth-century pamphlets resembles what the Elizabethans might have referred to as 'rhapsody' or, more pejoratively, 'gallimaufry', and the French as 'bigarrure' or 'marqueterie'.[1] The word 'rhapsody' meant what *rhapsoidia* meant to the Greeks: a stitching together of diverse material; it also implies, as Fr Ong points out, an oral method of composition which proceeds by aggregation and makes a literary medley from established themes and illustrations.[2] (The difference in the low style in Elizabethan comic prose is that these *topoi* are parodied or supplanted by preposterously base allusions and images.) The discursive essay is born from this technique, and it is worth considering what Montaigne himself has to say about this aspect of his style. In the first place it is illogical and colloquial, 'un parler informe et sans regle, un jargon populaire et un proceder sans definition, sans partition, sans conclusion . . .'[3] ['a shapeless, rule-less way of speaking, a common patter and a way of proceeding without definitions, partitions or conclusion . . .']. It is a bundling together, as of kindling wood: 'Ce fagotage de tant de diverses pièces'[4] ['This bundling-up of so many different pieces']. It is all-embracing: 'Il n'est subject si vain qui ne merite un rang en cette

18

rapsodie'[5] ['No subject so trivial but it finds a place in this concoction']. And, finally, it spawns the grotesque:[6]

> [L'oisiveté] m'enfante tant de chimères et monstres fantasques les uns sur les autres, sans ordre et sans propos, que pour en contempler à mon aise, l'ineptie et l'estrangeté, j'ay commancé de les mettre en rolle.
> [My idleness gives birth to so many chimeras and fantastic monsters one on top of the other, without order or direction, that I have decided, so as to contemplate their foolishness and strangeness at my leisure, to start keeping a record of them.]

These comments fit oddly with our conception of the essay as a form exemplified by the rigidly compartmentalised, purposeful writings of Bacon. But they are highly appropriate to a work such as Nashe's *The Terrors of the Night* (1594). Bacon erected barriers between the various areas of human activity which Nashe and Montaigne had restlessly explored, but the grotesque can flourish only in writing where 'Toutes choses se tiennent par quelque similitude'[7] ['Everything connects with everything else by some kind of similarity'], and where a continual kaleidoscoping of images and ideas brings the unexpected into juxtaposition with the familiar. Like Montaigne's 'chimères', Nashe's nocturnal demons emerge from this associative, rhapsodic technique:[8]

> Everie one shapes his own feares and fancies as he list. . . .
> And as the firmament is still mooving and working, so uncessant is the wheeling and rolling on of our braines; which everie hower are tempring some newe peece of prodigie or other, and turmoyling, mixing, and changing the course of our thoughts.

Rhapsody requires a kind of indolence (cf. Montaigne's 'oisiveté'). But it is not torpor. Rather it is a relinquishing of intellect in its structuralising capacity, and a surrender to the endless commotions of a sensitive, even febrile imagination.

'Residual oral techniques', as Fr Ong calls them, are associated with the grotesque in another way. An important element of Nashe's style, and that of his imitators such as Dekker and the young Middleton,[9] is the manipulation and inversion of standard rhetorical procedures. Burlesque and parody are a common source of the grotesque. This may seem a bit obvious; I think, though, that an example will show a close, but perhaps unfamiliar, relationship between the terms. The *blason*, used as a rhetorical term,[10] is the itemisation of a person's physical charms; a burlesque or *contre-blason* will use roughly the same terminology, but will switch it about for the purpose of detraction. Sidney gives us an illustration:[11]

Her forhead jacinth like, her cheekes of opall hue,
Her twinckling eies bedeckt with pearle, her lips of Saphir blew:
Her haire pure Crapal-stone; her mouth O heavenly wyde;
Her skin like burnisht gold, her hands like silver ure untryde.

But the grotesque inversion of the *blason* is the anatomy, whether simply listed, like Rabelais's anatomisation of Quaresmeprenant:[12]

> Les ventricules d'icelle, comme un tirefond.
> L'excrescence vermiforme, comme un pillemaille.
> Les membranes, comme la coqueluche d'un moine.
> L'entonnoir, comme un oiseau de masson.
> [The ventricles of it (his brain), like a cooper's hook.
> The vermiform excrescence, like a tennis-racket.
> The membranes, like a monk's hood.
> The funnel, like a mason's hod.]

or placed in a different framework, as in Middleton's description of Lucifer's will in *The Blacke Booke* (1604). To 'Barnaby Burning-glass arch-tobacco-taker of England, in ordinaries' he bequeaths:[13]

> a brain well sooted, where the Muses hang up in the smoke like red herrings; and look how the narrow alley of thy pipe shows in the inside, so shall all the pipes through thy body. Besides, I give and bequeath to thee lungs as smooth as jet, and just of the same colour, that when thou art closed in thy grave, the worms may be consumed with them, and take them for black puddings.

Like Arcimboldi's grotesque heads, these characters are pieced together from items plundered from the butcher's shop and the kitchen.[14] The use of a laudatory form for purpose of comic disparagement is burlesque; the absurdity of the images, and their relation to the body, is grotesque.

On occasions, literary composition itself could be thought of as a grotesquely physical enterprise, indicating that book titles which proposed an 'Anatomy' of this or that were not based merely on a dead metaphor. John Eliot,[15] the author, or compiler, of *Ortho-Epia Gallica* (1593), describes the work, aptly enough, as 'a fantasticall Rapsody of dialogisme';[16] it is, in fact, a manual for students of French. And it is Eliot's account of his method in compiling the work which is of interest:[17]

> The truth is I turned over some few French authors, and where I espied any pretie example that might quicken the capacitie of the learner, I presumed to make a peece of it flie this way, to set together the frame of my fantasticall Comedie, pulling here a wing from one, there an arme from another, from this a leg, from that a buttocke . . .

The association of heterogeneous material which is called 'rhapsody' has become, in Eliot's mind, a surgical operation; the verbal components of his book have become flesh. The notion does not appear to be prompted by anything else in Eliot's preface. What it demonstrates is the way in which the Elizabethan grotesque springs from an oddly physical concept of literary composition itself.

The emergence in Elizabethan literature of burlesque forms, and their grotesque extensions, is closely linked to the growth of satire generally in England. This dates roughly from the Marprelate controversy of 1588–9, which had a considerable effect upon English comic prose style.[18] On the one hand it brought into literature the imagery and idioms of everyday life, along with its more sordid aspects, so that by 1602 the modish undergraduate who wrote *The Returne from Parnassus* can dismiss Drayton as *passé* because 'he wants one true note of a Poet of our times, and that is this, hee cannot swagger it well in a Taverne, nor dominere in a hot-house.'[19] On the other hand, it produced a new and dazzling kind of speed in colloquial prose itself; the grotesque images in Nashe's writing seem to flash cinematically past the eye. A certain amount has been written on why Harvey was so thoroughly at a disadvantage in his quarrel with Nashe, but the best answer, I think, is provided by Nashe himself, stressing the physical properties of language: 'He hath some good words, but he cannot writhe them and tosse them to and fro nimbly, or so bring them about that hee maye make one streight thrust at his enemies face.'[20] Faced with

this kind of highly mobile, gymnastic verbal performance, there is
a pathetic and wholly misplaced confidence in Harvey's petulant
comment, 'There is logicke inoughe, to aunsweare Carters Logicke.'[21] In Nashe's first reply to Harvey in *Strange Newes* (1592)
he springs immediately upon that old-fashioned belief in the standard debating procedures, hence, 'Heere beginneth the first Epistle
and first Booke of *Orator Gabriell to the Catilinaries or Phillip-
picks*.'[22] Harvey's stolid, oratorical constructions ('To be over-
bould with one, or two, is something: to be sawcy with many, is
much: to spare fewe, or none, is odious: to be impudent with all
is intollerable.'[23]) are quite unserviceable; he did not understand,
tucked away in Pembroke College in Cambridge, that a marmoreal
style is hardly appropriate to ephemeral writing. And as Bacon's
Senecan staccato sharpened English ears after the soporific, rolling
periods of Hooker, so Nashe's agile satirical techniques drew attention to the stilted and old-fashioned style of Harvey.

Among these satirical techniques the stylistic feature which best
epitomises the grotesque in Renaissance literature is the 'base
comparison'. It is as central a feature in the passages by Rabelais
and Middleton quoted above as in the writing of Nashe. And if
the anatomy is the grotesque inversion of the *blason*, elaborate
base comparisons are the grotesque inversion of Euphuistic embellishments by similitude. Erasmus had sanctioned the use of what
looks like grotesque imagery in satire in the *Ecclesiastes* where he
discusses *imago* and *effictio*, both types of similitude:

> Imago tantum ab animantis forma ducitur, & ad rem vel
> amplificandam, vel oculis subiciendam facit: ut si hominem
> rapacem ac virulentem depingas: similem iubato draconi.
> [*Imago* is taken from the form of a living creature, and used
> in order either to amplify the subject, or to put it clearly
> before the eyes of the reader: as for example if you wish to
> depict a greedy and violent man, you will compare him to a
> crested dragon.]

To another you can give 'venter prominens, crura distorta, pedes
utroque claudicantes' ['a prominent belly, twisted legs, feet limping
on either side']. But he adds: 'Illud tantum admonebo, curandum
ut Similitudo quadret ad id cui adhibetur, ne sit sordida aut ob-
scoena.'[24] ['I should insist here that care be taken that the similitude
be fitting to the thing to which it is applied; it should not be sordid

or obscene.'] And Hoskyns, whose *Directions for Speech and Style*
(1599) bears much resemblance to the format of the *Ecclesiastes*,
writes: 'As I said before that a metaphor might be too bold, or too
farr fetcht, Soe I nowe remember that it may be too base;
As ... they that say a red herring is a shooeing horne to a pott of
ale.'[25] Elsewhere Hoskyns cavils at the vogue for abuse, and he is
obviously attempting to 'maintain standards' after the London
literary world had been delighted first by the ribald style of the
Marprelate controversy, and then by the boisterous invectives of
Nashe and Harvey. But the base comparison or metaphor had
already been assimilated into the drama – *Henry IV*[26] and *Every
Man In his Humour* were performed shortly before the publication
of Hosykns's work – and in the early years of the seventeenth
century it was to be a major characteristic of Jonson's fibrous,
colloquial language in the urban comedies.

While it would be inaccurate to describe the satirical sketches in
Nashe's *Pierce Penilesse* (1592) as the earliest English examples of
social typification etched in by the grotesque, there is little in earlier
prose or drama which could act as a precedent. Perhaps the closest
we come to Nasheian grotesque is in certain plays of Lyly, with
whom Nashe became friendly.[27] Here is Motto, the barber, offering
a trim in *Midas* (c. 1589):[28]

> wil you have your beard like a spade, or a bodkin? a pent-
> house on your upper lip, or an allie on your chin? a lowe curle
> on your head like a Bull, or dangling lock like a spaniel? your
> mustachoes sharp at the endes, like shomakers aules, or hang-
> ing down to your mouth like Goates flakes? (III. ii. 38–43)

But this stiffly repetitive construction has none of Nashe's speed
and energy; we may compare his description of the 'upstart' in
Pierce Penilesse:[29]

> You shall see a dapper Jacke, that hath been but over at
> *Deepe*, wring his face round about, as a man would stir up
> a mustard pot, & talk English through the teeth, like *Jaques
> Scabd-hams* or *Monsieur Mingo de Moustrap*.

And it is this kind of startling vignette on which Jonson's *Every
Man Out of his Humour* is based:

> hee lookes like a shield of brawne, at *Shrovetide*, out of date,

and readie to take his leave: or a drie poule of ling upon
Easter-eve, that has furnisht the table, all *Lent*, as he hath
done the citie this last vacation   (IV. iv. 109–13)

says Carlo Buffone of Puntarvolo. The unlikely analogies, the vigorous, physical contortion suggested by the stirred mustard pot,
and the mildly unpleasant metamorphosis of Puntarvolo into shrivelled, smelly fish, are typical of the grotesque. One might compare
Rabelais's description of Jupiter in the prologue to the *Quart Livre*
(with the Nashe piece, especially): 'Jupiter, contournant la teste
comme un cinge qui avalle pillules, feist une morgue tant espou-
vantable que tout le grand Olympe tremble'[30] ['Jupiter, turning his
head from side to side like a monkey swallowing pills, made such
a hideous face that all great Olympus trembled with fear']. But the
novelty of this mode in England in the 1590s lies in its showing
the professional writer improvising, with the materials closest at
hand, a series of similitudes adequate to hit off the more prepos-
terous aspects of the London scene. Erasmus and the dog-eared
commonplace book remain on the shelf; the urban imagery of the
ancient world is not that of Elizabethan London. And from the
satirical point of view we notice that the more familiar and the
more specific the image (mustard pot or dried-up fish), and the
more surprising its context, the more incisive and memorable is its
satiric effect.

The last stylistic feature conducive to the grotesque to which I
want to draw attention is the coinage.[31] In Nashe, at least, coinages
are of two kinds – the base, and the extravagant. The first derives
from the improvising techniques of the professional writer who
makes use of his immediate surroundings, gathering material from
the tavern conversation or the contents of a kitchen. But it improves
on the actually colloquial by inventing a quasi-idiom: hence, phrases such as 'two blunderkins, having their braines stuft with nought
but balder-dash'[32] or 'Peters successour was so in his mulliegrums
that he had thought to have buffeted him'[33] use neologism not
because imaginative pressure is such that the writer is forced to go
beyond the known world of words, but because the writer is
attempting to be super-colloquial, super-idiomatic. The journalist
has to be the man on the spot; he must pick up the latest off-beat
slang – even if it means making it up for himself – to avoid
tediousness: 'Newe Herrings, new, wee must crye, every time wee

make our selves publique, or else we shall be christened with a hundred newe tytles of Idiotisme',[34] claims Nashe in *Pierce Penilesse*.

The 'extravagant' neologism Nashe discusses himself:[35]

> The ploddinger sort of unlearned Zoilists about London exclaim that it is a puft-up stile, and full of prophane eloquence: others object unto me the multitude of my boystrous compound wordes, and the often coining of Italionate verbes which end all in Ize, as mummianize, tympanize, tirannize.

Christs Teares over Jerusalem, in which this passage appears, was written in the year after the publication of R. D.'s translation of Colonna's *Hypnerotomachia* (1592). Nashe certainly read this work at some stage, admiring its exceptionally extravagant style,[36] and I think it probable that fanciful coinages such as 'inglomerate', 'remigiall' and 'mustulent' in R. D.'s translation are the model for Nashe's 'boystrous compound wordes'. However, there seems little point in hunting for borrowings to prove this. Nashe was not that kind of plagiarist. Rather, he imitates the spirit of these bizarre verbal embellishments, reproducing the gaudy and intricate language of the *Hypnerotomachia* in Christ's oration in *Christs Teares*, and, in the description of the banqueting house in *The Unfortunate Traveller*, its involved architectural fantasies. But what is peculiar to Nashe is the combination of both base and extravagant word-mongering; it is typical that he should refer, in his defence of words like 'mummianize', to the *'ploddinger* sort of unlearned Zoilists'. As in the case of imagery, the dragging together of incongrous verbal elements is a major feature of the grotesque.

In a fascinating article on Rabelais, Leo Spitzer has argued that 'grotesque comedy is precisely the horror that emanates from a void that was, only a minute ago, solid ground' and that the neologism pushes out into 'the no-man's land of the non-existent'. But the joviality of Pantagruelism 'is still able to neutralise the fear of nothingness which every neologism arouses'.[37] As the grotesque crosses the boundaries between areas of experience whose imagery we normally keep apart, advancing 'sans définition, sans partition, sans conclusion', it does inevitably encounter 'the no-man's land of the non-existent' in a verbal sense. However, many of Nashe's coinages and images are designed, like 'ploddinger', to fill that void by rendering in solid terms what was previously a purely abstract

concept, and to make that concept comically palpable. Indeed, it
is one of Nashe's coinages – 'palpabrize' ('they cannot grosslie
palpabrize or feele God with their bodily fingers'[38]) – which perfectly articulates Nashe's transmutation of the verbal into the physical. And his sense of the gross corporality of the coinages of others
can elicit a fantasia of ridicule which nevertheless spawns further,
grotesque neologism: ' "*Tropologicall!*" O embotched and trucu-
lent. No French gowtie-leg, with a gamash upon it, is so gotchie
and boystrous.'[39] Where neologism does instill a sense of the void
is rather when it careers towards nonsense. Nashe's producing
'Gogmagognes'[40] from the concept of 'greatness' makes the mind
reel in the way I think Spitzer is describing, and invites a comparison with Sterne or Joyce. The grotesque in this case, deriving from
seemingly impossible verbal connections, evokes that sense of insubstantiality and lack of solidity which Vasari described, rather
than the gross physicality we associate with Bruegel. It is the
grotesque in the latter sense which I shall be exploring in chapter 3.

2   ARETINO AND NASHE

In the remainder of this chapter I want to consider the possibility
that the Italian writer Pietro Aretino had a major influence on
Nashe's style. The matter is worth exploring not only because
Nashe's own writing is of central importance in the development
of the low style in Elizabethan comic prose, but also because
Aretino himself enjoyed a notorious reputation among the Elizabethans both as a political satirist and a pornographer. Attempts
to show to what extent Aretino may have influenced Elizabethan
comic literature have been curiously inconclusive. McKerrow, in
his great edition of Nashe, suggests that he may have seen manuscript translations of Aretino's work, but leaves the question very
much in the air: 'I must confess that my knowledge of the Italian
satirist is but superficial.'[41] In 1931 O. J. Campbell made a convincing claim for Aretino's comedy *Il Marescalco* as a source for
Jonson's *Epicoene*, but his projected work on the importance of
Aretino to Elizabethan writers[42] appears never to have been completed. Perhaps the impressive researches of Meyer, who collected
five hundred references to Aretino from twenty years (1585–1605)
of English literature,[43] seemed rather daunting. Some of these al-

lusions have been discussed by David McPherson, and he makes it clear, by extensive quotation from the two English writers, that Aretino's style was a contentious issue in the debate between Nashe and Harvey.[44] But since he quotes virtually nothing from Aretino's own writing, we are not invited to decide whether it bears any significant resemblance to that of Nashe. So I shall concentrate on presenting the main stylistic features of the two writers by fairly broad quotation and comparison.

The question of influence arises mainly because Nashe himself claimed such an influence. In the preface to *Lenten Stuffe* (1599) he says that 'of all stiles I most affect & strive to imitate *Aretines*'[45] (Thomas Lodge had earlier referred to him as 'true English Aretine'[46]). It would be perverse to dismiss such a statement out of hand, unless it could be shown that, for some reason, Nashe could *not* have read Aretino. Objections of that kind can be dealt with fairly quickly.

The first, of course, concerns the availability of Aretino's works in England during the 1590s. We know that the London publisher John Wolfe issued the first and second parts of the *Ragionamenti* as a single volume in 1584; in 1588 he published *Quattro Comedie* (*Il Marescalco, La Cortigiana, La Talanta* and *Lo Ipocrito*) and, in the following year, the third part of the *Ragionamenti* (*Ragionamento de le corti* and *Le Carte parlanti*).[47] The flood of references to Aretino begins shortly after the appearance of the first of these, which was clearly successful: it remained in print for five years and was reissued five times before 1660. How many – and which – Elizabethan writers understood Italian must remain a matter for speculation. Lady Wouldbe in *Volpone* implies that many could:

> All our *English* writers,
> I meane such, as are happy in th' *Italian*,
> Will deigne to steale out of this author [Guarini]. (III. iv. 87–9)

Many young Englishmen had, by the 1590s, travelled to Italy, and these were not all young aristocrats: Greene and Munday, for instance, found the means to get there.[48] Furthermore, the appearance of grammars and language manuals from 1550 onwards indicates an increasing interest in the study of Italian,[49] and hence a potential market for works of such guaranteed popularity as those of Aretino. Ultimately, though, one is bound to ask that if young, professional writers like Nashe, with a university education and living in the London literary world, did not read Aretino, then who did? And why were his works so popular?

The second factor in an argument of this sort is the matter of what constitutes an 'influence'. The direct verbal echoes and apparent textual borrowings noted by respectable Renaissance scholarship are very often commonplaces, *sententiae* (usually of classical origin), for which two or more writers are indebted to a common source, often a compilation. The 'influence' of Montaigne upon English writers is a case in point,[50] and Nashe himself alludes to this practice of relying on compilers when he mocks Harvey's '*Licosthenes* reading (which showes plodding & no wit)'.[51] Now a major strength of the prose styles of both Aretino and Nashe lies in their force as instruments of satirical journalism: this entails spontaneity, improvisation, parody, a fascination with the topical and the local, and a vigorously physical use of language. And if the manner of their writing is journalistic, its literary effects are those of the grotesque; that is to say, the effects are both comic and disgusting in the measure that the squalid paraphernalia of contemporary, urban life are revitalised and exaggerated for satirical purposes. It is hardly surprising, therefore, that we do not, in Nashe, find borrowings from Aretino of the conventional sort. The style in which they were writing put a premium upon originality, and it is only in manner and technique that Nashe 'affects and strives' to imitate Aretino.

In the prologue to *La Cortigiana* – and it is in this same prologue that we find Nashe's only direct borrowing from Aretino[52] – a gentleman tells a stranger to Rome, 'non vi maravigliate se lo stil comico non s'osserva con l'ordine che si richiede, perché si vive d'un'altra maniera a Roma, che non si vivea in Atene'[53] ['Don't wonder if the comic style is not observed with the order it requires, because we live differently in Rome from the way they did in Athens']. And by stressing that this is to be a play about contemporary life, he prepares us for the satirical journalism which is the first feature of Aretino's style: his vivid recreation in words of the ridiculous and sordid details of everyday life. Rosso, for instance, gives us a grotesque description of a servants' hall where 'È ben vero che ci si dà in cambio de i frutti quattro tagliature di provatura sì arida e sì dura, che ci fa una colla su lo stomaco, così fatta che ammazzarebbe un Marforio'[54] ['It's quite true that, instead of fruit, they give us four slivers of a cheese so hard and dried up it gives

us a stomach ache that would murder a Marforio']. Marforio was
a dilapidated statue in the Campus Martius on which vicious political lampoons were hung. This sort of writing, with its invective
tone and absurd, physical exaggeration, is carried to further heights
of fantasy in the first part of the *Ragionamenti*. Here – to pick one
example from many – we are told of a dildo which resembles 'la
lucertola così terribile ch'è appiccata nella chiesa del Popolo' or
'quelle spine bestiali del pesce che rimase in secco a Corneto'[55]
['that terrible lizard that hangs on the church *del Popolo*' (i.e. a
water-spout) . . . 'those monstrous spines of the fish that was left
high and dry at Corneto']. The same verbal tactics are used by
Nashe: in *The Unfortunate Traveller* he describes Vanderhulke, an
orator, as having 'eyes lyke two Kentish oysters, a mouth that
opened every time he spake, as one of those old knit trap doores';[56]
in the same work, 'I thought verily my palat had bin turned to
pissing Conduit in *London*'[57] and in *Have With you to Saffron-
Walden* (1596) the wretched Gabriel Harvey's complexion is likened to 'restie bacon, or a dride scate-fish'.[58] We can see from these
examples that what both Aretino and Nashe are doing is improvising, using the materials at hand, to appeal to the reader's familiarity with his immediate environment ('*quelle* spine bestiali del
pesce', 'one of *those* old knit trap doores') and its local landmarks
(Marforio and the pissing Conduit). And, equally, they are using
such familiar material for the purposes of ludicrous and repulsive
comparison, which is the chief art of satirical journalism.

A style which aims at garish visual effects naturally lends itself
to caricature, and some of the most memorable pieces of Aretino
and Nashe take this form. Caricature requires not only a keenly
observant eye, but also an awareness of the potential for grotesque
exaggeration in the physical detail. The virtuosity of Aretino's
caricature of the mother of discipline in a convent is of this kind:[59]

> ella avea in capo da venti capelli simili a quelli di una spe-
> latoia . . . e pareano le sue mascelle un pettine d'osso da
> pidocchiosi con duo denti; i labbri secchi e il mento aguzzo
> come il capo d'un genovese: il quale avea per sua grazia
> alcuni peli che spuntavano fuora a guisa di quei d'una leona,
> ma pungenti (mi penso io) come spine . . . Vero è che ella
> avea intorno al pisciatoio una ghirlanda di foglie di cavoli

che parea che fossero stati un mese nella testa a un tignoso. . . . Le cosce erano fuscelli ricoperti di carta pecorina. [on her head she had about twenty hairs like the bristles of a brush . . . and her jaws looked like a bone comb for raking out lice, with two teeth; her lips were withered, and her chin was as sharp as a Genoese's skull; it had been granted the favour of a few whiskers, sprouting forth like a lioness's, but as prickly (I imagined) as thorns. . . . It is true that she had a garland of cabbage-leaves around her pee-hole which looked as though they'd been a month on the head of some scurfy wretch. . . . Her thighs were spindles covered with parchment.]

We find continually in Nashe the same relish for exaggerating repulsive minutiae to the realm of the absurd. His portrait of Harvey with 'a beard like a Crow with two or three durtie strawes in her mouth, going to build her neast'[60] relies for its effect partly on the fantasy of the image, and partly (as does Aretino's 'pettine . . . con duo denti') on its ridiculous specificity. And both writers call upon the resources of the kitchen to swell the riot of sordid detail: Nashe's usurer in *Pierce Penilesse* with his 'garnish of night-caps',[61] or, a few pages further on, Dame Niggardize, who wears 'a sedge rug kirtle, that had been a mat time out of minde . . . and an old wives pudding pan on her head',[62] echo Aretino's image of the 'ghirlanda di foglie di cavoli'. Moreover, the unlikely garb of the mother of discipline, we are told, looked as if it had seen long service in a different capacity. The same technique of exaggeration is used by Nashe in his reference to the kirtle.

This sort of style may offend sixteenth-century notions of literary decorum, but it is not anti-rhetorical. The 'low' style has its own system of conceits and amplification, of which the type is the 'base comparison'. We have seen examples of this already in the context of journalistic techniques and those of caricature, but it is worth considering further, because it illuminates the comments of contemporary writers on the peculiar rhetoric of Aretino and Nashe. These comparisons are the staple of their writing. They seem to be an instinctive reflex of the business of composition. Aretino, when about to tell us how a woman murders her husband, begins 'ed ella, che parea un caratello da tonnina per essere più larghe che lunga, postogli un guanciale in su la bocca'[63] ['and she, who looked like a barrel of tunny-fish, broader than she was long, crammed a pillow over his mouth']. Nashe's writing, too, thrives upon such gratuitous, satirical embellishment. Complaining about the stinginess of patrons, he likens them to Spaniards 'with *Cales* beards as broad as scullers maples that they make cleane their boates with',[64] which is wonderful, but hardly to the point. This is a deliberate abuse of standard *copia* techniques; the amplifications are decorative, but quite the reverse of the sort suggested by the rhetoric manuals. Narrative is being distended for the sake of bizarre, local effects, and it is surely to this sort of thing that Montaigne is referring when he calls Aretino's style 'bouffie et bouillonnée de pointes'[65] ['blown-up and bubbled with witty sayings']. Similarly, Harvey, comparing Aretino and Nashe, talks of their 'capricious and transcendent witte',[66] their 'fantasticall mould'[67] and their 'surmountingest amplifications';[68] from what we have seen of Aretino and Nashe so far, there is, I think, a strong indication that Harvey knows what he is talking about.

Similes of this sort, however, are not always wholly incidental to the narrative in Aretino and Nashe. Nor are they always grotesque. Both writers have a taste for the more extended simile, which is best described as mock-heroic. In the *Ragionamenti* a sharp knock at the door of a monastery disturbs the inmates from their decidedly unmonastic activities:[69]

> il safruganio del vescovo protettore del monistero era quello che con il *tic tac toc* ci spaventò come spaventa le rane poste in un greppo, a testa alta fra l'erba, una voce o il gittare d'un sasso, al suon del quale si tuffano nel rio quasi tutte in un tempo.
> [it was the suffragan of the episcopal protector of the monastery who with the *tic tac toc* startled them as frogs are startled, crouched on a river-bank, their heads poking from the grass, by a voice or a thrown stone, at the sound of which they seem all to plunge into the stream at once.]

Jack Wilton's shock in falling through a trap door into Zadoch's cellar is similarly described by Nashe in *The Unfortunate Traveller*:[70]

> over head and eares I fell into it, as a man falls in a shippe from the oreloope into the hold, or as in an earth-quake the

> ground should open, and a blinde man come feeling pad pad
> over the open Gulph with his staffe, should tumble on a
> sodaine into hell.

This is quite different from the gross, physical comparisons which
we have seen. The device (with an added nicety of detail in the
sounds: *'tic tac toc'* . . . 'pad pad') is that of classical epic, where
similes are often composed of a finely documented action complete
in itself. But the contexts here give them a mock-heroic quality.
Aretino's frightened frogs are, in fact, a group of monks and nuns,
who, a moment earlier, had been happily copulating, and the first
thing Jack sees when he hits the floor of the cellar is 'my Curtizane
kissing very lovingly with a prentise'. I should like to note, in
passing, a further similarity between these passages. Both writers
are fascinated, not merely by shocking images, but by images *of*
shock. In a more serious moment Aretino can achieve quite chilling
effects: 'La tradita de la sua bontà e da l'altrui tristizia, udendo
ciò, parve me quando, ne la selva di Montefiascone, in su l'alba
del dì, urtai con la spalla nel petto d'uno impiccato.'[71] ['When I
heard about the betrayal of her virtue and the other's wickedness,
I felt as when, in the forest of Montefiascone, just before day-
break, I struck my shoulder against the breast of a hanged man.']
Nashe, too:[72]

> The rest we take in our beds is such another kinde of rest as
> the wearie traveller taketh in the coole soft grasse in summer,
> who thinking there to lye at ease, and refresh his tyred
> limmes, layeth his fainting head unawares on a loathsome
> neast of snakes.

It is not difficult to see, in writers of such volatile imaginations as
these, how the burlesque manner may suddenly dissolve into something harsher and more disturbing. The precipitate style generates
unexpected images of terror.

I do not, however, wish to stress this aspect of their writing. The
sudden serious notes develop naturally from the spontaneous and
febrile character of their prose, but in the case of Aretino they are
infrequent. More central is the matter of burlesque. For Aretino
and Nashe both exploit the mock-heroic vein further to produce
burlesques of the elaborate personification associated, again, with
classical epic:

La Nanna e la Antonia si levaro appunto in quello che Titone becco rimbambito volea ascondere la camiscia alla sua signora perché il giorno roffiano non la desse nelle mani del Sole suo bertone. . . .[73]

Vi giunsero a punto che il Sole si avea messi gli stivali per gire in poste agli Antipodi[74]

[Nanna and Antonia rose just when that senile cuckold Titonus was trying to hide his wife's shift so that her pimp, the Day, wouldn't hand her over to her paramour, the Sun. . . . They got there just when the Sun had put on his boots to dash round to the Antipodes]

Nashe's parody in *Lenten Stuffe* bears a close resemblance to this:[75]

The sunne was so in his mumps uppon it, that it was almost noone before hee could goe to cart that day . . . he would not descend as hee was woont, to wash him in the Ocean, but under a tree layde him down to rest in his cloathes all night, and so did the scouling Moone under another fast by him . . .

We find here the same delight in the comic potential of the mundane which characterises their work as a whole. The early morning domestic tiff which Aretino describes is reproduced in Nashe's account of the surly carter refusing to go to work: as usual, it is the lowly world of everyday life which stimulates their imaginations.

The last stylistic area which I want to consider is the highly concrete and often metaphorical way in which both writers use language. Words and phrases are invested with a physicality which made the names of Aretino and Nashe bywords for verbal violence among their contemporaries. Both, for instance, have a strong feeling for the texture of things. Women, according to Ambrogio in *Il Marescalco*, 'non restano mai d'impiastrarsi, d'infarinarsi e di sconcacarsi' ['never cease plastering, and flouring, and besquittering themselves'], and their husbands, to keep them 'tagliuzzate, ed indorate, vanno più unti e più bisunti che i cortigiani'[76] ['chopped about, and gilded over, go around more greasy and super-greasy than the courtiers']. The succession of images – daubing with plaster, sprinkling with flour, and larding on excrement – or the contrast between 'tagliuzzate' and 'bisunti' is very Nasheian. An

old woman doing her face in *Pierce Penilesse* 'might have pild off
the scale like the skin of a custard' and 'these aged mothers of
iniquitie will have their deformities newe plaistred over';[77] in *Lenten Stuffe* the herring is claimed to 'embrawne and Iron crust'[78]
even the feeblest constitution; care-worn faces in *The Terrors of
the Night* are 'welked and crumpled'.[79] Sensitivity to physical surfaces is matched by a similarly metaphorical tendency in descriptions of physical action. Marescalco uses the word 'zazzeare'[80] of
hangers-on at court, which links the image of a gnat buzzing and
zig-zagging to the courtiers' flaunting effeminacy. More vigorously,
the phrase 'la gualcò come è gualcata della gualchiera una pezza
di panno'[81] ['kneaded her as a piece of cloth is kneaded by the
fulling-mill'] is employed in the *Ragionamenti* to describe the embraces of a lover. We enjoy the same vivacity in Nashe: Esdras in
The Unfortunate Traveller 'inscarft'[82] his hand in Heraclide's locks;
preachers in *Christs Teares* 'writhe texts lyke waxe';[83] Harvey's
verses 'run hobling like a Brewers Cart upon the stones'[84] in *Strange
Newes*. Both Nashe and Aretino also pursue metaphor into monstrous coinages. Aretino's 'forbiculate e mandragolate' (verbs
formed from *forbice*: earwig, and *mandragola*: mandrake) in *Il
Marescalco* recall Nashe's comments on his own 'boystrous compound wordes, and the often coyning of Italionate verbes'.[85] And
absurd terms of abuse such as 'ghiotticidio'[86] ['glutton-slaying'] or
'tira-corregge, gratta-porci, scanna-minestre'[87] ['fart-letter, hog-
scratcher, soup-slaughterer'] echo the ridiculous invective of
Nashe's innumerable epithets for Harvey.

   Given this vivid physicality in their use of language, it is appropriate that both Aretino and Nashe should view the business of
writing in comically concrete terms. One critic of Aretino's style
has decided that 'this habit of making things concrete, of bringing
every fact, every situation within the grasp of the faculties of
sensation, is common at every level of Aretino's work',[88] and the
figurative descriptions of the procedures of composition in both
writers suggest that they would have shared this judgment of their
own work. In the *Ragionamento de le corti* Piccardo begins a
breathless, headlong oration on vices at court thus: 'Essendo io il
cornucopia è forza abondare in nominativi hora con sopportatione
de le degnità e de la prosopopea de ciambellotti ...'[89] ['As I am
the horn of plenty I must now pour forth my denominations, with
a discourse of the dignities and characters of doughnuts ...'].

Verbal communication becomes a gastronomic experience. Nanna tells Pippa in the *Ragionamenti* that[90]

> io t'ho pizzicato il gorgozzule con lo albume de l'uovo, nel contarti le gaglioffarie dei gaglioffi: spetta pure che io ti porga inanzi il tuorlo e che io attachi agli uncinelli del tuo cervello i miei ditti, appuntando il saliscende de l'uscio de la mia memoria acciò che stia aperto.
>
> [I have only tickled your gullet with the white of the egg, telling you about the loutishness of these louts: but hold on for now I'm going to give you the yolk, and hang my sayings on the hooks of your brain, pinning back the swaying door of my memory so that it stays open.]

and that 'Infine io ho le cervella in bucato, io le ho nella stufa, io le ho date a sgranare i fagiuoli nel saltarti di palo in frasca.'[91] ['Anyhow, my brains are in the wash, they're in the stove, I've given them over to shell beans with all this jumping from one subject to another.'] The idea that words are edibles is thoroughly Nasheian: in *Lenten Stuffe* he tells his readers that 'I will cloy you with Herring before wee part',[92] and in the preface to that work says that the records of his experiences in Yarmouth 'like the crums in a bushy beard after a greate banquet, will remaine in my papers . . . when I am deade' from which 'hungry Poets shall receive good refreshing'.[93] Again, Piccardo's self-mockery is recalled by the dialogue in *Have With You to Saffron-Walden*: 'with a continuat *Tropologicall* speach I will astonish you, all to bee-spiced & dredged with sentences and allegories'.[94] We notice, too, the similarity of their descriptions of the workings of the brain. Nanna talks of it being 'in bucato' and of 'il saliscende de l'uscio' of her memory, while Nashe says that his brain is 'as poore and compendius as the pummell of a scotch saddle, or pan of a *Tobacco* pipe';[95] he tells how he 'tost his imagination like a dogge in a blanket'[96] and says that the pen shall 'wring our braines like emptie purses'.[97] The mind is seen as a purely physical object, and its activities as no more spiritual than anything else which forms the fabric of everyday life. This shared attitude to the business of talking and writing – the two are indistinguishable in Nashe and Aretino – provides us, I think, with one of the most persuasive signs of the similarity of their stylistic enterprises, and if Aretino can fairly be said to be the first European journalist, in English literature Nashe has the best claim to that title.

· 3 ·

Comedy and violence in Elizabethan pamphlet literature

It is time to consider the Elizabethan grotesque not in its merely satirical form, but in the form which it assumes when comedy encounters violence, and when religious or didactic themes collide with festive images and motifs. In this context the obvious point of reference is not Aretino but Rabelais. Rabelais, however, is unlikely to have had much direct influence on Elizabethan litera-ture;[1] where his work will help us is in providing a touchstone for a discussion of the grotesque in its more violent aspects. At the same time, the Marprelate controversy, which I have taken as a starting point for the development of the grotesque in Elizabethan comic prose, will provide a native model.

The writings of the controversy, unlike those of Rabelais, are important not so much for their literary achievement as for their literary influence. They fascinated the reading public of the time[2] and introduced swift, colloquial banter to a type of discussion previously conducted with depressing verbosity: 'a most senseless book, and I cannot very often at one breath come to a full point, when I read the same',[3] says Martin of Dr Bridges's *A Defence of the Government Established in the Church of England*. It intro-duced base coinages such as 'paltripolitans', 'bumfeg' and 'besoop',[4] which Martin's opponents were quick to seize upon, and it introduced a violent physicality to polemical and satirical writing which they developed to much nastier extremes than Martin's brandishing of his 'crabtree cudgel'.

Francis Bacon commented at the time upon these innovations in *An Advertisement Touching the Controversies of the Church of England*:[5]

it is more than time that there were an end and surseance made of this immodest and deformed manner of writing lately

37

entertained, whereby matters of religion are handled in the style of the stage . . . to turn religion into a comedy or satire, to search and rip up wounds with a laughing countenance . . . is a thing far from the devout reverence of a Christian.

The combination of jocular violence and theatre to which Bacon alludes is typified by a passage from *A Countercuffe given to Martin Junior* (1589), where Martin's countercuffers ruthlessly eviscerate their opponent. The passage is also reminiscent of Tripet's death in Rabelais's *Gargantua* ('Tripet . . . tombant rendit plus de quatre potées de souppes et l'âme meslée parmy les souppes'[6]) ['Tripet . . . as he fell brought up more than four potfuls of soup, and his soul mixed up in the soup'], and it will be useful to compare his grotesque violence with this kind of thing:[7]

> The Anotamie [sic] latelie taken of him, the blood and the humors that were taken from him, by launcing and worming him at *London* upon the common Stage . . . are evident to-kens, that beeing thorow soust in so many showres, hee had no other refuge but to run into a hole, and die as he lived, belching.

The play referred to is *The May-game of Martinisme*; no copy of it exists, but it is described in *The Returne of Pasquill* (1589).[8] What is happening is that the form of a festive game is being used as a blind in order to give a comic preview of the torture and execution of the Martinist writers, which did eventually occur. And that, too, is described by the anti-Martinists in the same grotesque manner; they vow 'to write him out of his right wittes . . . til we have brought *Martin* to the ablative case, that is, to bee taken away with *Bulls* voider'.[9] (The word-play is typical of the grotesque: a 'voider' was a basket or tray for removing the remains of a meal, and Bull was the Tyburn hangman until c. 1601.) I do not want to pursue the analogy very far, but it seems also that this sort of grotesque violence, which is both comic and disgusting, contained by the structure of game, has an important and long-standing precedent in the Corpus Christi drama. V. A. Kolve, for instance, shows how the *tortores* do their savage business with a ribald gusto, and in the context of a game which both controls the horror aesthetically and prevents them from understanding the full significance of what they are doing.[10]

Now grotesque of this invective and punitive kind is fundamentally different from the comic violence in Rabelais. In *The First Parte of Pasquils Apologie* (1590) we read:[11]

> howe like a good Generall the Archb. of Canterburie hath behaved himself with his battle-axe, and how the braynes of *Tho. Cartwright* flye thys way and that way, battered and beaten out, every bone in his bodie pittifullie broken, and his guttes trayling upon the grounde.

This has no literary value. The description of the violent revenge of the religious establishment upon its critics is too literally correct for it to be anything but disgusting. But the grotesque results of the Church Militant, in the person of Frère Jean, in Rabelais's account of the battle in the vineyard, are slightly different; it concludes[12]

> Es aultres tant fièrement frappoyt par le nombril qu'il leur faisoyt sortir les tripes. Es aultres parmi les couillons persoyt le boiau cullier. Croiez que c'estoyt le plus horrible spectacle qu'on veit oncques.
> [Some others he struck so hard in the navel that he brought their tripes out. Some others he pierced between the ballocks and straight up the bum. Believe me, it was the most horrible sight ever seen.]

Rabelais's anatomisation is closer to the concept of the grotesque I have been putting forward, because, while being grossly physical, the comic and the gruesome elements produce a more complex response. The facts are disgusting, but the pedantic chaos contrived by the absurdly specific detail, and the splendidly laconic conclusion, are funny.

It has been argued by Philip Thomson that, on account of the 'disorienting' effect of the grotesque, it 'is in this sense *anti-rational* and not conducive to the grasping of satiric points'.[13] This sounds right in theory, but a critical theory which takes little account of cultural-historical contexts will have a limited application. The imagery and modes of attack in Elizabethan satire are intensely physical; it is an anti-rational and invective genre. One strand of development in 1590s' satire, which derives from the kind of writing I have discussed in the Marprelate controversy, reaches a conclusion in the ferocious satirical weaponry of the verse-writers,

Marston and Guilpin. But this development diverges from what I am considering as grotesque. Marston's verbal incontinence is of a different kind from Nashe's. His endlessly tautological adjectives ('beastly', 'tainted', 'foule', 'brutish', 'vile', etc.), and parallels between sensuality and sewage, reduce descriptive art to an inundation of language which obliterates by monotony. The gist of the seventh satire in *The Scourge of Villanie* (1598), for instance, is contained in the last three lines:[14]

> Thou brutish world, that in all vileness drown'd
> Hast lost thy soule, for naught but Shades I see,
> Resemblances of men inhabit thee.

These soul-less shades are the wan creations of a writer with no eye for the ludicrous diversity of the physical; this is a quality continually present in Nashe's grotesque portraiture:[15]

> his [the Dane] apparel is so puft up with bladders of Taffatie, and his back like biefe stuft with Parsly, so drawne out with Ribands and devises, and blisterd with light sarcenet bastings, that you would thinke him nothing but a swarme of Butterflies, if you saw him a farre off . . . if an Englishman set his little finger to him, he falles like a hogs-trough that is set on one end.

The vitality of this description lies in the rapid switching between two images of the Dane – as a lump of meat, a swinish creature, but garnished with the ridiculous frippery of 'Taffatie' and 'sarcenet'; the grotesque incongruity of the fussy and delicate ('swarme of Butterflies') and the gross ('like a hogs-trough') serves to make the picture more amusing and more effective satirically than anything generated by Marston's flattening disgust.

Invective and disgust can, of course, be important accompaniments of the grotesque. Nashe's portrait of Harvey furiously writing up plague bills to pay off his debts to Wolfe, the publisher, at the height of the epidemic, is truly savage:[16]

> he beganne to Epistle it against mee . . . in the deadest season that might bee, hee lying in the ragingest furie of the last Plague, where there dyde above 1600. a week in *London*, inck-squittring and printing against me at *Wolfes* in *Powles Church-yard*.

Here the venom is expelled through a single grotesque image – 'inck-squittring' – into which is packed all the sense of frantic haste over a sordid business that Nashe is trying to convey. And typical of the grotesque is the yoking together of two quite disparate areas of human activity – writing and excreting – to produce a new and shocking image of the first.

But Nashe is not usually so unequivocally disgusting. More often in his work imagery is released from the narrow intensity of the scourging and purging vein of Elizabethan satire, and acquires that marvellous physical liberality on which the grotesque thrives. His imagery explores the whole gamut of the grotesque from comedy to horror, and emerges consistently from a fascinated sense of the body – its endlessly bizarre functions and metamorphoses, its absurd malleability. Characterising literary style itself Nashe makes comically palpable phenomena which are essentially mental. In *Strange Newes* (1592) he complains to Harvey that 'my stile, with treading in thy clammie steps, is growne as heavie gated, as if it were bound to an Aldermans pace, with the irons at Newgate cald the widows Almes',[17] where 'clammie' perfectly insinuates the laborious trudge of the second image. We notice, too, the restiveness of his imagination: the associations of 'clammie' suggest to us a stylistic slough of despond, but Nashe's mobile imagination generates a second, no less apt image to replace the hint of the first. Of this quality Nashe says himself, referring to the character Pierce Penilesse, 'He tels how he tost his imagination like a dogge in a blanket . . .'.[18] Stylistically self-conscious he is, but the expression is physical, and his tireless manipulation of stylistic effects is intimately connected with his exploration of the stranger realms of physical activity. Despising tonal rigidity, he whips the 'Italionat complement-mungers' in *The Terrors of the Night*[19]

> who would faine be counted the Courts *Gloriosos*, and the refined judges of wit; when if their wardrops and the withred bladders of their braines were well searcht, they have nothing but a fewe moath-eaten cod-peece sutes (made against the comming of Mounsier)

The domestic image of rooting through a wardrobe nicely deflates the literary (and, we guess, sartorial) ostentation of these Italians, and it is an essential characteristic of Nashe's imagination that the physical, 'the withred bladders of their braines', is put in the con-

text of another, 'homely' image. As we observed in the portrait of
the upstart earlier, the professional writer uses the materials closest
at hand; he improvises. The closest source of imagery is one's own
body, and, next, its immediate domestic surroundings. In his comments on literary style these materials are put to devastating use in
guying those addicted to a sublimer concept of artistic creation.

Further along the sinuous track of the grotesque, closer to Rabelais, and closer to the comedy of physical disgust, is Nashe's
delight in monstrous food imagery. His description of a man dying
of consumption in *The Terrors of the Night* – 'it is as a man should
be rosted to death, and melt away by little and little, whiles Phis-
itions lyke Cookes stand stuffing him out with hearbes, and basting
him with this oyle and that sirrup'[20] – reminds us of Panurge's fate
at the hands of the Turks: 'Les paillards Turcqs m'avoient mys en
broche tout lardé comme un connil'[21] ['The filthy Turks had put
me on a skewer, all larded like a rabbit']. Sharply aware of the
body's capacity for mutation, both Nashe and Rabelais use grotesque food imagery to remind us of the essential similarity between
our own flesh and the flesh we feed it with: the devourer is de-
voured. And, again, we are entertained by the nicety of Nashe's
image, 'melting away', pointing to the liquidisation of the basted
flesh. What goes into the stomach is linked in his imagination with
what is already inside it. Speaking of Harvey's *Pierces Supererero-
gation* in *Have With You to Saffron-Walden* (1596), he says:[22]

> But when I came to unrip and unbumbast this *Gargantuan*
> bag-pudding, and found nothing in it but dogs-tripes, swines
> livers, oxe galls, and sheepes gutts, I was in a bitterer chafe
> than anie Cooke at a long Sermon when his meate burnes.

This comic evisceration is subtler than the savagery of the anti-
Marprelate tracts. Giving a notional humanity to the fruits of
Harvey's literary labour – that 'unconscionable vast gorbellied
Volume'[23] – the book becomes a ludicrous surrogate for Harvey
himself: less nasty; more funny. We see also how food and clothes
rapidly associate in Nashe's mind ('unrip and unbumbast' are
clothes images and further help to personify the book), and take
us to the theme of inside-out and outside-in. In this way visceral
imagery turns a shade more unpleasant in *Lenten Stuffe* where we
learn that on long sea-voyages:[24]

Those that escape to bring news tell of nothing but eating Tallow and yong blackamores, of five and five to a Rat in every messe, and the ship-boy to the tayle, of stopping their noses when they drunke stinking water that came out of the pumpe of the ship, and cutting a greasie buffe jerkin in tripes and broiling it for their dinners.

The theme of guts as good for guts is a central part of Rabelais's conception of the physical cycle (cf. the passage on Gargantua's birth quoted in chapter 1); here, the syndrome of food, guts and clothes points to another image – that of disembowelment – which crops up again and again in satires on contemporary dress. Marston's version is typical: 'What he that's drawne, and quartered with lace?'[25] And in Nashe's piece the reference to cannibalism completes the cycle of slaughter for food and food for slaughter, which lies close to the heart of the grotesque physical cycle of Rabelais's world.

To say that there are themes of high seriousness in Nashe's writing is to suggest an explicit moral and philosophical concern which he plainly does not have to any great degree. But I am analysing a writer's imagination from the premise that its expression through imagery will reveal as much about his vision of life as will explicitly stated ideas and beliefs. Visceral imagery has a peculiar and revolting relevance to Elizabethan London, and Nashe's descriptions of Zadoch and Cutwolfe's executions in *The Unfortunate Traveller* would doubtless have been aided by first-hand experience (although the execution of Ruy Lopez for treason, which Nashe probably witnessed, was not until after the work had been written[26]). What we are treated to is a spectacle for public entertainment:[27]

Herewith all the people (outragiously incensed) with one conjoyned outcrie yelled mainely, Awaie with him, away with him. Executioner, torture him, teare him, or we will teare thee in peeces if thou spare him. . . . At the first chop with his wood-knife would he fish for a mans heart, and fetch it out as easily as a plum from the bottome of a porredge pot. He woulde cracke neckes as fast as a cooke cracks egges: a fidler cannot turne his pin so soone as he would turn a man of the ladder.

The grotesque elements of this description are plain: we are loth to admit the congruity of gutted human torsos and porridge pots; we are nervous about finding the trivialising culinary imagery funny; surely the equation of the executioner's professional expertise with that of the cook and the fiddler, purveyors of sensuous pleasure, is merely tasteless? But the cook and the fiddler are not, perhaps, entirely gratuitous comparisons, for they would have been the key men at any popular festivity – and this is such an occasion. The very first words of Cutwolfe's gallows speech, which immediately precedes the above quotation, are 'Men and people that have made holy day to beholde my pained flesh toil on the wheele'.[28] Festive brutality is something we also find in Rabelais, and the carnival motifs in the *Quart Livre* in which the Chiquanous is half-killed also give rise to culinary imagery: 'ils le festoirèrent à grande coups de guanteletz, si bien qu'il resta tout estourdy et meurtry, un oeil poché au beurre noir, huict coustes freussées . . . et le tout en riant'[29] ['they treated him to a feast of blows from their gloves, so that he was left all stunned and bruised, one eye poached in black butter, eight ribs crushed . . . and all in good part']. But whereas in Rabelais the licensed beatings of carnival are a pretext for more serious savagery, in Nashe's description suffering becomes a pretext for holiday, and, by keeping carnival associations present in our minds, he produces a piece of grotesque which is an apt climax to his best-known work. Grotesque of this kind makes us laugh, but our laughter chokes on an awareness of the scene's actual horror. Tugging us in two ways, the grotesque becomes a penetrating examiner of our concept of what is entertaining, what is festive.

It is, however, difficult to know how much of this ambiguity was apparent to Nashe. Sin and the devil had a much greater physical reality for him than for us; as he points out in *Christs Teares*, 'wee deeme it an impatient spectacle, to see a Traytour but halfe an houre groning under the Hangmans hands. What then is it, to live in threescore times more griding discruciament of dying . . . for ever.'[30] And no Elizabethan of Nashe's wildly active imagination would have been spared nightmares on this subject. It is fascinating to glimpse in his most subjective work, *The Terrors of the Night*, what anguish the realms of sleep might have held for him: 'Dreaming is no other than groaning, while sleepe our surgeon hath us in cure', he says, and continues:[31]

If a dogge howle, we suppose we are transported into hell, where we heare the complaint of damned ghosts. If our heads lye double or uneasie, we imagine we uphold all heaven with our shoulders like *Atlas* . . . I knew one that was crampt, and hee dreamt that hee was torne in peeces with wylde horses.

This proprioceptive ability, suggested by the Atlas image especially, is the source of Nashe's interest in physical behaviour generally, but it indicates, too, the degree to which the idea of an eternity of physical torment could have a real imaginative force for him. But, unlike Greene, who simply admitted to being half-paralysed with fear, Nashe is prepared to joke about his demons:[32]

Hereunto the Philosopher alluded, when hee said, Nature made no voydnes in the whole universall: for no place (bee it no bigger than a pockhole in a mans face) but is close thronged with them. Infinite millions of them wil hang swarming about a wormeaten nose

and 'The *Druides* . . . are reported to have beene lousie with familiars', he adds shortly afterwards. This is a quality of the grotesque, with its mingled comic and terrifying elements, which L. B. Jennings refers to as an exorcising of fear through 'the demonic made trivial'.[33] It is the other swing of the pendulum, not from mock-prognostication to apocalyptic sermon, but back again.

And yet, despite the necessary vacillations in the tone of the grotesque, this flippancy lies uneasily with the very real anxieties which emerge from Nashe's apocalyptic landscapes. Often by concentrating in purely imaginative terms upon the physical, Nashe reveals how like other matter human bodies are, and, ultimately, just how little a life can be. At the battle of Marignano Jack Wilton observes that 'all the ground was strewed as thicke with Battle-axes as the Carpenters yard with chips; the Plaine appeared like a quagmyre, overspred as it was with trampled dead bodies.'[34] Living individuals become splintered wood, and are then moulded into conglomerate, dead clay. Nashe reminds us, as Ver does Will Summers in *Summers Last Will and Testament* (performed 1592),[35] how easily human beings can become expendable physical substance. This is the sombre conclusion of the stages of anthropomorphism which the grotesque explores. The original festoons of plant, animal, and human life found in the grottoes at Rome take on a grimmer meaning in Nashe's most sensational and least comic work, *Christs Teares*, in which various kinds of physical extremity mutate the human into the elemental. The lively anthropomorphic imagery of Pantagruel's voyage to the island of Ennasin[36] in Rabelais's *Quart Livre* acquires an apocalyptic note. Jerusalem is punished by plague, fire, and such famine that 'Like an overhanging Rocke eaten in with the tyde, or Death that is nere picturd but with an upper chap only, so did theyr propendant breast-bones imminent-overcanopy theyr bellies',[37] and Gargantuan food imagery is replaced by the spectacle of Miriam making a meal of her own baby. Ultimately, people themselves, in one form or another, can supply most human needs – even road repairs: 'withered dead-bodies serve to mend High-waies with'.[38]

Sensationalism is the nadir of this kind of grotesque, and this is chiefly what a pamphlet like Samuel Rowlands's *Hells Broke Loose* (1605) derives from Nashe's *Christs Teares*. I do not want to dwell much longer on an area of the grotesque which, as literature, is of doubtful interest, but I would like to end this discussion of physical mutation in Nashe's work by referring again to the analogy between microcosm and macrocosm which I touched on earlier. Towards the end of *Christs Teares* Nashe mentions the following portent of the plague:[39]

> The vulgar menialty . . . talke of an Oxe that tolde the bell at *Wolwitch*, & howe from an Oxe hee trans-formed himselfe to an olde man, and from an old man to an infant, & from an infant to a young man.

Bodily distortion in the microcosm reflects disharmony in the body politic, or at least points to an imminent disharmony – the pamphlets which contained reports of such monstrosities are the grotesque equivalents of Ulysses' famous speech on degree in *Troilus and Cressida*. When Nashe speaks of sins as 'Monsters of nature',[40] he is metaphorically extending this idea, and the presentation of the seven deadly sins as 'monsters' in Lodge's *Wits Miserie* (1596) is based upon a similar analogy. Browne's curious piecing together of the broken symmetries of Elizabethan philosophy led him to remark that 'there are no *grotesques* in nature.'[41] But a grotesque vision of the world had much to thrive on at this time: in Bullein's *A Dialogue of the Fever Pestilence* a long conversation on monstrous portents is interrupted by Civis's comment 'Oh God! How is nature repugnant to herself!'[42] And, given the constant emphasis upon analogy in Elizabethan thought, grotesque imagery must often imply a warping of the natural order which in turn has connotations of vast social destruction.

The plagues of 1592–3 and 1603–4 were the climax of this tide in Elizabethan thought, and plague-jokes the epitome of the comic-horror elements of the grotesque. There was a sense of apocalypse – certainly this was God's just retribution on a wicked society. The portents were right. Many fled the city: there was little fresh food to be had, and the grass grew on Cheapside; at night, bodies were spirited away under cover of darkness, and the wretched constable ran the risk of being clawed by manic, diseased vagrants. As the healthy servant disdained his contaminated master, or the wife her husband, the plague could be seen to destroy the most vital bonds of social order, and the plague pit became the ultimate social leveller.[43]

Dekker remained in London and wrote *The Wonderfull Yeare* (1603), believing, as he says in the dedication, that 'mirth is both *Phisicall*, and wholesome against the *Plague*'.[44] But beneath the flippancy there is a real feeling for the suffering and social abandonment caused by the plague. After a rhapsody of grotesque anecdotes, he concludes:[45]

> Neither will I speake a word of a poore boy (servant to a Chandler) dwelling thereabouts, who being struck to the heart by sicknes, was first caryed away by water, to be left any where, but landing being denyed by an army of browne bill-men that kept the shore, back againe was he brought, and left in an out-celler, where lying groveling and groning on his face (amongst fagots, but not one of them set on fire to comfort him) there continued all night, and dyed miserably for want of succor.

Dekker's style is so often a poor imitation of Nashe's; here he is completely himself. Indeed, there is nothing of a similar compassion in Nashe which he could imitate. Grotesque elaboration is foregone, and the language pared down to accommodate the pathetic detail ('servant to a Chandler', 'amongst fagots') and the quiet, factual tone; this, and the tenderness of 'struck to the heart by sicknes' contrasting with the bleak futility of the journey and final abandonment, give the passage a dignity which is hard to find in Nashe's treatment of human suffering.

The pressures of urban life moved a writer like Dekker from the grotesque to a less equivocal kind of social realism. But the more documentary style underlies *The Wonderfull Yeare*, rather than characterises the work as a whole, which does rely heavily upon grotesque humour. Perhaps recalling Nashe's portrait of the Dane in *Pierce Penilesse*, Dekker writes of the terrified Londoners:[46]

> those that could shift for a time, and shrink their heads out of the collar (as many did) yet went they (most bitterly) miching and muffled up and downe with Rue and Worme- wood stuft into their eares and nosthrils, looking like so many Bores heads stuck with branches of Rosemary, to be served in for Brawne at Christmas.

The grim association of the plague with that festive occasion has the same force as the grotesque combination of execution and festivity in the Marprelate writings and in Nashe. Nor does the comic appearance of the citizens remove the sacrificial implications of being 'served in for Brawne' – elsewhere Dekker speaks of 'this *Anthropophagized* plague'.[47] The image of a man being gutted and cooked is developed further in this description of an inn-keeper trying to avoid the plague in a more energetic manner; finding what he takes to be an infected corpse, he takes to his heels[48]

> as nimbly, as if his guttes had bene taken out by the hangman: out of the house he wallowed presently, beeing followed with two or three doozen of napkins to drie up the larde, that ranne so fast downe his heeles, that all the way hee went, was more greazie than a kitchin-stuffe-wifes basket.

The malleability of his flesh, its capacity for decomposition, makes this 'gorbelly Host' a victim of the grotesque truth that human bodies have a disturbing tendency to resemble, then become, rather baser matter.

I find this truth epitomised by Dekker's story of the drunk who falls into a plague pit, which seems to provide an image for the way the grotesque operates in much of the writing I have discussed. Dekker was obviously fascinated by it, too: he uses it at the end of *The Wonderfull Yeare*, and repeats it without comic elements in *The Meeting of Gallants* (1604). This is the first version:[49]

This setter up of malt-men, being troubled with the staggers, fell into the self-same grave, which stood gaping wide open for a breakfast next morning, and imagining (when he was in) that he had stumbled into his own house, and that all his bedfellowes (as they were indeede) were in their dead sleepe, he, (never complaining of colde, nor calling for more sheets) soundly takes a nap till he snorts againe.

What is unsettling about this comedy is that it depends upon the diversity between such homely and comforting images as 'breakfast' and 'bedfellowes' and the horror of the actual circumstances: the grave is a devourer, and human flesh its food. Mass graves are the ultimate grotesque leveller, converting individual lives into stacked, dead matter, but the image of the bedroom plucks us back to the warm centre of human security which it is the function of the grotesque to undermine. The suddenness of his fall, like the swiftness of the disease, underlines the grotesque vision of the perilous fabric of humanity. Dekker's plague-pit is the ghastly inversion of Rabelais's festive grotesque, a hideous reflection upon the community of physical experience. Our laughter sticks on this irony.

· 4 ·

Nashe and the beginning of satirical journalism

1   PREACHING AND SATIRE

It is impossible to consider the beginnings of satirical journalism
in the last fifteen years of Elizabeth's reign without some reference
to the admonitory literature of the sermon and moral tract. The
comic prose pamphlet develops directly from the didactic material
which had aimed to produce that garish mixture of sensational
news (plagues, civil wars, monstrous births), accounts of urban
'vice' (plays, fashions in dress) and good counsel, which the middle-
class Elizabethan found so palatable. In the first place, the comprehensive function of this kind of literature meant that any journalistic enterprise made independently of the pulpit would, in its
early days at least, cover many of the areas which had been for-
merly the preserve of the preacher or self-appointed moralist.
Stubbes's fascinated censures of elaborate clothing in *The Anatomie of Abuses* (1583)[1] are aped by Nashe in *Christs Teares over
Jerusalem*, though he had previously realised the comic grotesque
potential of the subject in *Pierce Penilesse*. Usury and drunkenness,
the topics of two of Henry Smith's immensely popular sermons in
1591[2] – the year before the publication of *Pierce Penilesse* – are
prominent features of that work. Furthermore, the didactic pamphlets could supply a basis for the comic grotesque which the
secular writers develop. In 1586 Robert Robinson published a
work in which ladies' clothing is compared to strange birds.[3] And
as late as 1617 William Jones's awesome warning against ruffs
told of a mother who, after wearing such monstrosities, bore a
child with 'a peece of flesh of two fingers thicke round about, the
flesh being wonderfully curled like a Gentlewomens attire: being
of a very blew collour like a turcke Locke'.[4] This sort of absurdity,
along with an extensive use of realistic detail (Stubbes is the most

50

keenly observant Elizabethan prose writer before Nashe), is a visible starting point for the more imaginative branches of topical prose satire.

In the second place, sermon literature offered a possible authorial stance or persona to the prose satirist. The formulation of a persona based on the satyr figure had served verse satirists,[5] but, as Marshall McLuhan has said, the roles of the popular prose writer in the sixteenth century remained that of either clown or preacher.[6] McLuhan goes on to suggest that the lack of a definite authorial role caused Renaissance writers to switch uneasily between personal and public utterances; the relevance of this to the alternative masks of clown and preacher is not immediately clear, and the point can, I think, be developed more effectively.

In the previous chapter I argued that the fusion of humour and festivity with macabre spectacles of violence is a fundamental source of the grotesque in Elizabethan comic prose; in particular, that Nashe's wild, physical clowning can rapidly shift to a much more hysterical note. Now it is precisely the absence of a satisfactory authorial role which accounts for this tonal unsteadiness, and hence for much that is grotesque in his writing. As clown, Nashe can parade the corpulent, the dandified and the deformed with the same coarse hilarity he pretends to condemn in Charles the Fryer, who likened noblemen 'to guilded chines of beefe, or a shoomaker sweating, when he puls on a shoo'.[7] As preacher, he becomes acutely aware with Stubbes (whom he also attacks) that hell is not a metaphor. The comically reductive physicality of the clown's imagination finds a sinister echo in the warnings of the preacher: 'in adulterie . . . the soule is made all flesh'.[8] The same ability to render life in wholly physical terms serves both clown and preacher, but in the latter the fleshing out of vice is a prologue to the reminder that the soul too may be palpably tortured. Any personal note associated with the duality of authorial role emerges, then, from the feverish mental activity which can produce comedy and horror from the same material. When Nashe writes:[9]

> There is no man put to any torment, but quaketh & trembleth a great while after the executioner hath withdrawne his hand from him. In the daye time wee torment our thoughts and imaginations with sundry cares and devices; all the night time they quake and tremble after the terror of their late suffering,

and still continue thinking of the perplexities they have
endured

we glimpse, in the extraordinary violence of the image, something
of the personal anguish which lies behind the proliferation of the
grotesque in Nashe's prose. And this imaginative instability is
fuelled, I suggest, by a consciousness of the instability of his persona: the clown mocks the preacher, but the preacher terrifies the
clown.

A further point of contact between sermon literature, the moral
harangue and the kind of comic prose developed by Nashe is their
polemicism, and the headlong quality of style which polemicism
breeds. The more tedious variety of invective that he lets loose on
Harvey (for instance, 'this mud-born bubble, this bile on the browe
of the Universitie, this bladder of pride newe blowne'[10]) is couched
in the language of the more histrionic kind of pulpit oratory; there
is almost a consistency between the satirical abuse of Harvey in
Strange Newes and the religious invective of *Christs Teares*. But a
detail from that second work may illustrate how Nashe can react
more interestingly to the sensational imagery of the polemical sermon. A passage in John Stockwood's lurid account of the destruction of Jerusalem – one of Nashe's sources – tells how, during
severe famine, 'the leather of the charrets, theyr own vomitte, and
(saving your reverence,) their own younge, became in the end very
good meat.'[11] In *Christs Teares* this becomes 'Many Noble-men
eate the Leather of theyr Chariots *as they ridde*'[12] (my italics).
Nashe literally sets the image in motion, epitomising his imaginative procedure as a whole. Like the Sorcerer's Apprentice he acti-
vates the world around him with a reckless energy, but cannot
bring it under control. He never really learnt how to conclude a
work. The hiatus between Cutwolfe's execution and Jack's speedy
return to the king's camp near Ardes in *The Unfortunate Traveller*
is bridged by the perfunctory observation that[13]

> Unsearchable is the booke of our destinies. One murder be-
> getteth another: was never yet bloud-shed barren from the
> beginning of the world to this daie. Mortifiedly abjected and
> danted was I with this truculent tragedie of *Cutwolfe* and
> *Esdras*. To such straight life did it thence forward incite me
> that ere I went out of *Bolognia* I married my curtizan, per-
> formed many almes deedes.

And *Lenten Stuffe* is brought to a halt by the statement that[14]

> My conceit is cast into a sweating sicknesse, with ascending
> these few steps of his [the red herring] renowne; into what a
> hote broyling saint Laurence fever would it relapse then,
> should I spend the whole bagge of my winde in climbing up
> to the lofty mountaine creast of his trophees?

Though written under the different guises of moralist and clown,
both passages speak of the uncontrollability of events, and both
are suggestive of the imaginative profusion which is a chief stimu-
lant of the grotesque. Nashe shares with Dickens a mixture of
buffoonery and moral stridency, and, as in Dickens, we sense that
it is often a horror at the uncontrollability of his own imaginative
creations that prompts the denunciatory tone.

I have emphasised the close links Nashe has with admonitory
literature in order to focus on the differences between the grotesque
features of his own writing and those of his imitators. I want to
argue that the dilution of these elements in the comic pamphlets
which follow Nashe is not just a result of their authors' lack of
real imaginative vigour, which in the case of Lodge is doubtless
true, but that the disappearance of the grotesque which derives
from an interrelation of comedy and violence is also caused by the
gradual secularisation of the medium around the turn of the century. The kind of comic journalism which Nashe created from the
religious and didactic material surrounding him compelled an
awareness of the ambiguity of his venture, and it is in this ambiguity that his grotesque manner flourishes. The development and
imitation of this manner in Lodge's *Wits Miserie* (1596),
Middleton's *The Blacke Booke* and *Father Hubburd's Tales* (both
1604), and Dekker's *Newes from Hell* and *The Seven Deadly
Sinnes of London* (both 1606) reveals a basic indifference to its
origins in admonitory literature.[15] Even though Lodge and Dekker
retain the format of a pageant of monstrous vices, there is no sense
of crisis in the authorial persona adopted. Consequently, one of
the first things we notice when reading their works is their relatively
coherent structures. Abandoning the restless shifts of tone and style
which characterise Nashe's writing, they relapse into a comfortable
compartmentalisation of their predecessor's material; hack journalism begins when the role of the journalist is resolved.

If this was the whole story it would not be worth dwelling

further on the subject. In fact, the streams of grotesque imagery which engage the reader so avidly in Nashe and, to a lesser extent, Dekker's plague pamphlets, do not vanish altogether. There is conscious imitation of Nashe in each of the works mentioned above – he is cited by name in all but Dekker's *The Seven Deadly Sinnes* – but the grotesque elements are used in a different way. Of central importance is the switch towards direct social criticism uncluttered by the more histrionic kinds of moral fervour, and this is the main factor in the secularisation of the comic prose pamphlet at this time. As I suggested at the end of the last chapter, the description of the dying chandler's boy in Dekker's *The Wonderfull Yeare* discloses a mixture of steady, compassionate reporting which is alien to Nashe's writing.[16] Second, the disappearance of the continual authorial intrusions and 'rhapsodic' structures of oral composition, which is the method employed by preachers, polemicists and performers, allows the city itself to move into the centre of the canvas. Hence, it is the elaborate caricature, the lively sense of topography and the teeming images of vice and squalor which typify *Pierce Penilesse* that Nashe's imitators seize upon.

These developments have a direct effect on the drama produced in the first years of the seventeenth century. The old type of dramatised 'social satire' relied heavily on moral diatribe: Jonas in Lodge and Greene's *A Looking Glasse for London and England* (1590) is a prophetic and admonitory figure – dreary, too – who has little in common with Jonson's more abrasively intelligent characters. The sermonising elements of popular pamphlet literature are cut away from the drama,[17] while the satirical and journalistic elements are extended in a novel attempt to dramatise the seamier aspects of contemporary social life. Even by 1600 the *Looking Glasse* must have seemed one of those 'Unpossible drie mustie Fictions' of which Marston speaks in *Jack Drums Entertainment*.[18] From the re-opening of the children's companies to about 1606 there are two closely related dramatic vogues which are noticeably influenced by the 1590s pamphleteers (and here we must include Greene's conycatching pamphlets).[19] The first was for plays with a large content of personal and topical satire, e.g. the Parnassus plays at Cambridge and the productions of the War of the Theatres; the second was for plays which aimed at a journalistic *exposé* of urban vice, e.g. *The Family of Love*, *Your Five Gallants*, *Eastward Ho*, and the several plays written c.1604 which deal with prostitution. Grotesque enters this drama partly as an expression of the abusive and physical quality of social life, but with it comes a sharper sense of the kind of sexual relations which the city fosters. It is the language of sexual greed, pervaded by an imagery based almost obsessively on the body's desire to feed and susceptibility to violation or decay, that will be the subject of the next chapter.

2   THE SCHOOL OF NASHE

First, however, I want to return to the prose pamphlets themselves. A glance at Lodge's *Wits Miserie*, the first of the pamphlets which consciously imitate Nashe,[20] might suggest that the shadow of the Elizabethan sermon had in no way receded from the genre by 1596. When we watch Lodge in earnest pursuit of thirteen arguments against dicing,[21] this is no doubt true. What, however, we do not find in this work is the oral style of composition common to the preacher and popular entertainer; the motif of the seven deadly sins provides the work's entire structure, and there is nothing of the live, personal quality of *Pierce Penilesse* where Nashe continually interposes himself in the parade of caricatures to offer us 'The Pasquil that was made upon this last Pope', 'An invective against enemies of Poetrie', or, wearing his solemn mask, a discourse on the nature of devils. Lodge is not a performer, but a ringmaster, trooping his deadly sins in orderly, stolid fashion through the pages of his encyclopaedic book. It is, basically, a compilation, and one half of its ancestry is the register of monstrosities in the manner of Lycosthenes's *De Prodigiorum ac ostentorum chronicon* (Basel, 1557); Lycosthenes, as we have seen, was a favourite standby for Renaissance writers low on inspiration. But Lodge's intention is not to present a series of deformed creatures as 'an admonition and a horror for mankind',[22] so much as to entertain the reader with the ins and outs of contemporary vice. His stance is a secular one, and we do not even know whether he accepts this doctrine concerning monsters – preachers certainly exploited it. The sciapod, for instance, featured in Lycosthenes, is described in *Wits Miserie*, significantly by the character 'Lying': 'he wil tel you of monsters that have faces in their breasts, and men that cover their bodies with their feet in steed of a Penthouse',[23] where the comparison of a monstrous, overhanging foot to a shop canopy adds a slight touch of the comic grotesque. And while Lodge does provide moralising appendices to his chapters, he is ironical about the sententiousness of these conclusions: 'Tut preachers can better teach this (say you) returne you to your devils.'[24] Not only has he explicitly distinguished his role from that of the preacher; even his devils are merely figurative.

A second feature of Lodge's settlement in the journalistic role is the consistency of his style of satirical portraiture. Nashe's creations move back and forth between Rabelaisian caricature and the Theophrastan character – between grotesque, bit-by-bit descriptions of physical appearance, and witty delineations of social behaviour. In *Pierce Penilesse* this means an alternation between the medieval tradition of personification ('Dame Niggardize', 'Greedinesse') and the up-to-date satire on specific social types ('The nature of an upstart', 'The pride of Marchants Wives'). Lodge's portraits are almost exclusively of the second category. While there are occasional flashes of Nasheian caricature elsewhere ('Bosting', for example, sports a beard 'cut like the spier of Grantham steeple, his eies turne in his head like the Puppets in a motion'[25]), it is really only in his descriptions of the usurer and the glutton that Lodge reminds himself of Nashe's true, grotesque manner. And these are the best passages in the book:[26]

> the chiefest ornament of his face is, that his nose sticks in the midst like an embosment in Tarrace worke, here & there embelished and decked with *verucae* for want of purging with Agarick; some Authors have compared it to a Rutters codpiece, but I like not the allusion so well, by reason the tyings have no correspondence . . . double chinned hee is, and over his throat hangs a bunch of skin like a mony bag . . . his spectacles hang beating over his codpiece like the flag in the top of a maypole . . . his gowne is . . . faced with foines that had kept a widows taile warme twenty winters before his time.

What is unusual here is the knowingness with which Lodge uses the range of base comparison; the absurd comment on the possible analogy of 'a Rutters codpiece' that 'the tyings have no correspondence' reveals an easy familiarity with a style which is already past the experimental stage. His portrait of the glutton shows a further stylistic development:[27]

> If you marke his gate in the streets, it is sausages and neats
> tongues: he shawmes like a cow had broke her forelegs: you
> shall ever see him sweating, and his landresse, I know, hath
> a good master of him, for the very pure grease of his hand-
> kerchiefe, is sufficient to find her candles for a winter time
> . . . from the wast to the foot of equall proportion . . . all
> pure beefe of twenty pence a stone, a dog would not eat it.

Similes have been compressed into metaphors (sausages and beef),
and Nashe's expansive, precipitate style straitened into something
much closer to the jerky and aphoristic modes of Jonson or
'Overbury' (in the full text colons precede the last two statements
quoted here). While Lodge retains something of Nashe's grotesque,
Wits Miserie is also a step towards the more clipped and compartmentalised forms of seventeenth-century prose.

In this respect Middleton's *The Blacke Booke* is a step backwards, but back into a style considerably more vivid and exuberant
than anything which Lodge could produce. It is the best of the
imitations of Nashe's grotesque manner, and captures much of his
imaginative velocity and expertise in physical caricature. The book
is a sequel to *Pierce Penilesse*: on receiving Pierce's gloomy supplication Lucifer disguises himself as a constable of the watch in
order to expose the vice and squalor of London's less salubrious
suburbs. His first stop is a stew in Picthatch:[28]

> there came puffing out of the next room a villanous lieutenant
> without a band, as if he had been new cut down, like one at
> Wapping, with his cruel garters about his neck, which fitly
> resembled two of Derrick's necklaces . . . his brow was made
> of coarse bran, as if all the flour had been bolted out to make
> honester men, so ruggedly moulded with chaps and crevices,
> that I wonder how it held together . . . his eyebrows jetted
> out like the round casement of an alderman's dining-room

The macabre touch of the first image, with the ironical 'necklaces'
(Derrick succeeded Bull as the Tyburn hangman), the lively feeling
for physical textures in the next, and the fantasy on domestic
architecture in the last are quintessential Nashe; so is the energy
of the verbs ('puffing' . . . 'bolted' . . . 'moulded' . . . 'jetted'). The
rapid, stylistic punches also include the kind of animation we
associate with Dickens: 'his crow-black muchatoes were almost

half an ell from one end to the other, as though they would whisper him in the ear about a cheat or a murder'[29] – a description remarkably similar to that of General Scadder in *Martin Chuzzlewit*, one of whose eyes 'had no sight in it, and stood stock still. With that side of his face he seemed to listen to what the other side was doing.'[30] In Dickens physical features are detached and invested with a ridiculous life of their own; Middleton's lieutenant with the talkative moustache and 'his red buttons like foxes out of their holes'[31] is a creation of the same habits of observation and fantasy.

Descriptive verve of this kind ensures for *The Blacke Booke* a fund of grotesque imagery based on caricature, but it is better integrated into the narrative structure than it is in Nashe's writing. For one thing, the grotesque elements are not confined to description, but enter the dialogue in the form of obliquely obscene banter: as the proprieter of the brothel tells his wife, 'Naud, go to bed, sweet Naud; thou wilt cool thy grease anon, and make thy fat cake.'[32] Sexual grotesque of this sort is beyond the range of Nashe; his pamphlet work was still too aware of its religious and didactic connections, while his desultory excursions into dramatic writing give us little clue as to how he would have managed his comic prose style in dialogue. Middleton, on the other hand, had already learnt this by 1604, and the two pamphlets published that year may simply have been a result of theatre closures during the plague.[33]

I want to pursue the Nashe–Middleton connection a little further chiefly to show how grotesque imagery can be deployed in a clearer narrative and dramatic framework than Nashe attempts to create, but, incidentally, to demonstrate that Middleton used quite specific material from Nashe in *The Blacke Booke*; for example: 'her fat-sagg chin hanging down like a cow's udder' (Bullen, VIII, 12), 'a sagging paire of cheeks like a sows pap that gives suck' (McKerrow, III, 190); 'lay poor Pierce upon a pillow stuffed with horse-meat' (Bullen, VIII, 25), 'a side of bacon that you might lay under your head in stead of a bolster' (McKerrow, I, 200); 'I would build a nunnery in Pict-hatch here, and turn the walk in Paul's into a bowling alley' (Bullen, VIII, 26), 'goe where you will in the Suburbes, and bring me two Virgins that have vowd Chastitie, and Ile builde a Nunnerie' (McKerrow, I, 216); 'he called his hose and doublet to him (which could almost go alone, borne like a hearse upon the legs of vermin)' (Bullen, VIII, 28), 'Rattes and Mise . . . carried it [a codpiece] in triumph, like a coffin, on their shoulders

betwixt them' (McKerrow, I, 168); 'a valiant buff doublet, stuffed
with points like a leg of mutton with parsley ... I marched to
master Bezle's ordinary' (Bullen, VIII, 29) and 'his back like biefe
stuft with parsley ... foule drunken bezzle' (McKerrow, I, 177–
8). In *Pierce Penilesse* these details supply Nashe's tableaux with
the grotesque colouring which is the real substance of the work;
the tableaux exist in order to display his imaginative virtuosity.
But Middleton works them into a narrative structure – albeit a
loose one – and gains an element of surprise. The pendulous flesh
of the bawd's 'fat-sagg chin', as she 'lay reeking out at the window'
at Lucifer in *The Blacke Booke*, gives an essentially dramatic situation sudden visual clarity; the grotesque description highlights,
rather than submerges, a point in the narrative. Better, Nashe's
incidental fantasies of the 'side of bacon' and building the nunnery
are picked out by Middleton to dramatise the wretched condition
of Pierce (presumably Nashe himself), as he lies asleep in a squalid
chamber three doors down from the brothel. The playful suggestion
of a bacon-bolster has become for Pierce the grotesque reality of
'a pillow stuffed with horse-meat', and as he rests on this revolting
object he dreams of zany redevelopments for London: a nunnery
in Pict-hatch, a bowling alley in St Paul's, and 'the Thames leaded
over, that they might play at cony-holes with the arches under
London bridge'.[34] The combination of these borrowings is inventive and powerful: the image produced, and the surrounding description of the 'pitiful ruins' of Pierce's lodgings, is perhaps the
first attempt in English prose actually to visualise what it is like to
be down and out in a large city. Whereas Nashe's descriptions of
sordid living conditions are confined to the allegorical portraits of
Greediness and Dame Niggardize, Middleton's account is of
Nashe's own circumstances. The shift, as with Dekker's plague
pamphlets, is towards social realism.

An important aspect of this shift is the use of grotesque imagery
as an agent of social criticism. It is not the diabolical nature of
monstrous ruffs that bothers Middleton; it is the contrast between
'prodigal glisterings' and squalor:[35]

> And are these so glorious, so flourishing, so brimful of golden
> Lucifers or light angels, and thou a pander and poor? a bawd
> and empty, apparalled in villanous packthread, in a wicked

suit of coarse hop-bags, the wings and skirts faced with the
ruins of dishclouts?

is the caustic observation of the lieutenant at the brothel on his
customers. Elsewhere, sartorial elegance can prompt in Middleton
the cutting irony for which his drama is now rightly admired. Here,
Lucifer is talking of his new disguise:[36]

> When returning home for the purpose, in my captain's ap-
> parel of buff and velvet, I struck mine hostess into admiration
> at my proper appearance, for my polt-foot was helped out
> with bumbast; a property which many worldings use whose
> toes are dead and rotten, and therefore so stuff out their
> shoes like the corners of woolpacks.

The hostess's admiration depends upon the primary use of bumbast
to fill and flaunt an extravagant set of doublet and hose; the
unpleasant alternative use implicitly provides a bitter indictment of
such ostentation, just as the final image of the woolpacks neatly
ridicules it. The whole thing is managed economically and trench-
antly – Middleton is not necessarily a more intelligent writer than
Nashe, but his intelligence is severer and less diffuse.

This is especially true of *Father Hubburd's Tales*. The first of
these deals with the degeneration of a nasty young gentleman, who
ruins himself, and, more to the point, the tenants of his estate, by
profligate living in the city. The piece has a tight narrative structure
and a social and economic awareness which Nashe does not
achieve. The sympathetic tone and sharp, social observation owes
more, I should guess, to Rouland's translation of *Lazarillo de
Tormes* (1586)[37] – a name which Middleton uses for a character
in *Burt, Master Constable*. Though written in a plainer style than
Nashe's (or 'Nasheian') pamphlets, this is a first-rate account of
poverty in a sixteenth-century European city (Madrid). The author
is particularly acute in his description of the effect of poverty on
a young aristocrat. In the following passage the narrator, who at
this point in the story is ostensibly in the service of such a gentleman, observes how he tries to maintain his dignity in the face of
starvation: 'and for to maintain his poore honor, hee was wonte
to take a straw in his hand, whereof also there was wante in our
house, and standing without the dore, would therewith picke those
which had little neede of picking, for any thing that had stucke in

them with eating'. And, like *Lazarillo de Tormes*, Middleton's tale is too astringently realistic to allow much in the way of comic grotesque. When it does appear, it has a marked, social point, as in the passage where the ploughman, who narrates the story, is summoned with his friends to the young gallant's room in the Strand. The fantastic appearance of their landlord amazes him:[38]

> All this while his French monkey bore his cloak of three pounds a-yard, lined clean through with purple velvet, which did so dazzle our coarse eyes, that we thought we should have been purblind ever after ... it drunk up the price of all my plough-land in very pearl, which stuck as thick upon those hangers as the white measles upon hog's flesh.

Reaching his spurs, the ploughman observes that 'they did so much and so far exceed the compass of our fashion, that they looked more like the forerunners of wheelbarrows.'[39] The gross comparisons nicely deflate this extravagance, and they are not random; they are, of course, the ploughman's attempt to translate something utterly foreign into the terms of his own experience. His own experience is farming, and it is particularly apt that his imagination should turn prodigal and useless ornaments into images of labour. And, as with Lucifer's remarks about the bumbast, irony is the vehicle which gives the grotesque image its social point.

The secularisation of the prose pamphlet, and, in the case of Middleton, its new perceptiveness about the economic bases of social life, introduce an unfamiliar note of compassion to popular literature. Suffering, rather than sin, becomes an object of concern. The soldier in the second part of *Father Hubburd's Tales*, discharged with one arm, one leg and no money, totters around London seeking charity; instead, he is jeered at:[40]

> some jesting at my deformity, whilst others laughed at the jests: one amongst them, I remember, likened me to a sea-crab, because I went all of one side; another fellow vied it, and said I looked like a rabbit cut up and half-eaten, because my wing and leg, as they termed it, were departed.

In Nashe the game of grotesque analogies had been played by the author himself; here, Middleton appropriates it to condemn the heartlessness of such mockery.

Dekker's *Newes from Hell*, another reply to Pierce's supplication, brings this kind of sensitivity into the caricature itself. The following passage describes a broken, old man who confronts the devil's messenger, and asks the way to hell:[41]

> When he spake his tongue smoakt . . . a wise man might have taken it for the Snuffe of a candle in a Muscovie Lanthorne: the Barber Surgions had begde the body of a man at a Sessions to make an Anatomie, and that Anatomie this wretched creature begged of them, to make him a body: *Charon* had but newly landed him: yet it seemde he stood in pittiful feare, for his eyes were no bigger than pinnes heads, with blubbring and howling.

The description proceeds from conventional caricature to a most unusual and witty way of exaggerating the old man's skeletal appearance. It is neat, but it is not unsympathetic ('this wretched creature begged'), and the suggestion of extreme vulnerability is then extended in the man's confused and terror-stricken state. But what is most surprising is that the person in question is a usurer. Not only has Dekker departed from the standard formulae (fox-fur, boil-ridden nose and coughing spasms), he has tinged with pity a subject which, more than any other, excited uniform disgust among Elizabethan writers. This departure from the norm in the direction of compassion is confirmed by *The Seven Deadly Sinnes*. Cruelty is not one of Nashe's deadly sins; nor is it one of Lodge's. For Dekker it is a universal social evil: 'No (you inhabitants of this little world of people) Crueltie is a large Tree & you all stand under it.'[42] Imprisonment for debt, ruthless employers, even forced marriages, are all condemned. There is no room in this kind of journalism for either the comic grotesque of *Pierce Penilesse* or the extravagant horrors of *Christs Teares*. Nor is Dekker an ironist like Middleton, and he could not easily use grotesque imagery for the purpose of social criticism. And though he continued to produce pamphlets such as *The Guls Horn-Booke* (1609) and *Work for Armourers* (1609), which retain some traces of the early influence of Nashe, Dekker's concern with the real social issues of the time reined in any desire to imitate the exuberant, sprawling grotesque of Nashe's writing. Nashe could see comedy in squalor and violence, but Dekker tended to see only the suffering. The beginning of socially critical journalism is also the end of the grotesque in popular pamphlet literature.

5

The grotesque and satirical comedy

1 SATIRE AND THE THEATRES

The emergence of satire at the beginning of the 1590s – the most striking feature of the prose and verse of that decade – did not immediately affect developments in the theatre. During these years the Chamberlain's Men were staging Shakespeare's histories and early comedies, while patrons of the Admiral's Men were being offered Kyd and Marlowe as staple fare at least until October 1597.[1] The children's companies were dormant. When they re-opened (Paul's Boys in 1599 and the Children of the Chapel in 1600), a shift in taste had already begun. The two parts of *Henry IV*, performed by the Chamberlain's Men in the winter of 1596–7, introduced to the 'sub-plot' of a history such vivacious and extravagantly colloquial comic prose as to undermine the dramatic priority of the events which formed the 'main plot', while in the mighty lines of Pistol further capital was made out of their rivals' tedious repertoire. Nashe's lost play, *The Isle of Dogs*, followed in the summer of 1597, and was thought to be libellous.[2] The loss is greater because it is the first we hear of Jonson as a dramatist, and since the play is also Nashe's only essay at dramatic satire, we are unable to estimate the extent to which he influenced the direction that Jonson was shortly to take. Henslowe, meanwhile, had discovered Chapman, who managed to force a more contemporary, satirical note into a play (*An Humorous Day's Mirth*, 1597) which still retained many of the conventions of earlier verse comedy. But it was Jonson who appropriated the idea of dramatic characterisation by 'humours' and married it to a comic prose style of sufficient brilliance and density to reflect the extraordinary surfaces of late Elizabethan London. And the years between *Every Man In His Humour* (1598) and *Eastward Ho* (1605) are dominated by the attempt of the stage to express something of the increasingly volatile and vicious aspects of urban life through the medium of vivid comic prose. The language and imagery of that prose, with its insistent physicality and constant attention to the uses and abuses of the human body, will be the subject of the present chapter. For the moment I shall concentrate chiefly on the Parnassus plays and the early drama of Dekker and Middleton, returning to the contributions of Shakespeare and Jonson to the genre in the second part of this study.

But, first, what precipitated satire into the theatres at this point? It is a commonplace to say that the comedies of the early 1600s were designed to entertain young men from the Inns of Court, but it is hardly an explanation of the vogue; the students would presumably have enjoyed this kind of drama quite as keenly had it been on offer when Justice Shallow was at Clement's Inn. Both general and specific answers can be given to this question. The general answer is that by the end of Queen Elizabeth's reign a spectacle of considerable social disintegration presented itself to the London dramatist. Upper-class prodigality and lust, and middle-class avarice, which are epitomised by the remark made by Quomodo in *Michaelmas Term* (1604) that 'They're busy 'bout our wives, we 'bout their lands' (I. i. 112), prompted rapid social mobility. In 1592 Greene's cony-catchers are still rogues and vagabonds, but Middleton's, a dozen years later, are erstwhile gentlemen;[3] conversely, the Allwits in *A Chaste Maid in Cheapside* (1613), having bled Sir Walter Whorehound, decide that they can afford to move to the Strand. But there are more specific answers: the first, which I have suggested already, is the enormous influence of Nashe in the years (1592–7) immediately preceding the débuts of most of the major Jacobean comic playwrights – Chapman, Jonson, Dekker, Marston and Middleton. The second is that, given this sudden influx of talent into a theatrical world barren of any first-rate author bar Shakespeare, the wave of internecine literary satire which followed in the 'War of the Theatres' can be seen as a natural struggle for professional superiority. Third, there is the fact of the Bishops' Injunction of 1599, which decreed that 'noe Satyres or Epigrams be printed hereafter' and that 'all Nasshes bookes and Doctor Harvyes bookes be taken wheresoever they may be found and that none of theire bookes bee ever printed hereafter',[4] but which did not prevent rancorous debates in the

Nashe–Harvey manner, or any other kind of satire, becoming a money-spinner for the theatres.

The other main factor in the shift to satirical drama was the reopening of the children's companies. Whether or not the Earl of Derby promoted Paul's Boys at this point chiefly to cater for the current enthusiasm for satire, the company quickly capitalised on that enthusiasm. The bishops' ban was issued on the first of June, and in the spring of the following year Paul's had secured the services of Marston, whose satires had been burned in the Stationers' Hall as a result of the new restrictions.[5] His first play for the company was *Jack Drum's Entertainment* (1600);[6] they must have decided that the author's reputation as a 'satirist' – the title alone, perhaps, glamorised by the recent prohibition – was enough to pull a crowd. The work itself has few interesting features, but one is the gesture towards Nasheian grotesque. Ned Planet, for instance, delivers the following rancid description of Camelia: 'her lips looke like a dried Neats-tongue: her face as richly yeallow, as the skin of a cold Custard, and her mind as setled as the feet of bald pated time.'[7] Marston does not usually interest himself in cumulative base comparisons, or, indeed, in emulating Nashe; this example, and a further allusion to the stages of drunkenness in *Pierce Penilesse*,[8] suggest that he is trying hard to produce the right formula for a first success on the commercial stage. That being the case, it looks as though Paul's were consciously setting out to provide a theatrical forum for the satirical vogue which the bishops had just tried to halt.

But we must also consider how far the children's companies really do offer a distinct and more satirical repertoire than the public theatres, and, what is more relevant to the present study, how far such a repertoire involves the grotesque. The distinction between public and 'coterie' dramatic styles outlined by Alfred Harbage[9] is convincing and still basically sound. But he underestimates the flexibility of writers for the public stage. Brian Gibbons has shown how *The Malcontent* (1604) was easily transferable from the Queen's Revels boys to the King's Men at the Globe,[10] while Shakespeare himself probably took the *exposé* technique in *Measure for Measure* (1604) – a disguised prince spying out the moral landscape of his kingdom – from Middleton's coterie play, *The Phoenix*, acted the year before. And it is important to remember that the Falstaff plays and Jonson's 'humour' plays, all of which exploit the comic potential of low life in the city, were written before the children's companies were reformed. Nevertheless, any discussion of the drama between 1599 and 1606, or later, must be aware that there were two sets of theatre-goers, and that those who preferred the coterie repertoire preferred a more topical, and usually more cynical, kind of play.[11] The second question is more complex. While Elizabethan literary grotesque is, as we have seen, intimately linked with techniques of prose satire made fashionable in the 1590s, the children's companies with their more concentratedly satirical repertoire seem to have inherited little of Nashe's stylistic legacy. Nor could they have taken for their own the whole range of low, comic imagery which forms the sub-soil of Elizabethan popular speech – the literary presentation of it, at any rate. In relating the grotesque to types of satirical comedy one basic distinction, at least, must be drawn. This is between the dramatised personal conflict which employs satirical techniques such as caricature and gross physical invective, and authorial satire on a general social scene. Jonson gives Carlo Buffone most of the grotesque lines in *Every Man Out of his Humour*, but presents his social satire through the mask of Asper-Macilente. Similarly, the second part of Dekker's *The Honest Whore* (1605) contains a fund of grotesque imagery, particularly in the exchanges between Orlando and Matheo in act three, but the play itself is not really of the genre of satire. So, while plays in the manner of *Michaelmas Term* predominate in the coterie repertoires, this is no guarantee that they will employ the kind of language in which we are interested.

There is, however, one aspect of the private theatres which does add a further dimension to a discussion of the grotesque in the drama. This is the fact, often too glibly recorded, that their plays were acted by children. The nebulous matter of 'taste' returns – inevitably a difficult area of cultural history, and more so, in this case, because we know so little about Elizabethan acting styles. The comic grotesque treatment of violence and suffering does not seem to have offended Elizabethan taste, and the participation of children in a drama of that kind would probably have made little difference. The Marprelate affair gives us a useful pointer. The play in which Martin was 'sundrie waies verie curstlie handled; as . . . wormd and launced, that he took verie grievouslie, to be made a Maygame upon the stage'[12] was probably acted by Paul's Boys in 1589 and the company closed as a result.[13] The public theatres

were also engaged in anti-Marprelate satire, but they managed to
escape official sanctions. Harbage suggests only that 'they were at
least self-preservingly discreet'[14] (whereas the children, presumably,
were not 'discreet'). Bearing in mind Bacon's indictment of 'this
immodest and deformed manner of writing lately entertained
whereby matters of religion are handled in the style of the stage'[15]
and the fact that the players were, after all, choristers, the most
likely explanation of the closure of Paul's Boys in 1590 is that it
was considered most unfitting for children to be mixed up in a
religious controversy. Religious issues were scrupulously avoided
by the company after 1599, as in general were unpleasantly blood-
thirsty scenes, but that does leave one area which is consistently
exploited for its grotesque comedy, and which would be offensive
to a modern audience: this is the enacting of obscenities by children. Boyish precocity was much enjoyed by the Elizabethans, as
Moth's role in *Love's Labour's Lost* testifies, but the relentless
sexual innuendo of the coterie drama goes way beyond impudence:
some of the language in Middleton's *Your Five Gallants* (1605),
for instance, is quite startlingly obscene. And it does seem that the
contrast between the angelic appearance and tone of the boys and
the rankness of the dialogue, often heightened by the inclusion of
songs, was emphasised at any cost. As early as 1559 an entry in
the Revels accounts records that a Chapel play had contained 'such
matter that they were commanded to leave off'.[16] Perhaps the
audience found such a contrast *piquant*. How many found it tasteless we cannot say. But the effect itself, comic and, at the same
time, disgusting – produced by a heterogeneous combination of
theatrical elements – is precisely that of the grotesque.

A word more must be said about the way dramatic conditions
affect the use of the grotesque in comic prose dialogue, without
reference, this time, to either public or private theatres. In the last
chapter I discussed the function of authorial persona, how it moves
from that of sermonist to that of journalist, and how this alters
both the tone and scope of the grotesque elements in such literature.
Drama obliges authorial persona either to recede completely, or to
take on the disguise of one character among many, hence the
presenter figure in 'comicall satyre'. The language of a play is the
language of its separate characters, and the grotesque, in the form
of imagery and verbal mannerism, becomes a means of defining
character. There is a considerable difference between the exuberant

physicality of Simon Eyre in *The Shoemaker's Holiday* (1599) and Matheo's violent execrations in the second part of *The Honest Whore*; even between the obscene banter of Doll Tearsheet, the bawd, in *Northward Ho* (1605) and that of Primero, the bawd-gallant, in *Your Five Gallants*. Dramatic dialogue employs the grotesque not only in the form of satirical portraiture, which is usually reserved for the satirist figure in the play, but also to enforce distinctions of character in a non-visual way; to charge the speech of certain characters with a physicality which expresses kinds of relationship, rather than individual appearances.

Consequently, one of the chief roles of the grotesque in satirical comedy is the formulation of conflicts in which abuse and vilification are raised to extravagant levels of artistry. Two basic styles of abuse are discernible, though, obviously enough, they intermingle freely: one bears witness to the fashionable enthusiasm for base comparisons in the manner of Aretino; the other to the enduring corporality of oaths, which is part of a much older and less traceable folk tradition. In fact, the substance of almost all Elizabethan execration is the figurative violation of the body, whether in the sophisticated manner of Tucca, ridiculing Minever in Dekker's *Satiromastix* (1601): 'thy teeth stand like the Arches under London Bridge' (III. i. 201),[17] or in the more popular style: 'I will make a brown toast of thy heart, and drink it in a pot of thy strong blood' (*Blurt, Master Constable*, IV. iii. 101–3), which is Lazarillo's furious reaction to being drenched in urine by Frisco. The common principle is a reductive physicality which involves the dehumanising or dismembering of the object of scorn. It is a living language of abuse, and a literary one: living, because the folk-culture which nourished this kind of physical invective had not entirely disappeared by the late sixteenth century, and literary, because the oaths are not (in contrast to our own) merely reflexive formulae; their power depends upon the inventiveness of the execrator. Reviewing an anthology of Elizabethan prose for *Scrutiny* in 1934, L. C. Knights made the pertinent remark that[18]

> Not only was the relation of word and thing, of word and action, far more intimate than in a society that obtains most of its more permanent impressions from books and news-papers, a large number of Elizabethan words and phrases are the direct equivalent of action – gestures of sociability, con-

tempt or offence (the Elizabethans had a particularly rich vocabulary of abuse).

How, then, does this densely physical vocabulary of abuse participate in the vogue for satirical comedy between c.1597 and c.1606? The distinction offered earlier between the satirical techniques used in a dramatised personal conflict and authorial satire on a general social scene might seem to compel a quite separate discussion of the two things. I believe that they cannot be considered apart chiefly because the physicality which is the typical idiom of social relationships in that drama, and which generates imagery of violent execration, is itself the object of satire in one crucial area, i.e. sexual behaviour. Sex provokes little in Nashe that could be called grotesque; in fact, he is surprisingly reticent on the subject (excepting the amusingly salacious poem, 'A Choice of Valentines', of which McKerrow grimly remarks: 'There can, I fear, be little doubt that this poem is the work of Nashe').[19] But the satirical drama of the period thrives on the sensual, dealing variously with prostitution, male lechery and the lust of citizens' wives: *The Family of Love* (1602), *The Honest Whore* (1604–5), *The Dutch Courtesan* (1604), *Westward Ho* (1604) and *Northward Ho* (1605) are all part of this trend. The chief agent in the linking of the vocabulary of violent abuse and the vocabulary of sex in these and similar plays is what I shall call the 'syndromic' character of Elizabethan low-comic imagery; that is to say, a number of different ideas associate naturally with certain types of image to produce a series of comic reverberations: oaths suggest slaughter, slaughter suggests food, food suggests sex, sex suggests disease, and so on. These comic reverberations are one of the most characteristic features of the prose style of late Elizabethan comedy. Moreover, their 'syndromic' character is the root of the techniques of heterogeneous association which are a fundamental element of the grotesque. And it is the physicality of Elizabethan prose, deriving from an exploration of the grotesque world of the body, with which this study as a whole is primarily concerned.

2   STUDENT DRAMA; DEKKER; MIDDLETON

The three Parnassus plays – *The Pilgrimage to Parnassus* and the first and second parts of *The Return from Parnassus* – were per-

formed at St John's College, Cambridge, probably in the winters
of 1598–9, 1599–1600 and 1601–2, respectively. Their author(s)
is unknown.[20] The first of these is brief, stilted and of little interest,
but the two parts of *The Return*, though crudely constructed in an
episodic manner, are a mine of contemporary parody and pastiche.
Elizabethan undergraduates were as earnestly modish as those of
later eras and, consequently, the plays are a sensitive pointer to
fashionable literary trends. In general, this means satire; the theme
of *The Return* is an attack on the social and economic conditions
which force young scholars to seek work in such degrading occupations as acting and writing for Shakespeare's company. In particular, it means Nashe and Nasheian invective. Ingenioso is the
character more or less based on Nashe (it is unnecessary to say he
is Nashe), and at his first appearance his prose style establishes him
as a touchstone in the current literary ambience which the plays
also examine. His account of his own literary activity is expressed,
in the Aretinian manner, as the basest of bodily functions: 'It
pleased my witt yesternighte to make water, and to use this goutie
patron in steed of an urinall' (*The Return*, part one, 214–16). But
the crudeness conceals a dangerous virtuosity, or so he claims to
his patron's servant:

> Why man, I am able to make a pamphlet of thy blew coate
> and the button in thy capp, to rime thy bearde of thy face,
> to make thee a ridiculous blew sleevd creature, while thou
> livest. I have immortalitie in my pen, and bestowe it on
> whome I will. (249–53)

The last sentence contains the novel recognition of the power of
language not merely to immortalise author and subject by Petrar-
chan idealisation, but also to fix a person for posterity in the
grotesque posture of a caricature. It is novel in England, at least,
though the lines seem to reiterate the notorious claims of Aretino:[21]

> Without a master, without a model, without a guide, without
> artifice I go to work and earn my living, my well-being and
> my fame. What do I need more? With a goose-quill and a
> few sheets of paper I mock myself of the universe?

And this is the connection between the social criticism and the
invective style: the pen becomes the unaccommodated writer's
lethal weapon, an instrument of revenge. Ingenioso goes on to

prove his point, describing the arrival of his patron in a quin-tessentially Nasheian manner:[22]

> I was faine to take paines to washe his doges face with a few
> good tearmes; & then he steps and brings out Signiour Bar-barisme in a case of nightcapps, in a case of headpeeces all-to-bewrought like a blocke in a seamster shopp. (358–62)

The philistine and stingy patron, 'Signiour Barbarisme', emerging from his slovenly doze, has to be courted, but in the last resort he can be transformed by caricature into an eternal object of ridicule.

In the second part of *The Return* contemporary writers are discussed in a scene which presents Ingenioso with an alter-ego, Judico. This character speaks in roughly the same style as Ingen-ioso, and is introduced partly to give the impression of a debate, but chiefly to confer the authority of Justice on the figure of the prose satirist. The mellifluous vein is obviously outmoded: Drayton and Shakespeare are censured,[23] Davies and Jonson applauded, and Marston is advised to abandon 'his oylie tearmes' and follow 'plaine dealing *Aretine*'[24] (*The Return*, part two, 202–335). What I chiefly want to draw attention to here is not the judgments themselves (though they are of considerably more interest than the list of writers in Meres' *Palladis Tamia* [1598], which has been quoted *ad nauseam* by literary historians), but the stream of low comic imagery which precedes them. Judico begins:

> Would it not grieve any good spirritt to sit a whole moneth
> nitting over a lousy beggarly Pamphlet, and like a needy
> Phisitian to stand whole yeares tooting and tumbling the filth
> that falleth from so many draughty inventions as daily
> swarme in our printing house? (142–6)

The first image describes the critic's dismal task as one of, literally, 'nit-picking'. (Leishman compares Nashe's 'I have here tooke the paines to nit and louze over the Doctours Booke', McKerrow, III, 14; cf., also, a version of the image in his description of the book as a cheese with 'the purest *Parmasen* magget Phrases therein', *loc. cit.*) But the dead metaphor of 'nit-picking' was still conspicuously alive in 1601. First, it leads in to the image of a doctor sifting through a patient's excrement to diagnose his complaint; a few lines later, the image of excrement 'swarming' with microbial life sparks off another: these literary hacks turn out 'Slymy rimes, as thicke as flies in the sunne' (151). (Leishman is puzzled by 'slymy'; the point is, surely, that these pamphlets are spontaneously engendered in corruption, like certain kinds of animal.[25]) Ingenioso then develops the aspect of seething activity: 'Such barmy heads wil alwaies be working, when as sad vineger witts sit souring at the bottome of a barrell' (158–160) – again, we notice a currently dead metaphor, 'barmy', in an earlier and more energetic state. The image finally reappears towards the end of the scene to describe hack writers as 'the botts and glanders of the printing house' (322), which transforms them again into swarming parasites. This brief example reveals, I think, just how active such low comic imagery can be, working within this intensely physical idiom, and the presence of the two dead metaphors reminds us how correspondingly inert our own use of such language is.

A short detour at this point will enable me to place this kind of satirical abuse in a slightly wider context. The reason for allowing *Wily Beguiled* (1601–2?) into a discussion of the Parnassus plays is that Greg thought that it might be 'in its origin at least a Cambridge piece of the circle of Parnassus'.[26] He may have been influenced by the fact that Hazlitt places it immediately after the second part of *The Return* in the 1874 edition of Dodsley's *Old English Plays*. Baldwin Maxwell's argument, however, that the play is not a Cambridge play, but a revised version of the Merton College, Oxford, *Wylie Beguylie* (1566–7), acted on the London stage in the winter of 1601–2, is more convincing.[27] For one thing, that would explain the curious mixture of satirical invective styles which it offers (though in fact Maxwell does not discuss this). Will Cricket is the nearest equivalent to Ingenioso; he has a sympathetic relationship with Sophos, the poor scholar who is trying to marry a rich farmer's daughter, and he also has most of the grotesque lines. But he is more like an old clown than a young wit: 'Now Ile clap me as close to hir as *Jones* buttocks of a close stoole, and come over hir with my rowling, rattling, rumbling eloquence' (633–5) is his elegant way of saying that he plans to court Peg Pudding, the nurse's daughter. The style is altogether more primitive (Maxwell suggests a connection with mumming, e.g. the Revesby sword play) than the Aretinian or Nasheian manner. So too is this grotesque oath: 'let blind *Hugh* bewitch him, and tourne his bodie, into a barrel of strong Ale, and let his nose be the Spigat, his mouth the Fosset, and his tongue a Plugge for the bunge hole' (1657–60).

The item-by-item caricature is a feature of the grotesque we have encountered before; the difference here is that it is regarded not as a weapon of the satirical journalist, but of a male witch – a fascinating detail which returns satire to its most basic roots in folk-culture.[28] On the other hand, the Nurse's description of Sophos is as fashionable and sophisticated a piece of satire as there could be in 1601–2: 'hee lookes like a red herring at a Noble mans table on *Easter* day, and he speakes nothing but Almond butter and suger Candie' (1465–7). The influence, of course, is Jonson,[29] and Jonson, as we know from the Parnassus plays, was much in vogue among the devotees of Nashe. The amalgamation of the styles bears out Maxwell's contention of a revision. It also indicates how older, more clownish styles of satirical abuse still, presumably, retained colloquial force when set beside a more up-to-date mode.[30]

The other point of contact between *Wily Beguiled* and the Parnassus plays is the conflict – though this is predictable enough – between the poor scholar and the rich philistine. The latter is represented in *Wily Beguiled* by Ploddall, the farmer, whose wooden attempts at aphorism (scholars without money are 'like puddings without suet', 414) contrast sharply with the language of Sir Raderick, the salacious country gentleman in the second part of *The Return*. The love element in *Wily Beguiled* is the sentimental one of rivalry; Sir Raderick's attitude is far from sentimentality: he grumbles about scholars and satirists, the two being synonymous in his mind, and longs for the time when 'an old knight may have his wench in a corner without any Satyres or Epigrams' (1233–5). His views on the restrictions of marriage are expressed as follows: 'there's no pleasure alwayes to be tyed to a piece of Mutton; sometimes a messe of stewd broth will do well, and an unlac'd Rabbet is best of all' (1484–7). These lines encapsulate the kind of sexual grotesque which became fashionable in the comic drama of the early 1600s: 'mutton' is a fairly comprehensive colloquialism for woman as a sexual object (in this case, a wife); 'stewd broth' comes to mean a prostitute via the pun on 'stew', i.e. brothel, and a rabbit is a young girl (virgin?). The translation of sex into terms of food produces a satirical image of the speaker not so much as predator, but as glutton. The basis of the image syndrome is not the equivalence of woman and the hunted animal, but of woman and food prepared for eating, and just as there is a grotesque coalescence between food and the violated human body

in scenes of violence, so the comic dramatists exploit the same
equivalence to describe and satirise sexual behaviour. Balurdo in
Marston's *Antonio and Mellida* (1600) illustrates the point:[31]

> I wold have you paint mee, for my device, a good fat legge
> of ewe mutton, swimming in stewde broth of plummes (boy
> keele your mouth, it runnes over) and the word shall be;
> *Holde my dish, whilst I spill my pottage.*

And the painter whom he is commissioning replies, 'Twoud sent
of kitchin-stuffe too much' ('kitchen stuff', in Elizabethan parlance,
meaning the greasy detritus of cooking). Marston has adapted the
fashion of the 1580s and 1590s for the burlesque *impresa* to the
current trends: the grotesque device satirically defines Balurdo's
swaggering, gluttonous sexuality. What is more, Marston (writing
for children, perhaps *because* he is writing for children) drives the
images to a more indecent conclusion than the author of Sir
Raderick's lines; I take it that, in the context, 'Holde my dish,
whilst I spill my pottage' is a grotesque periphrasis for copulation.
The synthesis of food and sex is not peculiar to Elizabethan slang,
but the comic prose of that period does exploit the association to
a quite extraordinary degree, and I shall be discussing further
elements of the sex–food syndrome in the remainder of this
chapter.

In turning to Dekker we turn to a writer whose taste for grotesque sexual repartee was generally subservient to his taste for
comedy of a more homely kind. But at the turn of the century
when competition between professional dramatists was at its fier-
cest he could hardly ignore the current trends, and the result is
sometimes an uneasy mixture of scabrousness and bourgeois
morality.

His first unaided play that we still have is *The Shoemaker's
Holiday*, and it is also the only play of his that is at all frequently
performed or anthologised. The critical taboo on discussing comic
prose runs into difficulties here; nobody, I think, could argue that
the verse scenes which contribute the sentimental element to the
drama are the source either of the play's relative popularity, or of
its literary interest. Its distinctive characteristic is the language of
Simon Eyre and his assistants. This is usually described as 'racy',
'boisterous', or something of the kind. But there is, in the first
place, a considerable difference between Eyre's language and that

of Sybil or Firke. Mindful of the new trends in comic prose, Dekker turns these two into abrasive caricaturists. Sybil, for instance, can imitate Macilente in *Every Man Out*: 'Milde? yea, as a bushel of stampt crabs, he lookt upon me as sowre as verjuice' (I. ii. 37–8). And she can echo Nashe: 'I lookt as pale as a new cheese to see him' (II. ii. 4), cf. the Essex lagman 'with a visage as pale as a peece of white leather'[32] in *Lenten Stuffe*. Firke's manner is very similar: 'he speakes yawing like a Jacke daw, that gapes to be fed with cheese curdes' (I. iv. 84–5) is his comment on Lacy in his Dutch disguise. These barbed epitomes of speech and gesture find no equivalent in the language of Simon Eyre, which belongs to an older tradition of comic vituperation. He speaks in the style of the Shrovetide celebrant, a Rabelaisian mixture of festive abuse and excitement at the prospect of feasting. His speech is littered with goods from the kitchen – tripes, gravy, puddings, mutton and custards. His long-suffering wife is sent about her business with a volley of culinary epithets: 'Away you Islington whitepot, hence you happerarse, you barly pudding ful of magots, you broyled carbonado, avaunt . . .' (V. iv. 46–7). Earlier, he curses his wife's and servants' idleness, claiming that 'they wallow in the fat brewisse of my bountie' (I. iv. 2), i.e. like lumps of bread in gravy. But the festive climax of the ringing Pancake bell turns abuse into celebration; abandoning his caustic, satirical style at the anticipation of food, Firke cries:

> venson pasties walke up and down piping hote, like sergeants, beefe and brewesse comes marching in drie fattes, fritters and pancakes comes trowling in in wheele barrowes, hennes and orenges hopping in porters baskets, colloppes and egges in scuttles, and tartes and custardes comes quavering in in mault shovels. (V. ii. 189–94)

Shrovetide abuse transforms people into puddings, sops, and joints of meat, while Shrovetide celebration animates the foods which are the centrepiece of that festival. It is this grotesque reciprocation in the imagery that defines the 'boisterous' quality of the play's comic prose, and supplies the festive context of the drama.

The other aspect of the play I want to consider is the way in which that context strips the imagery of the sexual associations which accompany references to food in more satirical works. The activity of preserving meat and offal, pickling and salting, provides a legion of comic innuendo in Elizabethan prose. Salt is suggestive of lechery, cf. the reference to Angelo's 'salt imagination' (*Measure for Measure*, V. i. 399); the pickling or powdering tub is a slang term for the sweating tub used to treat venereal disease, cf. 'the powd'ring tub of infamy' (*Henry V*, II. i. 73), and 'powdered flesh', with its cosmetic overtone, signifies an old prostitute, cf. 'every one his wench, and every weeke a fresh one: weele keepe no powderd fleshe' (Beaumont and Fletcher's *The Scornful Lady*, I. ii. 115–16). The sexual ramifications of the image are almost endless. But although Eyre twice refers to his wife and servants as 'powder-beefe-queanes' (I. iv. 4 and II. iii. 63), the sexual echo is faint. In the first instance, Firke takes up the image of pickling a few lines later in an entirely different way; told by Eyre to wash his face, he retorts 'Let them wash my face that will eate it, good maister send for a sowce wife, if youle have my face cleaner' (I. iv. 15–16). Any sexual association vanishes and is replaced by a grotesque, self-abusive oath in which Firke likens himself to butcher's offal.[33] In the second instance, a similar remark of Firke's, 'Fooles? nailes if I tarry nowe, I would my guts might be turnd to shoo-thread', prompts a series of connected images. Eyre reminds his wife of her humble past ('have I not tane you from selling tripes in Eastcheape') and calls her 'kitchinstuffe', 'powder beefe queane' and Firke a 'chitterling'; he rounds off by serving beer to the work-force, and telling them to 'wash your livers with this liquor' (II. iii. 53f.). The images are loosely agglomerated by Margery Eyre's former occupation: the souse-wife and tripe-wife – the trades were much the same and considered equally degrading[34] – were responsible for washing and pickling offal. But the preparation of flesh remains innocent of sexual connotation at Shrovetide; it is the occasion for a different kind of physical indulgence. What is more, Shrove Tuesday was also the day on which brothels were broken into and whores carted, as if to show that feasting disowns lechery.[35] When sexual innuendo does appear in the play, it is in the absence of Eyre, the master of ceremonies. Firke's comment on Margery is nastier than any of her husband's: 'she lookes like an old musty ale-bottle going to scalding' (III. ii. 10–11) – a slang term for the cure for venereal disease – and Margery herself, in the same scene, mocks Rafe about the possible venereal origins of his infirmity. In neither case, though, does food play any part in the raillery. That is reserved for its festive purpose.

Such innocence did not survive involvement with Marston. Drawn into his company by Jonson's ridicule of them both in *Poetaster* (1601), Dekker speedily adopted a more satirical manner and wrote *Satiromastix* for Paul's Boys, grafting an incoherent mixture of contemporary comic prose styles on to an old play refurbished for the occasion. Pantilius Tucca, an imitation of the character in *Poetaster*, is a particularly muddled creation. Like Jonson's Tucca he attacks satirists (IV. ii. 52–9), but unlike that character he speaks in their own language; Mistress Minever, he tells Sir Quintilian Shorthose, 'lookes like a bottle of ale, when the corke flyes out and the Ale fomes at mouth, shee lookes my good button-breech like the signe of Capricorne, or like Tiborne when it is cover'd with snow' (III. i. 109–12). The abuse is continued to her face, and, deprived of either festive context or personal motivation, it becomes as pointless in dramatic terms as the word games in *Cynthia's Revels*. Nasheian base comparisons mingle with sexual grotesque reminiscent of Marston's Balurdo: Minever is an 'Oyster-pye' and Sir Quintilian is told not to 'put thy spoone into that bumble-broth (for indeede Ide taste her my selfe)' (III. i. 143–4), where these slimy foods have a different connotation from the 'kitchen-stuff' which clings to the ex-tripe-wife in *The Shoemaker's Holiday*. Figurative eviscerations also come within Tucca's stylistic compass. Challenged by Asinius, an epigrammatist, he poses as a low comic Tamburlaine: 'thou seest my red flag is hung out, Ile fill thy guts with thine owne carrion carcas, and then eate them up in steed of Sawsages' (IV. ii. 29–30), food, as usual in Elizabethan satire, linking the realms of sex and violence. His final display of stylistic versatility is the caricaturing of Horace: '*Horace* had not his face puncht full of Oylet-holes, like the cover of a warming-pan' (V. ii. 257–8). Amusing though this is, it adds to our impression of Tucca as a mere repository of different satirical modes, hastily imitated and inefficiently used. They do not help to define the character so much as to assure the audience that the author is quite at home in the latest styles.

By contrast, the two parts of *The Honest Whore* (1604–5) are a considerable achievement. The theme of patience in adversity was close to Dekker's heart, but the tendency to sentimentality in, say, *Patient Grissil* (1600) is checked and stiffened – perhaps through Middleton's influence[36] – by the virulence of some of the language. The moral regeneration of Bellafront, the 'honest whore', and the consecutive degeneration of her husband, Matheo, in the second part of the play, is graphically expressed by their speech mannerisms. Bellafront's first appearance is a masterful piece of writing, and the precision of the stage directions suggests that Dekker took some relish in perfecting the realistic detail of this scene. Her language is nervous and belligerent as she alternately curses and coos at her pimp, Roger, while the longer outbursts are a cynical characterisation of her own trade:

> [of a tight-fisted client] hee's made like an Aldermans night-gowne, fac'st all with conny before, and within nothing but Foxe: this sweete *Oliver*, will eate Mutton till he be ready to burst, but the leane-jawde slave wil not pay for the scraping of his trencher. (*I Honest Whore*, II. i. 105–9)

A prostitute's flesh is saleable meat, a butcher's commodity, and this image reverberates through the play. When Bellafront mends her ways she begins to speak in bland and fluent verse, but echoes of her 'kitchen-stuff' imagery are provided by the very basest characters in the play, Bots and Mistress Horseleach, whose names alone sustain the theme of living off flesh: 'We have meates of all sorts of dressing; we have stew'd meat for your Frenchmen, pretty light picking meat for your Italian, and that which is rotten roasted, for *Don Spaniardo*' (*2 Honest Whore*, III. iii. 12–14), which is Bots's reply to the enquiry 'what flesh have you at home?'. Bellafront, however, is at this stage confronted with the irony that, having abandoned the trade of selling her own flesh, she doesn't have the means to buy food. In the scene following Bots's account of the *menu du jour* we find her lamenting that

> I am not worth a dish to hold my meate;
> I am yet poorer, I want bread to eate (IV. i. 141–2)

– previously, she herself had been both meat and trencher.

Matheo, meanwhile, who has been forcibly married to Bellafront for having been her initial seducer, has sunk from an easy-going, swaggering gallant to the depths of cruelty and boorishness. His language shows a similar degeneration. In the first scene of part one his discouragement of Hippolito's call to arms is jocular, not savage: 'youle bleed three pottles of Aligant, by this light, if you follow em, and then wee shall have a hole made in a wrong place, to have Surgeons roll thee up like a babie in swadling clowts'

(I. i. 80–3). Here, the image of Hippolito as an infant is affectionate, almost tender, but after his marriage to Bellafront the strivings
after wit begin to bristle with barbarity. On receiving a present of
fashionable clothes he comments ungratefully, 'we whose Pericran-
ions are the very Limbecks and Stillitories of good wit, and flie hie,
must drive liquor out of stale gaping Oysters' (2 *Honest Whore*,
IV. i. 17–19). Wit has not deserted him – there is a Nasheian touch
in that effusion – but it mingles now with the grotesque ferocity
of popular execration. Orlando Friscobaldo, Bellafront's watchful
father, is his butt:

> I could teare (by'th Lord) his flesh and eate his midriffe in
> salt, as I eate this: – must I choake – my Father *Friscabaldo*,
> I shall make a pittifull Hoglouse of you *Orlando*, if you fall
> once into my fingers. (IV. i. 174–7)

Ravaged by real, not sexual hunger, Matheo's language switches
from that of the witty gallant to the barbaric threats of a yeoman
like Tom Stroud in Day's *The Blind Beggar of Bednall Green*
(1600). And this kind of oath, figuratively violating the object of
scorn by debasing the body into flesh-food, is the counterpart of
the sexual grotesque which characterises the language of
Bellafront's own fallen state.

As the play reaches its climax this image syndrome is extended
into darker areas. Matheo is to hang for robbery, and the Duke
has ordered a round-up of all the whores in the city. Throughout
the last scene verbal echoes of Bellafront's exchanges with Roger
in the first part of the play remind us of her situation when the
story began.[37] Matheo cruelly presses the point; faced with execution, he decides to implicate Bellafront in the robbery: 'Oh, Sir,
you love no quarters of Mutton that hang up, you love none but
whole Mutton; she set the robbery, I perform'd it' (V. ii. 121–2).
Then, referring to her as a whore, he adds that she is 'A sixe-penny
Mutton Pasty for any to cut up' (V. ii. 149). The first remark
means, presumably, 'you don't want to hang one member of the
gang and let the others get away', but the image of quartered meat
points also to the savage realities of grotesque judicial execution.
The sexual reflection of the image in the second remark forms
further grotesque links between sex, food and slaughter – a connection epitomised by Mistress Honeysuckle's laconic observation
in *Westward Ho*; asked why a man need be faithful to a single

woman, she replies, 'Troth tis true, considering how much flesh is in every Shambles' (II. i. 167–8). The association of gallows, brothel, kitchen and slaughter-house through the constant ramifications of grotesque, physical imagery makes an assault not just on the integrity of the body, which is the basis of almost all grotesque imagery, but also on the integrity of social life in the city. Satirical drama is concerned with social volatility, the interchangeability of roles, as well as the exposure and castigation of corruption; the grotesque complements this concern by forming disturbing alliances of imagery within the language of the drama. And though, strictly speaking, *The Honest Whore* is less a satirical comedy than the drama of a heroine's endurance (a motif of romantic comedy), its placing that motif in the context of a satirical picture of urban life, where the body is sexual food and butcher's meat, courtiers turn robbers, and bawds turn city dames, submits a potentially sentimental plot to more testing acerbities than the theme of 'adversity' usually offers.

The Honest Whore is followed almost immediately by two collaborations with Webster which are Dekker's most deliberate attempt to write sophisticated city comedy in the manner of Jonson or Middleton. *Westward Ho* (1604) and *Northward Ho* (1605) were both performed by Paul's Boys, presumably with considerable success, for they induced Jonson, Marston and Chapman to join forces in a rival production, *Eastward Ho*, for the Queen's Revels. (The Children of the Chapel, the other boys' company, became The Queen's Revels in 1604.) For once Dekker was in the vanguard of fashion. Both plays deal almost exclusively with the rather tepid sexual intrigues of married citizens and lecherous gallants, and both attempt an urbanity in attitudes to sexual morality that we associate with Restoration comedy: as Birdline declares at the opening of *Westward Ho*, 'Many are honest, either because they have not wit, or, because they have not opportunity to be dishonest' (I. i. 89–91). Thoroughly Elizabethan, however, is the endless chatter about London topography – Charing Cross, Westminster Bridge, the 'wry-neckt Monument' and so on – which capitalises on the new sense of the city as literary material inaugurated by Nasheian satirical journalism. Conversation of this sort is encrusted with the comic grotesque detail of the pamphlet literature; Bellamont in *Northward Ho*, for instance, talks of seeing 'in the goose market a number of freshmen, stuck here and there, with a graduate: like cloves with great heads in a gammon of bacon' (I. i. 44–6). But where Dekker departs from the standard procedure is in giving such speeches not to the young wits but to the elderly or middle-aged citizens. Bellamont is of this class, and so too are Justiniano and Honeysuckle in *Westward Ho*. Honeysuckle can even turn his own ageing features into a subject for jazzy self-caricature: 'Gods my pitty, my forehead has more cromples, then the back part of a counsellor's gowne, when another rides uppon his necke at the barre' (II. i. 11–13). Even at his most consciously modish Dekker seems to be wavering in his allegiance to fashionable comic prose styles. The solid middle-class virtues, for which he had much respect, are insulated by the transfer to the citizens of those stylistic devices with which they were normally satirised.

When Bellamont's age becomes itself an object of sexual ridicule, Dekker merely resorts to the grotesque theme of *The Honest Whore*. Doll Tearsheet, the prostitute in *Northward Ho*, derides his physique with the remark, 'A legge and a Calfe! I have had better of a butcher fortie times for carrying! a body not worth begging by a Barber-surgeon', to which Bellamont replies, 'Very good, you draw me and quarter me, fates keepe me from hanging' (IV. i. 139–42). But there is a gratuitousness about the image here which is not at all the case in *The Honest Whore*. There is an awareness in both the *Ho* plays of the need for this kind of verbal display in satirical comedy, but little awareness of its function. It is not convincingly linked to character and still less so to plot; the plays' complicated social intrigues resist effective integration with the more static verbal displays of pamphlet literature, and the consequent diffuseness is, perhaps, Dekker's major fault as a dramatist.

During his association with Marston, Middleton and Webster the grotesque elements of Dekker's dramatic prose vacillate oddly between an asexual physical exuberance, which is partly his own and partly Nashe's, and more uneasy attempts to reproduce the cynical commentaries of his contemporaries on erotic behaviour. It would be impossible to state exactly what contribution these writers, each of whom had a harsher and more thoroughly satirical view of society, made either to his overall development as a dramatist or to individual plays. Work on the latter is still largely inconclusive.[38] It remains true, however, that during his early period (1599–1605) his plays became progressively more concerned with a satirical treatment of urban life, especially in the area of sexual relations, and that after the vogue for this kind of comedy had reached its height he returned to the more traditional subjects for which he seems to have had a natural preference. At no time did he produce a work consistently critical of middle-class morals: *his* citizens' wives ultimately retain their chastity. In this respect, while Dekker uses the stylistic techniques associated with Elizabethan satirical comedy, the grotesque combinations of sex, food and violent abuse, he is not a satirical dramatist in the way that Jonson and Middleton are. While he had both social compassion and a considerable feeling for the physical richness of contemporary comic styles, he lacked the critical intelligence of those writers.

Dekker's excursions into satirical comedy are obeisances to fashion; Middleton's work is the embodiment of that fashion. But as Middleton developed as a satirical dramatist his links with the comic prose writing of the 1590s became more tenuous. As a conclusion to this chapter therefore, I shall briefly illustrate his use of a grotesque theme which will be of central importance to my discussion of the grotesque in Shakespeare and Jonson.

The theme is the conflict between the fat and the lean. This rudimentary physical antithesis originates in the perennial combats between Carnival and Lent celebrated on the streets, and in fiction, throughout the medieval period. A work such as the thirteenth-century French poem, 'La Bataille de caresme et de charnage',[39] is the remote ancestor of the great sixteenth-century treatments of the subject: in Rabelais's *Quart Livre*, the most pictorial of the five books, where the greasy forces of the chitterlings unite against the common enemy, Quaresmeprenant, and in Bruegel's *Battle between Carnival and Lent*. (The poem itself is a parody of the *chanson de geste*, in which 'Quaresme le felon,/Qui moult est fel et anieus' ['The wretch, Lent, who is very cruel and spiteful'] is soundly defeated by Carnival.) The focal point of the imagery is, naturally, the conflict between meat and fish, and it is worth bearing in mind that the relative merits of these foods was a subject of far greater importance then than it is now. Elizabethan dietaries insisted that fish and salted meat offered little nourishment, and fish in general was considered to be the poor man's food. 'As Avicen saythe salte flesshe nourysheth but lyttel and it is gross and engendreth yll bludde' is Paynell's comment; Thomas Elyot's only judgment is that 'it dothe not moche nouryshe, and it doth soner

passe out by vapors', while Thomas Cogan says that 'as for red
hearinges and sprattes they be much worse, and they give as good
nourishment to the bodie, as restie bacon.'[40] Thus Bruegel's engravings of the kitchens of the rich and the poor nicely invert their
modern equivalents; the bloated rich are shown guzzling sausages
while the poor remain gaunt and hungry on a diet of oysters. And,
given these traditional associations, the increase in Elizabeth's reign
in the number of mandatory fish days to 3 a week outside Lent[41]
was enough to ensure the survival of the popular imagery connected with Carnival and Lent in its most basic form at least.

The growth of satirical comedy in England at the end of the
1590s affects this residual imagery in a quite specific way. The
theme of the fat and the lean, while retaining its Carnival or
Shrovetide associations, begins to acquire, through the sexual connotations of grease and fatty foods, an implicitly sexual meaning.
Middleton's *Blurt, Master Constable* (1601–2), though undoubtedly a minor dramatic work, is a fascinating example of this development. Love is the subject of the play's main plot, and lust of
the sub-plot; it is chiefly the language of the sub-plot that I want
to consider. The second scene of the play introduces us to Lazarillo,
a lecherous, itinerant Spaniard, and his starveling page, Pilcher,
who at once begin to play with the double meaning of 'flesh':
'*Lazarillo*: I pine away with the desire of flesh. *Pilcher*: It's neither
flesh nor fish that I pine for, but for both' (I. ii. 3–5). In his de-
hydrated state, Pilcher is suitably caustic about his master's excitement over the 'moist-handed' courtesan, Imperia, but when he is
accosted at the end of the scene by two more robust servants, he
finds himself abused in turn: 'Pilcher! thou'rt a most pitiful dried
one . . . I wonder thy master does not slice thee and swallow thee
for an anchovies' (I. ii. 194–6). Once this contention between the
fat and the lean has been established, the theme starts to permeate
the sexual encounters in the play. When we meet Imperia at the
beginning of the second act, she is awaiting her clients and dripping
grease with Falstaffian profusion. Curvetto, an aged courtier, is a
disappointment: 'I wonder what this gurnet's head makes here!
Yet bring him in; he will serve for picking meat' (II. ii. 179–81).
But softening his lean and withered flesh into sensuality proves to
be an unrewarding business, and he is dismissed with the contemptuous remark, 'I do not love to handle these dried stockfishes,
that ask so much tawing' (III. iii. 16–18). At this point Lazarillo

reappears and, attempting to woo Imperia and her ladies with a speech in praise of female dominance, is at first greeted warmly; 'I'll have a cut of that roast' (III. iii. 69), one of them says. But, like Curvetto, his lecherous plans do not meet with much enthusiasm from Imperia, whose parting shot reduces him to the same condition as Pilcher: 'So, so, so, I will be rid of this boiled red sprat, that stinks so in my stomach' (III. iii. 205–6). This strongly visceral revulsion from a sexuality which is expressed in terms of edible flesh, fat and lean, climaxes in Imperia's vengeful dampening of Lazarillo's lust. Trying to satisfy his hunger by creeping along to her chamber, he is welcomed with the waste products of many hearty meals, first by falling through a trap-door into a cess-pit, and then by being drenched with urine. The retribution is deeply traditional,[42] but in this play the reiterated imagery of fat and lean foods gives it a grotesque logic. Physical abuse and the comic grotesque treatment of sexuality marry in excrement.

The stream of imagery even spills into the ostensibly more romantic main plot. Act one ends with a meat–fish debate between Pilcher and the other servants and a kind of roundelay in which he laments his emaciated state. The next act begins with a conversation between Fontinelle, a French gallant held captive in Venice after the wars, and the page to the lady he desires. Fontinelle is the sexually successful character in the play, though this is not yet in evidence, and he is given the following advice by Truepenny:

> your hat nor head are not of the true heigh-ho block, for it should be broad-brimmed, limber like the skin of a white pudding when the meat is out, the facing fatty, the felt dusty, and not entered into any band. . . . I tell you, monsieur, a lover should be all loose from the sole of the foot rising upward, and from the bases or confines of the slop falling downward. (II. i. 24–32)

In immediate contrast to the description of astringency in the previous scene, the imagery here is suggestively unctuous, but in such a fanciful way as almost to constitute a piece of clothes caricature in the pamphleteering vein. Such passages lend weight to D. M. Holmes's judgment that the theme of the play is that love is 'a tawdry, glandular business'.[43]

Holmes also considers this theme to be peculiarly Middletonian (and not at all typical of Dekker). This is true, and it is also true that Middleton reiterates the sexual associations of Carnival and Lenten imagery, of fatness and leanness, elsewhere in his drama. *The Family of Love* (1602?) exposes the sexual hypocrisy of a Puritan sect and mixes gross, medical imagery with comments such as this: 'Love is like fasting-days, but the body is like flesh-days; and tis our English gallants' fashion to prefer a morsel of flesh before all the fasting-days in the whole year' (I. i. 42–6). But the play in which this kind of imagery assumes an essential role in the drama as a whole is *A Chaste Maid in Cheapside* (1613). In the setting of a meat market during Lent an illegitimate baby is hidden under a joint of mutton, a party of drunken Puritans suck 'long plums' and 'wriggle-tail comfits' at a christening, a childless woman is thought to be craving for calf's head and bacon, and the 'promoters' (the Lenten spies and searchers) use their ascetic duties as an opportunity for a riot of gluttony and sexual indulgence. Much of this is ably discussed by R. B. Parker in his edition of the play, and there is no need to repeat it here.[44] Oddly, however, Allwit's memorable description of the promoters does not figure in his discussion of the 'themes and imagery'; it is certainly worth quoting:

This Lent will fat the whoresons up with sweetbreads,
And lard their whores with lamb-stones; what their golls
Can clutch goes presently to their Molls and Dolls:
The bawds will be so fat with what they earn,
Their chins will hang like udders by Easter-eve
And, being stroak'd, will give the milk of witches. (II. ii. 64–9)

These lines knot together in astonishing physical density the main images of the play: the mingled suggestions of obesity and pregnancy, of gorging and discharging, and of an incontinence which even in satiety provokes the flesh to sensuous activity, are pinned to the paradox that the stimulus to such grotesque luxury is a time of abstention. It is 'carnal strictness' (II. ii. 73) that is the spur to orgy.

In a note to his remarks on the 'soiled Saturnalia' of the *Chaste Maid*, Parker writes that 'The closest critical term would seem to be *grotesque*, as defined by Arthur Clayborough, *The Grotesque in English Literature* (1966)'.[45] And elsewhere he argues that the grotesque is an important technique of Middleton's social criticism, citing not only the christening feast in the *Chaste Maid*, but also Dampit's death in *A Trick to Catch the Old One* (1606) and

Tangle's purging of legal terms in *The Phoenix* (1603).[46] These are fair observations, and I do not want to argue with Parker on his use of the term. However, it is important to point out that such instances are 'grotesque' in terms of the kinds of dramatic spectacle they present, rather than the language in which they present it. With the exception of the *Chaste Maid* Middleton rarely integrated language and spectacle in the way that Jonson did in *Bartholomew Fair*, and his concentration on grotesque theatrical imagery, as opposed to verbal imagery, effectively severs his connections with the mainstream of comic prose writing inspired by Nashe.

A Chaste Maid in Cheapside was written nearly ten years after the height of the fashion for satirical comedy and 'brothel drama'. Comic prose grotesque has been transmuted into a peculiar poetry in which the influence of Nashe is no longer felt and which has few contemporary parallels: the closest comparisons of language and imagery are with *Bartholomew Fair*, but, predictably, Jonson considered prose to be the appropriate medium for this kind of subject. Middleton's last links with Nashe and the kind of comic prose developed in pamphlets and drama during the last years of Elizabeth's reign appear in *Your Five Gallants* (c. 1605). This is a loosely structured, episodic play which is clearly based on pamphlet literature, particularly of the cony-catching variety. Soliloquies quite incidental to the plot give the gallants a chance to swing into the familiar, Nasheian caricature, now combined with a farrago of sexual connotation:

> he's in his third sweat by this time, sipping of the doctor's bottle, or picking the ninth part of a rack of mutton, dry-roasted, with a leash of nightcaps on his head like the pope's triple crown, and as many pillows crushed to his back, with O-the-needles! for he got the pox of a sempster, and it pricked so much more naturally. (I. ii. 323–9)

But this breathless cramming together of physical detail in prose is something which Middleton more or less abandons in the subsequent city comedies. Just as Dekker's social concerns forced out comic grotesque detail from his later pamphlets, so Middleton's acid delineations of social vice began to exclude from their tightly structured plots the irresponsible profusion of grotesque imagery in which Nashe delighted.

Part II

6

Shakespearean grotesque: the Falstaff plays

1 NASHE AND SHAKESPEARE

The first part of this study has been primarily concerned with the origins and development of the comic prose styles which Nashe made fashionable during the 1590s. It is Nashe who plays the major part in the evolution of those styles from their nebulous beginnings in the sermon and folk humour to their employment first in the earliest examples of satirical journalism in England and then in satirical comedy. This process can, roughly speaking, be said to occupy the years from 1588 to 1604. Before 1588 there is almost nothing in English literature that could be described as 'comic prose': the jest books furnish no stylistic models for Nashe, or for anyone else – their comedy, such as it is, lies solely in the incident – and the calculated preciosity of Euphuism and Arcadianism is seldom capable of humour.[1] After about 1604 and the appearance of a new generation of professional writers, comic prose styles grow increasingly diffuse and echoes of Nashe increasingly fainter. But within this period pamphlet literature and the drama rapidly absorbed a variety of stylistic techniques to create a comic prose of immense vitality and colour. Anyone who has struggled through some of the drab little farces in *A Hundred Mery Talys* (1526) or *The Jestes of Skogyn* (c. 1570) and then turned to the Falstaff scenes of *Henry IV* will have witnessed a literary revolution quite as remarkable as the revolution in dramatic verse which occurred between Preston's *Cambises* (1561) and Marlowe's *Tamburlaine* (1587). But the feeling persists among many critics of Shakespeare that non-romantic comedy is in some sense an inferior genre, and that comic prose is beneath critical attention. For Ifor Evans the language of Shakespeare's plays means simply the language of their verse; for Caroline Spurgeon and W. H.

Clemen Shakespeare's imagery means his poetic imagery.[2] The fact
that Falstaff, one of Shakespeare's two or three finest creations of
character, is known to us entirely through the medium of comic
prose has scarcely disturbed these assumptions.

Milton Crane's dogged account of *Shakespeare's Prose* (1951)
is an attempt to fill the gap; unfortunately, that is all it is. The
book offers a descriptive catalogue of the prose passages in Shakespeare, and the level of critical interest in these is indicated by the
fact that, in his discussion of *Henry IV*, all of the seven quotations
are passages of verse. And Crane's own comment on *The Merry
Wives of Windsor* exposes the fraud: the play 'is almost wholly in
prose, and, for this very fact, is of comparatively slight interest'.[3]
Brian Vickers's *The Artistry of Shakespeare's Prose* (1968) is much
more ambitious but still makes no attempt to discuss the importance of Nashe and other non-dramatic prose writers, and it is by
ignoring these contemporary developments that Vickers is able to
follow the desiccated path of school rhetoric quite so relentlessly.
The book updates Abraham Fraunce's compilation of rhetorical
figures, *The Arcadian Rhetorike* (1588), encouraging the notion
that the finest Elizabethan prose consists of pre-fabricated sections
which can be fitted together and taken apart like a children's game.
Superficial elegance of this kind was certainly fashionable during
the 1580s, but by the end of the decade we begin to hear of a new
prose style – innovative, anti-logical and anti-rhetorical:[4]

> [Martin] hath chosen such a method as no man else besides
> hath done. Nay, his syllogisms, axioms, method and all are
> of his own making; he will borrow none of those common
> school rules, no not so much as the common grammar

remarks the author of *The Just Censure and Reproofe of Martin
Junior* (1589). In his anti-Marprelate tract *Pappe with an Hatchet*
(1589) even Lyly briefly abandoned his gilded periods for a style
which was both more spontaneous and more brutal, and by 1592
Greene was exchanging his own Arcadian rhetoric for Nasheian
caricature (almost certainly with Nashe's help) in *A Quip for an
Upstart Courtier*. Nashe himself was adopting the Marprelate posture of the anti-rhetorician; the first great assault on Harvey begins,
mockingly, 'The learned Orator in this Epistle *taketh precise order*
he will not be too eloquent, and yet it shall be (L,) *as well for
enditing unworthie to be published, as for publishing unworthie to*

be endited',[5] and later in *Strange Newes* he echoes Martin's claims to stylistic originality with the boast that 'the vaine which I have (be it a *median* vaine, or a madde man) is of my owne begetting'.[6] It is in this kind of literary climate that Shakespeare began his writing career, and while nobody would deny that rhetorical patterning is an important element in his prose, an exclusive application of the criteria of school rhetoric to the comic scenes of the Falstaff plays must disregard the very innovations which make those scenes the masterpieces they are. To tackle the prose style of *Henry IV* in the same way as one might analyse that of *Euphues and his England* is to pretend that Wolfe's Aretino, the Marprelate controversy, Nashe, and the vogue for satire in general, had never happened.

A considerable while ago, L. M. Buell, asking whether there was 'a prose period in Shakespeare's career', pointed out that 'eleven of the twelve plays usually ascribed to the years between 1596 and 1604 show each over 1000 lines of prose',[7] but he added that his conjectures as to why this should be so he would keep to himself. The period is, of course, the hey-day of satirical comedy: 1596 saw the publication of the first pamphlet clearly inspired by Nashe (Lodge's *Wits Miserie*) and 1597 the staging of the first 'humours' comedy (Chapman's *An Humorous Day's Mirth*). But there is no need to re-tread the ground covered in the previous two chapters. What I am now concerned with is the central question of Shakespeare's debt to Nashe and the extent to which the comic prose of the two *Henry IV* plays and *The Merry Wives of Windsor* displays the various aspects of the grotesque which I have been considering.

The first question we must ask is the likelihood of such an influence. It is worth noting, for a start, that Nashe does appear to have had some connection with the Chamberlain's Men. In his letter to William Cotton, written, significantly, in late 1596, he says:[8]

In towne I stayd (being earnestly invited elsewhere) upon had I wist hopes, & an after harvest I expected by writing for the stage & for the presse, when now the players as if they had writt another Christs tears, are piteously persecuted by the L. Maior & the aldermen, & however in there old Lords tyme they thought there state setled, it is now so uncertayne they cannot build upon it.

And we should remember, too, the immense prestige – or notoriety – which Nashe enjoyed at this time. After the deaths of Greene (1592) and Marlowe (1593) he was the most celebrated professional writer in London: *Pierce Penilesse* went through at least five impressions between 1592 and 1595; in 1597 even an enemy was prepared to 'graunt that you are famous, and that the Countrey reports you wise',[9] and by the end of the decade he had become the hero of the students who wrote the Parnassus plays. In the absence of any considerable drama, bar that of Shakespeare, in the middle years of the decade the literary battle between Nashe and Harvey provided spectacular entertainment of a different kind. It was a re-run of the Marprelate controversy conducted at a more sophisticated stylistic level. There is a self-consciousness about the pamphlets which certainly recommends their description as flyting, and there is a stagy, exhibitionist quality in the exchanges which is strongly suggestive of theatrical dialogue. The quarrel, in fact, attempted to turn journalism into drama, and its influence, along with the influence of Nashe's other pamphlets, is felt almost immediately in the growth of satirical comedy – drama which thrived on the low realism and invective techniques of the pamphleteers. In these circumstances it is highly improbable that Shakespeare was unaware of what Nashe was doing, and in writing *I Henry IV* in the winter of 1596–7, with its rhapsodies of grotesque abuse and its splendid evocation of low life in the city, he seems to be deliberately following that lead. After all, his instincts as a writer of comedy before this time were thoroughly romantic; Falstaff, though not without prototypes, declares a sharp switch of direction. One begins to wonder, thinking again of Nashe's hopes of 'writing for the stage' in autumn 1596, not whether, but how closely, he and Shakespeare were associated.

Nor is there a lack of Nasheian echoes and allusions in the Falstaff plays. Dover Wilson in his edition of *I Henry IV* devoted an appendix to 'Parallels from Nashe' in the two plays (and F. P. Wilson added a couple more in his revision of McKerrow). Dover Wilson, however, was curiously reticent about his findings: 'I have no explanation to offer', he writes, 'though making a few general observations on the problem in *The Library*, June 1945'.[10] These observations amount to the single suggestion, in the case of Nashe, that he may have had a hand in *The Famous Victories of Henry V* (c. 1588) which became one of Shakespeare's sources for *Henry IV*. Dover Wilson is at a loss here because he appears to have no interest in the literary developments of the decade: he cannot see why Nashe is, in a sense, *the* literary figure of the 1590s. And he cannot see this because he hates Nashe: 'We . . . happen to detest his style', he declares in his introduction to *Love's Labour's Lost*.[11] It is hardly surprising that Nashe's importance as a comic writer has been unrecognised when the scholar who has painstakingly discovered so many 'parallels from Nashe' is also the critic who discourages any further discussion of the subject.

But does anything in Shakespeare before *Henry IV* have a Nasheian flavour? Dover Wilson attributes the Jack Cade scenes in *Henry VI*, part two (1590–1) to Nashe, and while the weight of modern opinion is against this view[12] it is not difficult to see why he held it. The low scenes in the play sparkle with the comic devices which fascinated Nashe – absurd parodies of rhetoric, abuses of logic, festive motifs and the use of grotesquely physical language. In his first attempt at rabble-rousing, for instance, Cade 'vows reformation' in the illogical, saturnalian manner which Nashe enjoyed so much: 'There shall be in England seven half-penny loaves sold for a penny; the three-hoop'd pot shall have ten hoops; and I will make it felony to drink small beer'[13] (IV. ii. 62–6). The festive obedience of law to pleasure and the theme of licensed excess are expressed in a very similar way in the preface to *The Unfortunate Traveller*: 'It shalbe flat treason for anie of this fore-mentioned catalogue of the point trussers once to name him [Wilton] within fortie foote of an alehouse: marry, the taverne is honorable.'[14] The voice of Falstaff on the rampage, declaring that 'the laws of England are at my commandment' (*2 Henry IV*, V. iv. 134–5), is not far off, nor is the saturnalia of *Bartholomew Fair*.

Festive motifs in the Cade scenes, in Nashe, and in the Marprelate controversy have been excellently described by C. L. Barber in *Shakespeare's Festive Comedy*, though in the case of Nashe he is concerned exclusively with *Summer's Last Will and Testament*. I add merely this suggestion: behind a figure like Cade, or Nashe's John Leiden in *The Unfortunate Traveller*, or in the characterisation of Martin Marprelate by his opponents, is the tradition of the comic religious leaders who flourished in popular risings during the sixteenth century and for a while after; as D. G. Allan puts it, they were 'combinations as it were, of biblical saviours and lords of misrule'.[15] One such character is described by Edmond Howes in his account of the 1607 riots against enclosures. These were led by a certain Captain Pouch, who boasted that 'hee was directed by the lord of Heaven', and was so called[16]

> because of a great leather powch which he wore by his side, in which purse hee affirmed to his company, that there was sufficient matter to defend them against all commers, but afterward when hee was apprehended, his Powch was searched and therein was onely a peece of greene cheese.

Nashe would have delighted in such a deflation – claims to divine authority reduced to a lump of cheese – and there is much of that spirit in the Cade scenes, as the rebels' derisive comments on Cade's pretensions (IV. ii) show. But it is the Marprelate controversy which perhaps offers the clearest literary parallel in its constant association of religious protest and saturnalia, and is the immediate precedent for similar characters in Nashe and Shakespeare. And, when placed in the tradition of the religious leader as clown or fool, Martin Marprelate clearly stimulates that transition from sermon to satire during the 1590s in which Nashe played such a central part.

The other feature of the Cade scenes which links them to the Marprelate controversy, and hence to Nashe, is their treatment of violence. The rebels have a fund of abattoir humour which reduces their warlike aspirations to a grotesque extension of their more humble daily occupations. As they congregate at Blackheath, Bevis observes of 'Best's son, the tanner of Wingham' that 'He shall have the skins of our enemies to make dog's leather of' (IV. ii. 21–3), and after the fight with the Staffords Cade compliments Dick the butcher on his professional skills: 'They fell before thee like sheep and oxen, and thou behavedst thyself, as if thou hadst been in thine own slaughterhouse' (IV. iii. 3–5). He promises to reward him with a licence to kill during Lent. While these violent quips are thoroughly in the vein of the anti-Marprelate pamphleteers it is only in so far as he may have formed part of that group that Nashe is likely to have had any influence on Shakespeare at this stage. The most Nasheian moment in the play is Cade's swaggering defiance of Iden, the Kentish landowner in whose garden he has

been hiding out: 'Steel, if thou turn the edge, or cut not out the
burly-bon'd clown in chines of beef ere thou sleep in thy sheath,
I beseech God on my knees thou mayst be turn'd to hobnails'
(IV. x. 55–9). The sheer pace of this grotesque travesty of heroic
invocation, its vigorous alliteration and low imagery all combine
to produce an oddly unShakespearean effect. But if we accept the
basic integrity of the *Henry VI* trilogy then that unShakespearean
quality can best be attributed, again, to the influence of the Marprelate controversy. The word 'burly-bon'd', for instance, was
coined by the author of *An Almond for a Parrat* (1589–90) and is
not found elsewhere in Shakespeare; it is, however, used twice by
Nashe[17] and Nashe probably wrote *An Almond for a Parrat* in the
first place. But without further entangling the issue I think we can
conclude that, whether or not Shakespeare was responsible for
Henry VI in its entirety, and he probably was, he was certainly
aware of the stylistic innovations of the Marprelate controversy,
and that he realised the literary potential of these. The extent to
which he was indebted specifically to Nashe depends upon the
extent of Nashe's involvement in that controversy – a fact which
we cannot determine.

Two or three years later, however, we do have what looks very
like a pastiche of Nashe in *Love's Labour's Lost* (1593–4):[18]

> No, my complete master; but to jig off a tune at the tongue's
> end . . . with your hat penthouse-like o'er the shop of your
> eyes, with your arms cross'd on your thin-belly doublet, like
> a rabbit on a spit, or your hands in your pocket, like a man
> after the old painting; and keep not too long in one tune, but
> a snip and away. (III. i. 10–17)

The speaker is Moth, a precocious and evidently voluble page boy,
and an extraordinary amount of scholarly energy has been ex-
pended in demonstrating that he 'is' or 'is not' also Nashe.[19] Why
the play should demand *à clef* interpretations of this kind is uncertain. What is clear is that Shakespeare has appropriated Nashe's
style, in a play which sparkles with verbal ingenuity and display,
to sketch a picture of the brash sophistication of a youthful word-
spinner. Moth may not be Nashe, but he has read the highly
fashionable *Pierce Penilesse*, and learnt a certain deftness in using
the urban detail (penthouses) and the grotesque (spitted rabbits)
for the purposes of caricature. The other aspect of Nashe which

appears in *Love's Labour's Lost* is the Nashe of the anti-Harvey pamphlets. *Strange Newes* had recently been published, as had Harvey's reply, *Pierces Supererogation*, and much of the interest in the uses and abuses of language which pervades the play can be attributed to the stir these pamphlets caused. The extraordinary coinages ('infamonize' is Armado's distortion of Nashe's 'infamize'[20]), the quibbling and parody, elaborate abuse such as Costard's 'thou halfpenny purse of wit, thou pigeon egg of discretion' (V. i. 62–3), and the constant testing of formal rhetoric as a vehicle for truth are the immediate product of the Nashe–Harvey flyting. Their pamphlets harp endlessly on matters of style – individual words, modes of expression. *Love's Labour's Lost* continues this vein, and the joint opinion of Moth and Costard on the insatiable pedantry of Holofernes and Armado is couched in suitably scathing, and Nasheian, terms:

> *Moth.* [*Aside to Costard*] They have been at a
>   great feast of languages and stol'n the scraps.
> *Cost.* O, they have liv'd long on the alms-basket
>   of words. I marvel thy master has not eaten thee
>   for a word. (V. i. 33–6)

The solidification of language into food, of incontinent talking into hungry feeding, is a comic grotesque device which bears an unmistakably Nasheian stamp.

But *Love's Labour's Lost* is not a play which generally reveals much interest in the physicality of language. True, there is sexual innuendo, but the sexuality is submerged; the surface is intricate, rather than dense, and the imagery fanciful. What the play chiefly derives from Nashe is his fascinated probing of the varieties of literary construction and, above all, a self-consciousness about the misuse of language which is quite untypical of earlier dramatists. This is not the case with *The Taming of the Shrew* (1594–5): flyting in *Love's Labour's Lost* is shadow boxing; in this play verbal vituperation is indivisibly fused with physical punishment. Even the title – *The Taming of the Shrew* – is suggestive of an Elizabethan invective pamphlet such as *The Trimming of Thomas Nashe*, and the play itself is full of Nasheian mannerisms. It is the first play to occupy some common ground with the early satirical journalism, as opposed to merely echoing it. The stinging flurry of puns which Petruchio and Katherina exchange at their meeting (II. i) bears out the style of intercourse suggested earlier by Grumio:

> I'll tell you what, sir: and she stand him but a little, he will throw a figure in her face, and so disfigure her with it that she shall have no more eyes to see withal than a cat. (I. ii. 109–13)

(Compare Nashe's remark on Harvey in *Strange Newes*, 'he hath some good words, but he cannot writhe them and tosse them to and fro nimbly, or so bring them about, that hee maye make one streight thrust at his enemies face', McKerrow, *The Works of Thomas Nashe*, I, 282.) And Petruchio's role in the play is to act the part of the fashionable 'railing' character, though rarely with the imaginative verve of Nashe, it must be admitted. 'A whoreson, beetle-headed, flap-ear'd knave!' (IV. ii. 142) is fairly typical of the standard of his abuse.

Apart from railing, Petruchio's strategy of domestication consists of depressing Katherina's spirits through exhibitions of squalor. And, as the first prose-poet of the sordid and disreputable, Nashe comes inevitably to Shakespeare's mind. On his wedding day Petruchio arrives in a state of piece-meal dilapidation reminiscent of a caricature from *Pierce Penilesse*:

> Why, Petruchio is coming – in a new hat and an old jerkin; a pair of old breeches thrice turn'd; a pair of boots that have been candle-cases, one buckled, another lac'd; an old rusty sword ta'en out of the town armoury, with a broken hilt, and chapeless; with two broken points; his horse . . . with a half-cheek'd bit, and a head-stall of sheep's leather which, being restrain'd to keep him from stumbling, hath been often burst, and now repaired with knots; one girth six times piec'd, and a woman's crupper of velure, which hath two letters for her name fairly set down in studs, and here and there piec'd with pack-thread. (III. ii. 41–59)

Milton Crane is puzzled by this passage, finding it to be 'not Shakespeare's familiar comic prose style';[21] it is, of course, an imitation of Nasheian 'gallymaufry' and echoes the descriptions of Dame Niggardize, which we have seen already, and, more closely, John Leiden:[22]

That day come, flourishing entred *John Leiden* the Botcher
into the field, with a scarffe made of lysts like a bow-case, a
crosse on hys breast like a thred bottome, a round twilted
Taylors cushion buckled like a Tankard-bearers device to his
shoulders for a target, the pyke whereof was a pack-needle
. . . and on his head for a helmet a huge high shooe with the
bottome turnd upwards, embossed as full of hob-nayles as
ever it might sticke.

This is remarkably similar to the Shakespeare passage, where the
elaboration of shabby domestic paraphernalia pressed into cavalier
service (old jerkins, candle-cases and pack-thread are typically
Nasheian lumber), and the inflation of each successive period with
a new excess of detail, produces a set piece in the low style. And
it is a set piece which, in terms of contemporary literature, is
consciously modish. During the early and middle part of the decade
Shakespeare seems to be tentatively exploring the comic potential
of garrulity: the preciosity of Arcadian rhetoric is gradually being
tested against the sprawling energy of Nashe's prose. The infusion
of physicality into displays of wit, the increasing prominence of
flyting as a dramatic element,[23] and a sense of the crowdedness of
language are signals, in these early plays of Shakespeare, of a
stylistic development which is to culminate in the Falstaff plays.

The development of the low style in these earlier plays is ultimately reflected in their attention to the comic uses of incongruity.
The background of festive comedy sanctions the burlesque which
up-ends the social hierarchy, turning labourers into aristocrats,
aristocrats into knaves. Jack Cade's regal aspirations threaten to
topple that hierarchy, but they are also constantly undercut by the
ineptitude of his language. The humbler characters in *Love's
Labour's Lost* try vainly to portray the greatest heroes of antiquity
in their little show, and Christopher Sly in the introduction to *The
Taming of the Shrew* wakes from a drunken stupor to find that he
is no longer a tinker from Burton-heath but a great lord. Petruchio,
on the other hand, socially degrades himself, disguising his nobility
with a show of boorish and slovenly behaviour. In their various
ways these characters all foreshadow Falstaff while remaining
merely shadows of that incomparably greater figure; but the closest
parallel is perhaps Nashe's cider merchant in *The Unfortunate
Traveller* ('his great velvet breeches larded with the droppinges of

this daintie liquor, & yet he was an old servitor, a cavelier of an ancient house'[24]) in whom the two elements of addiction to drink and disgraced nobility are combined. But the use of the low style to dramatise incongruities of this sort is not (*pace* Vickers, pp. 26–7) intended to be simply a vehicle for ridicule – unambiguous ridicule is not, anyway, a tone which Shakespeare frequently adopts. These experiments are a prelude to the fully developed comic prose of the Falstaff plays, and it is the richness of his language which magnifies, rather than diminishes, Falstaff himself. The incongruities which are the basis of burlesque, distended by images drawn from the world of the body, become grotesque.

2   THE DRAMA OF THE BODY: *Henry IV, part one*

I Henry IV is the first English play to find a major imaginative stimulus in the disreputable. While the prodigal son plays, which were performed throughout the sixteenth century, did venture into the world of tavern and brothel, they did so chiefly by implication, paying scant attention to the physical detail of those worlds; to do otherwise, even had it been possible, would have brought into question the function of the disreputable as a goad to moral indignation. But with the beginning of satirical journalism the disreputable begins to acquire what is almost a comic poetry of its own, severed, if not always from the moralistic (since its function is now satirical), at least from the homiletic. Greene's cony-catching pamphlets, tavern scenes – and much else – in Nashe, and some of Harvey's more malicious gossip about the social lives of those two authors provide the raw material for the comedy of *Henry IV*. One thinks of Harvey's account of Greene's death following a 'banquet of pickle herring' and of 'his riotous and outragious surfeitinge; his continuall shifting of lodginges [and] . . . his imployinge of Ball (surnamed cuttinge Ball) . . . to guarde him in daunger of Arrestes'.[25] And there is Richard Lichfield's description of Nashe and a crony called Lusher down and out in London:[26]

> you remember the time when your fellowe *Lusher* and you lay in coleharbour together, when you had but one payre of breeches betweene you both, but not one penie to blesse you both, and howe by course hee woore the breeches one day,

and went cunny-catching about for victuals, whilest you lay in bedde, and the next day you wore the breeches to goe begge whilest he lay in bed; for all the worlde like two bucketes in one well.

Passages like these convey something of the new feeling for the less salubrious urban life styles; in both there is a strong element of bohemianism, and it is 'the chimes at midnight' that we hear echoing in the background.

This bohemian quality is the first thing that would have struck a contemporary audience of *I Henry IV* as novel. After a fairly conventional opening, scene two begins with a shock. A major character, a nobleman, is introduced lying on the floor in a drunken doze, waking, at last, to address the heir to the throne with the words 'Now, Hal, what time of day is it, lad?'. And the prince replies:

> What a devil hast thou to do with the time of the day? Unless hours were cups of sack, and minutes capons, and clocks the tongues of bawds, and dials the signs of leaping-houses, and the blessed sun himself a fair hot wench in flame-coloured taffeta, I see no reason why thou shouldst be so superfluous to demand the time of the day.

Falstaff's physical excesses sabotage the carefully punctuated routines of respectability, but his disreputable behaviour is not a cause for moral concern. Nobody could mistake the tone here: mock-aggressive, amused, indulgent; nor can we doubt Hal's reception of the remark that he and Falstaff are 'squires of the night's body . . . gentlemen of the shade' – 'Thou sayest well', he replies. Probably for the first time in English drama an audience is not expected to shake their heads in disapproval before an exhibition of prodigality. And this is due, in part at least, to Nashe's exploitation of the disreputable as a source of comedy. This first encounter between Falstaff and Hal is probably based on reminiscences of *Summers Last Will and Testament*: compare, for instance, 'What have we to doe with scales and hower-glasses, except we were Bakers or Clocke-keepers? I cannot tell how other men are addicted, but it is against my profession to . . . keepe any howers but dinner or supper. It is a pedanticall thing to respect times and seasons'; 'This is the last stroke my toungs clock must strike', and

'There is no such fine time to play the knave in as the night'.[27] And although the spirit of the old moral interlude remains in this play's judgment of the prodigals, Ver and Bacchus, there is also enough of Nashe's exuberant documentation of the bohemian way of life to establish a tone for Shakespeare.

The rest of the scene reveals a further aspect of the disreputable life style which Hal has adopted – a taste for lewd or grotesque word-play. And we are struck too, perhaps, by the sheer self-consciousness of the banter:

> *Prince* . . . is not a buff jerkin a most sweet robe of durance?
> *Fal.* How now, how now, mad wag! What, in thy quips and
> quiddities? What a plague have I to do with a buff jerkin?
> (I. ii. 40–5)

Hal's obscene pun[28] eludes Falstaff at first, and he can only splutter a complaint about this verbal dexterity. The games continue with an exchange of grotesque similes to which Falstaff again draws attention: 'Thou hast the most unsavoury similes, and art indeed the most comparative, rascalliest, sweet young prince' and, finally: 'O, thou hast damnable iteration, and art indeed able to corrupt a saint'. Although Falstaff is himself a master of 'quips and quiddities' and also adept at palming off his own faults on to others, his characterisation of Hal as a rather risqué word-juggler is wholly accurate. What Shakespeare is doing here is dramatising the fashion for pungent verbal display which pamphlets and satires had already introduced. Hal's 'unsavoury similes', which he calls 'base comparisons' (II. iv. 243), are what Nashe calls 'comparative tearmes', and as I have argued above, they are a staple of the low style in Elizabethan comic prose and hence of the grotesque. This scene in particular, and the play in general, is the culmination of the developing taste for the low style that we find in Aretino, in the Marprelate controversy, in Donne's satires and, of course, in the Nashe–Harvey quarrel. Nashe describes it as 'a new kind of a quicke fight, which your [Harvey's] decrepite slow-moving capacitie cannot fadge with'.[29] It is just such a quick fight in which Hal and Falstaff are engaged, and it is natural that the younger man should at first appear to be the more dexterous of the two. Brian Vickers's argument that it is Falstaff who is being mocked for his grotesque word play is surely a misreading:[30] moralistic commendations of Hal based, retrospectively, on the rejection scene at the end of part two simply do not correspond with his portrayal at the beginning of part one. (I am not referring to the devious and unconvincing piece of self-justification at the end of I. ii.) Quite apart from the tone of Hal's language, we should remember that 'Where shall we take a purse to-morrow' (I. ii. 96) is his suggestion, not Falstaff's. To see in that and every other remark of Hal's concealed ironies which detach him from the licence of his companions and inoculate him against the moral corruption of his chosen style of life is to pretend that Hal does not actually enjoy that style of life. In Shakespeare's play he clearly does.

The typical form that the grotesque word games take in *I Henry IV* is flyting. The comic invective with which Shakespeare had been experimenting earlier in the 1590s now becomes a structural element in the drama. For flyting is not confined to the low world of Eastcheap: the extended skirmishes between Hal and Falstaff are reproduced in Hotspur's violent attacks on Glendower:

> O, he is as tedious
> As a tired horse, a railing wife;
> Worse than a smoky house; I had rather live
> With cheese and garlic in a windmill, far. (III. i. 159–62)

Hotspur's indignation explodes the rhythms of blank verse into the more segmented pattern of comic prose, and the low imagery, concluding with the ridiculous and fanciful 'windmill', indicates just how powerfully Nashe's influence is being felt. Just as Falstaff himself threatens to topple the main plot into a subsidiary position, so Nasheian modes of comic invective invade the blank verse of the play to an extent which would have been inconceivable a few years earlier. The conventional argument that Shakespeare uses prose to relegate his characters to an inferior dramatic status looks odd indeed when applied to *I Henry IV*.

One reason why flyting is such a pervasive dramatic element in the play is the stimulus of Nashe's masterpiece of vituperation, *Have With You to Saffron-Walden*, published shortly before-hand in 1596 – there are reminiscences of this, too, in the Hotspur scenes, as I shall show presently – and some of the more grotesque imagery which Nashe uses to compose his picture of Harvey is reworked by Shakespeare in Hal's battles with Falstaff. In *Have With You* Nashe brilliantly demolishes both Harvey and his book,

Pierces Supererogation, by contrasting the meagreness of the one with the sheer obesity of the other. The book is[31]

> an unconscionable vast gorbellied Volume, bigger bulkt than a Dutch Hoy, & farre more boystrous and cumbersome than a payre of *Swissers* omnipotent galeaze breeches. But it shuld seeme he is asham'd of the incomprehensible corpulencie thereof

and it is 'a *Gargantuan* bag-pudding' stuffed with tripes. Harvey himself, however, is mean and shrivelled, 'a dride scate-fish' and 'more channels & creases he hath in his face than there be Fairie circles on *Salsburie Plaine*'.[32] This is a superb inversion of the traditional notion of a 'dry' book, which transfers, instead, the desiccation to the author and expands his creation into a gross and unctuous monstrosity. Contrasts of this kind filter through much of the imagery of Hal and Falstaff's flytings. Falstaff the 'stuff'd cloak-bag of guts' sets his huge bulk against the 'starveling' Hal: 'you eel-skin, you dried neat's tongue, you bull's pizzle, you stock-fish', he fulminates (II. iv. 237–8). And Falstaff, well-oiled and well-liquored, is contrasted in part two with Hal, the drinker of small beer. The flytings are physical engagements, battles between the fat and the lean.

Shakespeare also redeploys Nashe's imagery of the fat and the lean to emphasise its festive connotations of Carnival and Lent, and it is through such connotations that moralistic interpretations of Hal and Falstaff's battles begin to appear irrelevant. The Lenten imagery associated with Hal (eel-skins, stock-fish and small beer) and used by Falstaff to describe an improbable alter-ego (herrings, bunches of radish, gurnets and peppercorns) forms the traditional army of Lent; likewise, the tripes, the ribs and tallow, and the 'sweet beef' (i.e. fresh and juicy, not salted or 'powdered') which fill the frame of Falstaff are the army of Carnival. The slower development of printing in sixteenth-century England has meant that, by comparison with the Continent, little popular literature of this kind now survives. However, the description of a battle between Carnival and Lent in John Taylor's *Jack a Lent, His Beginning and Entertainment* (1620) indicates that this was an English tradition. In most versions[33] of the battle Lent is the aggressor because she believes that Carnival is diminishing her power, and in most cases Lent is finally defeated. There is never any approval

of Lent's association with moral rectitude: in French versions of
the story she is 'le felon . . . fel et anïeus' or 'Triste, hydeux'[34] ['The
cruel and spiteful wretch', 'gloomy, hideous'] and Rabelais's Quaresmeprenant 'pleure les troys pars du jour'[35] ['weeps for three
quarters of the day']. Lent is defeated because her followers, fish
and vegetables, lack the restorative succulence of meat and wine
(compare Falstaff's speech in praise of sherris-sack) and are unable
to resist the warm vitality of Carnival. Consequently, Falstaff's
great harangue in the Boar's Head tavern:

> If sack and sugar be a fault, God help the wicked! If to be
> old and merry be a sin, then many an old host that I know
> is damn'd; if to be fat be to be hated, then Pharoah's lean
> kine are to be loved, No . . . Banish plump Jack, and banish
> all the world (II. iv. 445–63)

appears, in the context of the preceding imagery, as a splendid
affirmation of the power of Carnival. Hal's sour rejoinder in the
role of his sick and ageing father ('I do, I will') may remind us of
a different kind of power, the inflexible power of regal authority,
but in dramatic terms it does nothing to obliterate the sense of
triumphant obesity which Falstaff has created of his person, and
that sense remains undiminished throughout *I Henry IV*. The play's
view of the grossly physical is, like that of Rabelais, celebratory.

The coalescence in Falstaff of wit and gross physicality makes
him the supreme dramatic embodiment of the Elizabethan grotesque, and although he is a creation far beyond the dramatic
powers of Nashe he is nevertheless a product of Nashe's achievements in comic prose. Verbal ingenuity which takes as its counters
the baser aspects of the body, its fuel and waste, is a peculiar
species of wit because it operates at a level so far removed from
the purely cerebral that it assumes an almost plastic quality. And
it is a species of wit peculiar to the sixteenth century. Analogies
between Bruegel and Rabelais or Bruegel and Nashe are meaningful
because the writers are exploring the physicality of language and
its ability to work in a solid and visual way. Nashe's coinages
which attempt to reproduce the physical quality of the thing they
denote; Aretino's grotesquely concrete descriptions of the process
of literary composition; John Eliot's imaginative linking of corporal
dismemberment and plagiarism; even the frozen words in
Rabelais's account of the arctic voyate in the *Quart Livre*: all these

instances (see chapter two above) imply what could almost be called a non-verbal experience of language, or, at any rate, a driving of language from the mental to the physical. They represent an incarnative view of language, the word becoming flesh. The first word which Hal uses to describe Falstaff – 'fat-witted' – is of this kind. Literally, of course, the word simply means 'stupid', but Falstaff is not stupid; he is 'fat-witted' in a larger sense, and this the play goes on to reveal. (An image which neatly associates the verbal and the physical in Falstaff is Hal's 'Peace, chewet, peace!' (V. i. 29). A 'chewet' could mean both a jackdaw, and hence any chatterer, and a meat pie.) He is also an Elizabethan paradox. John Huarte echoes the accepted view of the relation of mental power to physical girth when he says that:[36]

> Galen alleageth a proverbe which sayth, A grosse bellie makes a grosse understanding, and that this proceeds from nothing else, than that the brain and the stomacke are united and chained together with certaine sinewes, by way of which they interchangeably communicat their dammages.

Falstaff's brain and stomach are united, but the one inspires the other; this fact is established by Hal when he exposes Falstaff's fantastic version of the robbery at Gadshill: 'These lies are like their father that begets them – gross as a mountain, open, palpable. Why, thou clay-brain'd guts, thou knotty-pated fool' (II. iv. 218–20). Again, Hal is only trying to say that Falstaff's blatant lies are foolishly conceived, but the way in which he says it tells us something about the comic language of the play. And the father of Shakespeare's attempts to render the word as flesh is Nashe: 'Had they been wittie lies, or merry lies, they would never have greev'd mee: but palpable lies, damned lies, lies as big as one of the Guardes chynes of beefe, who can abide?'[37] That borrowing argues an identity of purpose in the two writers more forcibly, I think, than any other. The paradox of Falstaff is exemplified by the paradox of Nashe's own comic prose in that it is a verbal medium which produces its grotesque effects from a striving towards physical embodiment.

The main focus of the comedy in *I Henry IV* is, of course, Falstaff's own body, and the different ways in which both Hal and Falstaff himself explore its monstrous substance form a compendium of the grotesque imagery scattered throughout the works of

Rabelais, Nashe and Nashe's imitators. The first of these image clusters I want to consider is that of sweat and grease:

> Falstaff sweats to death
> And lards the lean earth as he walks along (II. ii. 104–5)

says Hal after the ambush at Gadshill. He is mere 'tallow' (II. iv. 107), and then a 'whoreson obscene greasy tallow-catch'(221); when he drinks he resembles the sun melting a dish of butter (114–16), while being himself as 'fat as butter' (493). The dissolution of Falstaff's body into grease and its transformation into roasting meat[38] is typical of the grotesque metamorphoses which Nashe's victims of disease undergo. In his account of the sweating sickness in *The Unfortunate Traveller* we learn that 'Cookes that stand continually basting their faces before the fire, were now all cashierd with this sweat into kitchin stuffe';[39] the consumptive in *The Terrors of the Night* is described as if 'a man should be rosted to death, and melt away by little and little'.[40] But within the syndrome of images connected with grease Falstaff's malleable body occupies a less macabre area than either these or the dripping brawn of Dekker's plague victims. The sermonising element which forces the sinister tone in the pamphlets is rarely a feature of Shakespearean comedy. Nor does Falstaff in this play convert his kitchen stuff into the sexual greasiness of similar imagery in satirical comedy. One might, for instance, compare John Taylor's description in *Jack a Lent, His Beginning and Entertainment*:[41]

> Moreover, it is a goodly sight to see how the Cookes in great mens kitchins, doe fry in their masters suet, and sweat in their own grease, that if ever a Cooke be worth the eating, it is when Shrove Tuesday is in town, for he is so stued and larded, roasted, basted, and almost over-roasted, that a man may eate the rawest bit of him and never take a surfet.

The fatty foods of Carnival are celebrated in the style of *The Shoemaker's Holiday* rather than the style of *Blurt, Master Constable*, and it is Hal, the starveling, the Jack of Lent, who affirms this aspect of the Falstaffian grotesque in his description of Sir John's sweating to death. The image acquires, in its festive context, the richer connotations of fertility, and that fertility is the product of Falstaff's Carnival role in part one. The grease which is the token of his decomposition replenishes and gives life to 'the lean earth'; nothing better fits C. L. Barber's description of him as the Carnival lord whose ultimate sacrifice brings health to an ailing, sterile community.[42]

The other positive aspect of Falstaff's constant exudation is its natural association with laughter. In the sixteenth century, unlike the eighteenth century, laughter was considered to be a beneficial and therapeutic form of physical activity;[43] and at the Montpellier medical school, where Rabelais was a student and later a teacher, serious study was devoted to the subject. Laurent Joubert, a member of the same school, explains:[44]

> Cette meme chaleur, fait quelque chose d'avantage an la matiere de la graisse. Car il la cuit, & an cuisant l'epaissit, la randant de samblable couleur aus parties qu'elle s'attache. . . .
> Or si cela et, & la même chaleur humide (qui accompagne le sang copieus) nous rand anclins au Ris, comme cy dessus nous avons assegné, de même source procederont l'habilité à rire, & l'amas de la graisse.
> [This same heat does something further in the matter of grease. For it cooks it, and in cooking it thickens it, turning it to the same colour as the parts to which it is attached. . . . Now if that is so, and that same moist heat which accompanies copious blood makes us inclined to laughter, as we have said above, it is clear that a propensity to laughter and an excess of grease come from the same source.]

The notion of fat (suet) melting to produce grease (sweat) – the words were homophonic in English – is taken a stage further as Joubert attributes laughter, too, to the cooking process. The theory weaves another strand in the grotesque links between the happy, feasting body and its capacity to resemble the things it consumes.

Despite the festive associations of Falstaff's greasiness it is not a quality to which he draws attention himself in *I Henry IV*. His own inventions upon his body are more bizarre. The oaths he scatters offer a profusion of improbable images of himself: 'if manhood, good manhood, be not forgot upon the face of the earth, then am I a shotten herring' (II. iv. 123–4); 'if I fought not with fifty of them, I am a bunch of radish' (II. iv. 178–9); 'An I have not forgotten what the inside of a church is made of, I am a peppercorn, a brewer's horse' (III. iii. 7–9); 'If I be not ashamed of my soldiers, I am a sous'd gurnet' (IV. ii. 10–11). These are, in part, a continuation of the fat–lean, Carnival–Lenten theme in the play, with the astringency of the gurnet's vinegar providing a neat antithesis to the image of Falstaff as 'sweet beef', steeped in liquid fat. But their grotesqueness is not confined to that theme. In this most pictorial play the deliberate incompatibility of the thin and the tiny with that 'huge hill of flesh' (II. iv. 236) creates a sense of alternate shrinkage and dilation in the image of Falstaff's body, and both instability of physical form and the confusion of the relative size of things are important features of grotesque art. As Wolfgang Kayser observes, in the grotesque 'laws of statics, symmetry and proportion are no longer valid'.[45] Hence in Rabelais one can never be sure just how big the giants are; Pantagruel can be small enough not to sink the ship he sails in, yet large enough for another world to exist beyond the frontiers of his mouth. In Bruegel's drawings, especially those influenced by Bosch, tiny men appear from the orifices of huge, floating heads, and outsize penknives are wielded by diminutive soldiers. As the images of Falstaff oscillate between the monstrous and the minute we receive the same impression of grotesque size-shifting.

This brand of oath, which relies for its effect upon the comic incongruity of the image, is relatively undisturbing, but there is another kind which threatens the violation of Falstaff's body in a more alarming manner. Falstaff's witty exploitation of his own corpulence implies a fusion of mind and matter, a 'fat-wittedness', but the readiness with which he sees himself in non-human terms also severs the natural association of self and the physical case which self inhabits. When Hal tells him to lie down during the ambush at Gadshill and he replies, 'Have you any levers to lift me up again, being down?', the inert heap he creates of himself suggests a lack of any sense of his physical integrity. Consequently, the grotesque amplifications which issue from his devising mind run carelessly towards physical self-destruction: 'hang me up by the heels for a rabbit-sucker or a poulter's hare' (II. iv. 421–2) he declares, if Hal's impersonation of the king should outdo his own. And, as so often in Elizabethan grotesque, images drawn from the butcher's shop resurface in culinary form; by act five he is saying that if he comes voluntarily in Hotspur's way during the battle, 'let him make a carbonado of me'[46] (V. iii. 55; i.e. meat scored across and broiled). In the following scene the last stage in this series of grotesque transformations is reached. Feigning death, he hears Hal pay his last respects and promise to 'embowel' (thus to embalm) his own entirely sensible body. He 'riseth up' and, as he comes to life, protests to Hal in terms which land him from the food shop on to the dining table: 'Embowell'd! If thou embowel me to-day, I'll give you leave to powder me and eat me tomorrow'[47] (V. iv. 111–13). The point is that Falstaff, as much as Hal, is the author of these metamorphoses, and it is through his manipulation of his own physical parts that he achieves the rare status of comic hero. In comedy it is generally the clown who is the passive butt of pretended or actual physical violation, but he has no part in its authorisation, while in tragedy the hero mentally anatomises himself in a struggle towards wholeness. It is Falstaff's combination of these roles, as he dismembers and amplifies himself, which is the chief source of his greatness.

It is not Falstaff himself, however, but Falstaff's body which has a monopoly of the grotesque in *I Henry IV* and there is a further category of image, not of his own devising, whose function is to destroy the integrity of that huge hill of flesh. This is the kind of image which presents Falstaff as a vessel or container, the finest sequence being Hal's outburst in the Boar's Head: 'Why dost thou converse with that trunk of humours, that bolting-hutch of beastliness, that swoll'n parcel of dropsies, that huge bombard of sack, that stuff'd cloak-bag of guts, that roasted Manningtree ox with the pudding in his belly' (II. iv. 434–8). In each image Falstaff is distended and filled up with extraneous material; he is alterable – a barrel of diseases or a horn of plenty which can be exchanged and replenished in a moment. What is fascinating about this particular sequence, though, is the way in which the varying images pursue a definite course from the one to the other, and hence from the disgusting to the affectionate: the first three speak of 'humours', 'beastliness' and 'dropsies' and the second three of 'sack', 'guts' and puddings. The lines run the gamut of the grotesque from the physically repulsive to the physically exuberant, concluding with the unmistakable image of Carnival (taken from Nashe: 'All the rest of his invention is nothing but an oxe with a pudding in his bellie'[48]) to which Hal, in his dealings with Falstaff, cannot help but return. Furthermore, vessels of all sorts, because they can be stuffed with strange matter and thus violate the integrity of things, are a favourite grotesque device: Bruegel's fish oozing smaller fish

from their slit bellies, his huge eggs broken to reveal strange creatures, and his barrels which sprout legs are typical of the graphic
artist's attempt to create a sense of the foreign body within. So too
are the extraordinary figures which fill the little book called *Les
Songes drolatiques de Pantagruel* (Paris, 1565). Purporting to
illustrate characters from Rabelais and executed in the manner of
Bruegel (or rather in Bruegel's Boschian manner), these weird creations include a cauldron-man who spoons liquid from his own
pot-like belly and a barrel-man spouting from a self-inflicted
wound in his staves. In each instance it is a sense of the body's
organic unity which is being destroyed to create a different, grotesque vision of worlds within worlds. Whether it is the world
within Pantagruel's mouth, or Falstaff's 'stuff'd cloak-bag of guts'
with its suggestion of the stomach as pudding and the pudding as
stuffing for a roast, the vision is the same: the body is not an
integer.

I Henry IV is, then, in a variety of ways a drama of the body,
but before considering how this drama develops in part two, I
want to return to Hotspur and the 'high' scenes of the play. While
these scenes are, of course, written in verse they are infiltrated by
the language of the low scenes in a way which is perhaps unpre-
cedented in Shakespeare. Hotspur, the supposed antithesis of Falstaff and the object of Hal's scornful wit, is neither an inarticulate
oaf nor a sublime martial hero; in fact, the headlong violence of
his speech, its physicality and capacity for caricature are closer to
the language of Eastcheap than seems fitting to the noble figure
which Hotspur cuts in the eyes of some critics. We have noticed
already his taste for base comparisons, and he deplores verbal
gentility even in his wife:

> Not yours, in good sooth! Heart! you swear like a comfit-
> maker's wife . . . . Swear me, Kate, like a lady as thou art,
> A good mouth-filling oath; and leave 'in sooth' And such
> protest of pepper-gingerbread To velvet-guards and
> Sunday-citizens. (III. i. 248–57)

The advice is more in tune with the values of the Boar's Head than
the courtly circle in Wales, and so too is Hotspur's dazzling caricature of the effeminate courtier who was:

> Fresh as a bridegroom, and his chin new reap'd

Show'd like a stubble-land at harvest-home. (I. iii. 34–5)

The cumulative, stabbing detail and the derisive mimicry of his
'bald unjointed chat' is delivered in the same spirit as Hal's own
caricatures of Hotspur in II. iv; though Hal may like to think of
himself as a sophisticate by comparison with Hotspur, their command of the skills of ridicule and invective suggests a closer similarity between them than either would care to admit. (The passage
is too long to quote in full, but it is worth comparing Hotspur's
account of the courtier on the battlefield with Nashe's of clerks
who take dead soldiers' pay in *The Unfortunate Traveller*: 'their
sincere and finigraphicall cleane shirts and cuffes . . . their nere
bitten beards must in a devills name bee dewed everye day with
Rose-water . . . They would in no wise permit that the moates in
the Sunbeames should be full mouthd beholders of their cleane
phinifide apparel; their shooes shined as bright as a slike-stone;
their hands troubled and foyled more water with washing, than
the Cammell doth . . .'.[49]) Moreover, the 'world of figures' which
Hotspur inhabits can even approach the Falstaffian: engaged by
the timid excuses of a defector from his cause, he declares 'O, I
could divide myself and go to buffets for moving such a dish of
skim milk with so honourable an action!' (II. iii. 28–30). That
image of physical severance, with the two halves of the body
battling against each other, is so thoroughly in the style of the
comic grotesque that it is difficult not to associate the remark with
the begetter of similar self-abusing oaths; compare, for instance,
Falstaff's 'If I were sawed into quantities' (*2 Henry IV*, V. i. 57).
The feeling grows, the more we inspect the language of the play,
that the high and low elements are by no means divorced.

For there remains the matter of flyting. After the sparring match
between Hal and Falstaff in act one we have the fulminations of
Hotspur against the king; after the torrential abuse of the scene in
the Boar's Head we have the absurd wrangle between Hotspur and
Glendower. In the first instance only a hesitant comparison can be
made, but in the second the structural parallel is too close to be
merely coincidental. The festive abuse of the sub-plot is clearly
rebounding into the dissensions which permeate the main plot, and
instilling it with the same spirit of grotesque raillery. When Glendower grandly announces the awful cosmic disturbances which
attended his birth, Hotspur retorts:

Diseased nature oftentimes breaks forth
In strange eruptions; oft the teeming earth
Is with a kind of colic pinch'd and vex'd
By the imprisoning of unruly wind
Within her womb; which, for enlargement striving,
Shakes the old beldam earth, and topples down
Steeples and moss-grown towers. At your birth,
Our grandam earth, having this distemp'rature,
In passion shook. . . . (III. i. 27–35)

This puncturing of Glendower's self-inflation is strongly reminiscent of Nashe's mock nativity of Harvey in *Have With You to
Saffron-Walden*. Commenting on the word 'enlargement', Dover
Wilson writes 'Hot. hints that Grandam Earth brought forth a
windbag'.[50] The suggestion of a monstrous birth, that staple ingredient of the Elizabethan news pamphlet, and the accompanying
ridicule of astrological portents are the basis of Nashe's attack:
Harvey's mother, he claims, 'was delivered and brought to bed of
one of these kistrell birds, called a wind-fucker', and he goes on to
recount 'the miracles of his conception' and 'The wonders of my
great Grand-father *Harveys* progeniture'.[51] A. R. Humphreys offers
further connections between Hotspur, Harvey and Nashe; he cites
both Harvey's *Pleasant . . . Discourse of the Earthquake in Aprill
last* (1580), where those phenomena are described in terms of
wind-breaking, and Nashe's similar use of the word 'distem-
'prature' in his derision of 'an absurd *Astrologicall Discourse*' in
which the author seemed to have 'beene at the anatomizing of the
Skies entrailes'.[52] But while Shakespeare seems to have the Nashe–
Harvey dispute specifically in mind here,[53] he is also following a
tradition of grotesque satire which is peculiar to the fifteenth and
sixteenth centuries, and which does not seem to have a counterpart
in Roman satire: that is, the comic exploitation of certain analogies
between the workings of the human body and exterior physical
phenomena. The enormous eructation which Hotspur describes so
graphically is closer to the procreative farts in Rabelais (II. 27)
than it is to the more literal scatology of Persius or Juvenal. Similarly, the mock biography and the monstrous birth are favourite
satirical gambits of the anti-Marprelate team (see, for example,
Martins Months Minde), but are not, as far as I know, employed
in Roman satire.[54]

I Henry IV, then, is a drama of the body, and the use of the grotesque is not confined to the sub-plot. Nor is the theme of feasted flesh the prerogative of the celebrant Falstaff, for that theme extends to the play's most solemn recesses of political discussion. King Henry's description of his ousted predecessor, Richard II,

> That being daily swallowed by men's eyes
> They surfeited with honey and began
> To loathe the taste of sweetness (III. ii. 70–2)

is ominously reworked by Worcester when he admonishes Henry himself:

> And being fed by us you us'd us so
> As that ungentle gull, the cuckoo's bird,
> Useth the sparrow – did oppress our nest,
> Grew by our feeding to so great a bulk
> That even our love durst not come near your sight
> For fear of swallowing. (V. i. 59–64)

These speeches, with those of Hotspur, tell us enough to regard Milton Crane's opinion that 'Nowhere in Shakespeare are the boundaries of two worlds so clearly delimited by the use of prose and verse as in the *Henry IV* plays'[55] as extraordinarily superficial criticism. And we have also seen enough of these analogies between the human body and the body politic, which produce the more sensational varieties of grotesque in Elizabethan literature, to know that connections between festive comedy and moralising onslaughts on vice, political or otherwise, are not entirely fortuitous. In *I Henry IV* such connections are submerged; in *2 Henry IV* the fusion of the political and the low comic imagery, seen most clearly in the spectacle of Falstaff's so-called deterioration, is essential to the movement of the play.

3   THE BODY PURGED: *Henry IV, part two*

It is generally agreed that in the second part of *Henry IV* Falstaff does in some sense degenerate. Age and diseases encroach upon him, supplanting the carnivalesque image with warnings of decrepitude. But there is less agreement as to whether this process has any moral significance. Doggedly moralistic interpretations of the play assert that it has; in Brian Vickers's view, for instance, we have a Falstaff who is continually lumbering into 'traps' sprung for him by Shakespeare.[56] Few descriptions of the dramatic function of Falstaff in the play could be further from the truth. On his first appearance in *2 Henry IV* his own sense of the comic role he has to play flatly contradicts such a view:

> Men of all sorts take a pride to gird at me. The brain of this foolish-compounded clay, man, is not able to invent anything that intends to laughter, more than I invent or is invented on me. I am not only witty in myself, but the cause that wit is in other men. (I. ii. 5–9)

We agree, surely. And if we do agree, then we must also agree that Falstaff's shameless up-ending of the truth in his confrontation with the Lord Chief Justice – 'You that are old consider not the capacities of us that are young' – represents an absolute comic victory over the latter's sober admonitions. (Or do we shake our heads in disapproval of this outrageous lie?) Falstaff's awareness of the comic potential of his own monstrosity, and his willingness to exploit it, precludes moral judgment. Renaissance comedy does not operate in the cerebrally conceived moral universe of the Victorian novel, and Falstaff is not, like Lydgate in *Middlemarch*, a person of basically sound character but with little 'spots of commonness'.[57] We are not invited to judge Falstaff in this way; it is Hal, not he, who is faced with moral dilemmas, and it is Hal's dramatic subservience to Falstaff which forces those dilemmas into such stark isolation from the action of the play. Hal's conscientious reflections are concerned with Falstaff, but they do not impinge upon our vision of Falstaff. He is as large as the drama itself and, rather than talking of his degeneration or deterioration in *2 Henry IV* (with the unnecessarily moralistic connotations which those terms carry), I would prefer to talk of this process as an evolution. While remaining both witty in himself and the cause of wit in others, Falstaff evolves into an image of the play itself – an image which concentrates and embodies the themes of the play and unifies its separate plots.

The two parts of *Henry IV* present two quite distinct Elizabethan views of gluttony. Through the festive associations of Carnival, gluttony in part one is a celebratory theme and Falstaff's obesity a celebratory image; the darker tone of part two, on the other hand, can be epitomised by the proverbs 'in much meat shall be sickness' or 'Much meat, much malady', admonitions which gained popular currency in the sixteenth century through medical books, dietaries and homilies. Within this second context the grotesque ramifications of feeding and sweating abandon their ties with laughter and fertility, and tallow, the product of perspiration, becomes an image of physical waste. Falstaff's wit is triumphant in his fracas with the Lord Chief Justice, but the tone has changed:

> *Ch. Just.* What! you are as a candle, the better part burnt out.
> *Fal.* A wassail candle, my lord – all tallow. (I. ii. 147–9)

Despite Falstaff's attempt to reinforce a festive idea of himself by the reference to wassailing, the implications of passing time and physical decay persist (Hal reiterates the image later: 'You whoreson candle-mine', II. iv. 289). Before the Lord Chief Justice leaves, Falstaff himself admits to his age: 'If ye will needs say I am an old man, you should give me rest. . . . I were better to be eaten to death with a rust than to be scoured to nothing with perpetual motion'. The notion of the body as inorganic matter subject to attrition is new to Falstaff, as is the sense of the body's subjection to an inexorable process of decay. And the image now encompasses Falstaff's financial state: 'I can get no remedy against this consumption of the purse; borrowing only lingers and lingers it out, but the disease is incurable.' Conscious that his dissipated body is on the wane, Falstaff nevertheless retains his ingenuity and humour, though in a more cynical manner. Persistently opportunist, he refuses to allow disease to deprive him of his greatest comic asset: 'A good wit will make use of anything. I will turn diseases to commodity.' His parting shot defines the development of the grotesque in *2 Henry IV*.

If the atmosphere of part one is predominantly that of Carnival, part two is pervaded by a chilly, Lenten spirit in which Falstaff too is enmeshed.[58] Meagre fare replaces the 'sweet beef' of part one, and the talk is now of 'mouldy stewed prunes and dried cakes', withered 'apple-johns' and 'dry toasts'. (Stewed prunes were, in particular, a brothel snack.) Falstaff accuses Hostess Quickly of being indicted for 'suffering flesh to be eaten in thy house, contrary to the law', and the troop that he musters from

Feeble, Shadow and Wart ('a little, lean, old, chopt, bald shot') is reminiscent of the sapless and emaciated army of Lent in her battles with Carnival. Hal is reduced to drinking small beer, but after his separation from Falstaff's entourage it is Justice Shallow who plays the role of Jack of Lent and from whom Falstaff will devise matter:

> I do remember him at Clement's Inn, like a man made after supper of a cheese-paring. When 'a was naked, he was for all the world like a fork'd radish, with a head fantastically carved upon it with a knife. 'A was so forlorn that his dimensions to any thick sight were invisible. 'A was the very genius of famine; yet lecherous as a monkey, and the whores call'd him mandrake . . . you might have thrust him and all his apparel into an eel-skin; the case of a treble hautboy was a mansion for him, a court – and now has he land and beeves.
> (III. ii. 301–20)

It is this kind of writing which helps to mould the prose style of Jonson's early comedies; drier and more clipped in character than the writing in *I Henry IV*, the speech proceeds in the jerky, aggregative manner which Barish has noted as being a typical feature of Jonson's prose style.[59] The caricature is based on a series of amplifications and extensions ('a mansion for him, a court' is a peculiarly Jonsonian mannerism) and represents Elizabethan literary grotesque at its most elaborately pictorial. At the same time something of the rich consonance between the verbal and the physical, which we associate with Falstaff's language elsewhere, is lost, and this is appropriate to the bleaker environment of *2 Henry IV*. Carnival and Lent swap roles. Justice Shallow's Lenten compound of cheese-paring, radish and eel-skin is exchanged for 'land and beeves', while Falstaff visibly falls away; as a 'dead elm' and a 'withered elder' he has lost the power of natural lubrication which had fortified his earlier, festive self.

The tone of *2 Henry IV* is determined chiefly by the sense that the world of holiday is not timeless. More particularly, it is determined by the implications that Shrovetide, the time of physical indulgence, is a prelude to a period of physical mortification. As the scene changes from London to rural Gloucestershire (V. iii), the strains of Justice Silence's drunken rendering of 'welcome merry Shrove-tide' echo comfortingly around Shallow's orchard, but Shallow's self-deprecating dismissal of his estate rings out with equal clarity: 'Barren, barren, barren'. And the presence of Lent behind Carnival is dramatically affirmed in the following scene, as we return suddenly to the streets of London and find Doll Tearsheet and Hostess Quickly in the hands of the beadles. Shrovetide, as we saw in *The Honest Whore*, was a time of physical retribution for prostitutes. The battle against Lent, against the mortifiers of the flesh, is now in earnest, and the tone of the play's last flyting is desperate:

> *Doll*. I'll tell you what, you thin man in a censer, I will have
>   you as soundly swing'd for this − you blue-bottle rogue,
>   you filthy famish'd correctioner.... Come, you rogue,
>   come; bring me to a justice.
> *Host*. Ay, come, you starv'd bloodhound.
> *Doll*. Goodman death, goodman bones!
> *Host*. Thou atomy, thou!
> *Doll*. Come, you thin thing! come, you rascal!
> *1 Bead*. Very well. [*Exeunt*.] (V. iv. 19–31)

The beadle is the last of the emaciated, Lenten figures in *Henry IV* and it is he who has the last, complacent word. The scene indicates not merely the sourer side of Shrovetide, but the sourer side too of the bohemianism celebrated in *I Henry IV*. The chimes of midnight are distant indeed.

In its exposure of the less pleasant aspects of bohemianism − Pistol, for instance, has killed a man in the brothel − *2 Henry IV* moves closer to the genre of satirical comedy, and the language of the play reveals the multiple associations between sex, disease and gluttony which inform that kind of drama. Doll speaks in an altogether more rancid way than any of the characters in *I Henry IV*, and this spurs Falstaff to joining in the kind of sexual repartee which he had previously tended to avoid:

> *Fal*. You make fat rascals, Mistress Doll.
> *Doll*. I make them! Gluttony and diseases make them: I make
>   them not.
> *Fal*. If the cook help to make the gluttony, you help to make
>   the diseases, Doll. We catch of you, Doll, we catch of you
>   (II. iv. 41–5)

and he continues with the fashionable, but rather laboured, grotesque analogies between syphilitic boils and jewellery, copulation and warfare, where the wounded soldier represents the infected lover.[60] Here the image of Falstaff as 'sweet beef' is diffracted by the sexual implications of obesity; as Monck Mason pointed out, 'to grow fat and bloated, is one of the consequences of the venereal disease'.[61] The prophecy in the epilogue that Falstaff may 'die of a sweat' is, therefore, most ambiguous. It suggests, on the one hand, the festive picture of Falstaff larding the lean earth and expiring like one of John Taylor's cooks who 'fry in their masters suet, and sweat in their own grease'; on the other hand, it refers to venereal disease ('sweat') and the means of curing it (a 'sweating-tub'). Falstaff has become a 'wen' (nicely glossed by Bucknill as 'A monstrous fatty tumour'[62]) and 'surfeit-swelled', and his body's final metamorphosis is into rank flesh in need of purgation. So the scene in which Doll and Hostess Quickly are taken to Bridewell to be scourged is closely linked to the play's increasingly satirical view of the physical. Elizabethan satire was concerned not so much with moral correction by rational means as with physical purgation. (And it is surely no coincidence that 1597–8 was the period in which the most characteristically violent of the Elizabethan verse satires were published: Hall's *Virge-demiarium*, Guilpin's *Skialeth-eia*, and Marston's *The Scourge of Villanie*.) The sins of the flesh were regarded as actual physical diseases, as poisonous growths which could be expelled only through the mortification of the flesh, and it is to this notion that Barber refers when he writes of the 'recurrent expression of a laboring need to be rid of a growth or humor'[63] in *2 Henry IV*. This theme which originates with Falstaff, which is enacted in the fate of Doll and Hostess Quickly, finally expresses the state of England itself.

Developments in the imagery of *2 Henry IV* are responsible for its sourer tone. They are also responsible for the fusion of the political scenes and the comic scenes in a coherent vision of social degeneration and the means of its arrest. I have stressed throughout the basis of the grotesque in the heterogeneous association of physical images, and in order to understand the function of the grotesque in the play it should be placed within the wider context of the system of correspondences which permeates Renaissance political literature. The system has been so amply documented that it scarcely requires further elaboration here; one need only reiterate the well-known analogies between the state (the 'body politic') and the human body to establish a frame of reference for both the political and comic scenes of the play. The body politic of England is bloated with the diseases which disordered physical indulgence provokes, and this image of the state is elaborated by both factions in the civil war. The Archbishop of York comments:

> The commonwealth is sick of their own choice;
> Their over-greedy love has surfeited . . .
> Thou, beastly feeder, art so full of him [King Henry]
> That thou provok'st thyself to cast him up.
> So, so, thou common dog, didst thou disgorge
> Thy glutton bosom of the royal Richard;
> And now thou wouldst eat thy dead vomit up,
> And howl'st to find it. (I. iii. 87–100)

Henry himself, speaking to Warwick, uses similarly grotesque language:

> Then you perceive the body of our Kingdom
> How foul it is; what rank diseases grow,
> And with what danger, near the heart of it

and then, remembering the words of his deposed predecessor, Richard:

> 'The time will come that foul sin, gathering head,
> Shall break into corruption' (III. i. 38–40, 76–7)

But while Warwick attempts to mollify the king by suggesting that a little medicine will provide sufficient remedy, the Archbishop pursues the sterner line of the Elizabethan satirists:

> we are all diseas'd
> And with our surfeiting and wanton hours
> Have brought ourselves into a burning fever,
> And we must bleed for it. . . .
> Nor do I as an enemy to peace
> Troop in the throngs of military men;
> But rather show awhile like fearful war
> To diet rank minds sick of happiness,
> And purge the obstructions which begin to stop
> Our very veins of life. (IV. i. 54–66)

Even such extensive quotation fails to indicate how dominant this grotesque image of England as a gorged and disease-ridden trunk becomes in *2 Henry IV*; allusions to disease, gluttony and the need for purgative remedies are as frequent in the political scenes of the play as they are in the other world of Falstaff. The two plots become interdependent through the deployment of such imagery: England must be mortified as Doll and Hostess Quickly are mortified, and they are surrogates for the mortification of Falstaff.

The underlying themes of prodigality, surfeit and purgation provide the means by which the political and comic matter of *2 Henry IV* can be drawn into an artistic whole. These themes are also the themes of *Summers Last Will and Testament*, and if *1 Henry IV* is indebted to Nashe through its verbal echoes of bohemian attitudes in his work, *2 Henry IV* embodies the maxim which is central to Nashe's argument in that play:

> He must be purged that hath surfeited:
> The fields have surfeited with Summer fruites;
> They must be purg'd, made poore, opprest with snow.
> (ll. 1551–3)

Winter's articulation of the processes of seasonal change is transferred to a political context by Shakespeare, and the political developments of *2 Henry IV* are intimately linked by imagery to the wider themes of indulgence and mortification. The prodigal spring (Ver) in *Summers Last Will* epitomises the Falstaffian of life: 'What talke you to me of living within my bounds?' (l. 241), he complains. Falstaff lives beyond his bounds both in the sense of financial means and in the potentially grotesque sense of physical confines: he is a fleshly vessel filled to overflowing with extraneous physical matter. It is this image, the image of the prodigal as vessel or container, which gives us a final glimpse of the underlying imaginative unity of *2 Henry IV*. The comic portrayal of Falstaff as a 'globe of sinful continents' (pun on 'containers'), a 'hogshead' and a 'hulk' (cargo ship) is echoed by the play's political imagery. Lamenting the political uncertainties with which he has to cope, King Henry exclaims:

> O God! that one might read the book of fate,
> And see the revolution of the times
> Make mountains level, and the continent,
> Weary of solid firmness, melt itself
> Into the sea; and other times to see

The beachy girdle of the ocean
Too wide for Neptune's hips; how chances mock,
And changes fill the cup of alteration
With divers liquors! (III. i. 45–53)

The development of the metaphor from the geographical to the anatomical and alimentary indicates just how powerful is Falstaff's influence on the expression of the play's political themes. The girdle, hips, and brimming cup return the metaphor as a whole to the focal point of the Falstaffian body. A similar influence is exerted on the theme of the king's speech to his son, Thomas, in which he hopes Thomas may prove:

A hoop of gold to bind thy brothers in,
That the united vessel of their blood,
Mingled with venom of suggestion –
As force, perforce, the age will pour it in –
Shall never leak. (IV. iv. 43–7)

The hooped barrel of 'divers liquors' has shifted from its original Falstaffian associations with prodigality to bring an image first of instability, and here, of wished for security. Nevertheless, it is Falstaff from whom such images emanate. Madeleine Doran has ably discussed the dense and complex way in which Shakespeare's imagery works in *Henry IV*, but she confines her discussion to the verse.[64] I would argue that not only is the prose imagery of the sub-plot throughout *Henry IV* quite as complex as that of the main plot, but that in *2 Henry IV* it also informs the expression of the play's political themes through the pervasive influence of the Falstaffian grotesque.

What is clear, then, is that the two strata of *2 Henry IV* work in a close imaginative relationship with one another, more closely indeed than they do in *I Henry IV*, and that this results in a progressive integration of the subject matter of the play as a whole. The political vocabulary of *2 Henry IV* becomes almost indistinguishable from the comic vocabulary: 'surfeited' . . . 'beastly feeder' . . . 'glutton bosom' . . . 'rank diseases' . . . 'wanton hours' . . . 'diet rank minds' . . . 'cup . . . with divers liquors' – this is the language of tavern and brothel, and, above all, it is the language of the Falstaffian body. Alternating between the physically exuberant and the physically macabre, the grotesque lifts character from the moral to the symbolic level. Falstaff's physical development in *Henry IV* is from the one pole of the grotesque to the other, and his role in the play becomes increasingly symbolic as the language of the main plot assumes a gradually closer identity with the language of the sub-plot. The patterns of imagery developed through Falstaff have grown into a coherent symbol of the state of England. But this process does not entail his loss of humanity: as a character Falstaff remains immune from simple moralistic judgments because the moral themes of the play are expressed in terms of purely physical processes, and he retains our sympathy throughout because his essentially festive nature must elicit positive responses from us. In the end, Shakespeare was faced with the familiar problem of how (or whether) to control a character whose dramatic impact had grown disproportionate to his role in the plot. He tried to solve the problem not by diminishing Falstaff but by expanding him — expanding him to the point where his symbolic function as an image of England unites comedy and history, the festive and political elements of *Henry IV*.

4   THE DEATH OF FALSTAFF

Although we do not hear of his death until *Henry V* (1599), the consensus of critical opinion has been that the Falstaff of *The Merry Wives of Windsor* (1597)[65] is already little more than a ghost of his former self, albeit a rather substantial ghost. There has been little dissent from Bradley's view that 'Falstaff was degraded by Shakespeare himself. The original character is to be found alive in the two parts of *Henry IV*, dead in *Henry V*, and nowhere else.'[66] No longer the buoyant survivor, Falstaff is now a victim of his own obesity, the fat boy mercilessly baited by tricksters. The resilient flesh which had previously been the source of so much verbal inspiration has become a burden, the means of his humiliation, and he is powerless to challenge Page's contemptuous description of him as 'Old, cold, wither'd, and of intolerable entrails' (V. v. 147). While his wit is not entirely dimmed, his comic rhapsodies on the state of his body are tinged with self-pity, and the cumulation of physical indignities finally evokes the embarrassed confession, 'See now how wit may be made a Jack-a-Lent when 'tis upon ill employment' (V. v. 123–4). That he should turn upon himself his favourite weapon of abuse is a measure of the extent of his defeat.

Falstaff's diminished power in *The Merry Wives* is partly a result of the narrow social base of its characters and partly of the structural rigidity of its plot. The play's thoroughly bourgeois setting places it, despite the rural location, in the genre of citizen comedy, but it is citizen comedy without the broad social range supplied by the urban locations of other plays in that genre. There are no usurers, cheats and drifting gallants against which middle-class values can be tested and defined. Nor is there anything of the bohemianism of *Henry IV*, because that again is an essentially urban phenomenon. Consequently, Falstaff and his hangers-on seem merely out of place in the little world of Windsor; they are characters without a social context in a play which is dominated by the values of a clearly defined social group. Windsor is no more than a tiny corner of the great social and political panorama of *Henry IV*, and it is this shrunken social setting which prevents *The Merry Wives* from deriving a dramatically unifying pattern of imagery from the grotesque resources of Falstaff's body. The absence of a broad social range in the play precludes the inversion and rotation of social roles with which Shakespeare was experimenting in the figures of Jack Cade, Petruchio, and Christopher Sly, and which he made the basis of *Henry IV*. The absence of a political context inhibits the fruitful expansion of the grotesque into an informing symbolic pattern based on correspondences between body and state. In both respects, what *The Merry Wives* lacks is the sense of the multiple and heterogeneous associations of life upon which the grotesque so largely depends. This limitation reduces Falstaff's contemplation of his physical state to an essentially private act.

In the second place, Falstaff's more passive role in the play is determined by the structure of the plot. The motif which Shakespeare uses is the relatively inflexible, Italianate story of the young lover who is forced into ingenious hiding places to escape discovery by the jealous husband.[67] The variation offered in *The Merry Wives* is that, since Falstaff is old and fat, convention demands that he should be a sexual failure. But now a further and equally rigid plot motif (again Italianate) comes into operation. Falstaff becomes the physical victim of a series of *lazzi* (i.e. practical jokes) which culminate in the humiliation of public disclosure. This is the kind of thing that Jonson liked, and *The Merry Wives* is, perhaps, Shakespeare's most Jonsonian play; 'Falstaff knocked out of his humour' would be an adequate epitome of its action.[68] Moreover, the *lazzi* in which Falstaff is knocked out of his humour act as figurative expressions of his cramped dramatic circumstances. The oaths which in *Henry IV* produced bizarre counter-images of Falstaff as 'pepper-corn' or 'bunch of radish' are here enacted in his attempts to conceal his huge hill of flesh during the frantic searches of Ford. Crammed into a buck-basket, Falstaff is 'compass'd like a good bilbo in the circumference of a peck, hilt to point, heel to head' (III. v. 100–1); Ford says that 'he cannot creep into a halfpenny purse nor into a pepper box' (III. v. 1237), but at the next encounter with Mistress Ford and Mistress Page he is prepared to 'creep up into the chimney' while Mrs Ford suggests the 'kiln-hole' (IV. ii. 46, 48). His efforts to accommodate himself to such confined spaces are in ludicrous contrast with the sheer expansiveness of his role in *Henry IV*; the overflowing container is now also the contained.

Since it is of the nature of the comic butt to be an inarticulate sufferer, Falstaff's verbal talents are also severely hampered by the role which the plot-structure demands of him. The 'fat-witted' (in the fullest sense of the term) Falstaff of *Henry IV* is now, by his own admission, a mere Jack of Lent, and we have been prepared for this ultimate image of desiccation by his earlier, maudlin reflections upon vanished ingenuity. At first, after his dousing in the Thames, he complains that 'if I be serv'd such another trick, I'll have my braines ta'en out and butter'd, and give them to a dog for a new-year's gift' (III. v. 6–8). But when he is further deceived and, disguised as the fat woman of Brainford, is cudgelled by Ford, the last traces of oiliness evaporate from his conception of himself. If the court should hear of his humiliation he fears that 'they would whip me with their fine wits till I were as crest-fallen as a dried pear' (IV. v. 92–3). Finally, after his traumatic experience in Windsor Park, which can stimulate him to nothing more verbal than yelps and cries, he is driven to ask, 'Have I laid my brain in the sun, and dried it, that it wants matter to prevent so gross o'erreaching as this?' (V. v. 131–3). The erosion of Falstaff's verbal mastery in *The Merry Wives* is inseparable from his physical subjection; he is gagged as well as beaten. From his sending of the transparently insincere love-letter to his final admissions of witlessness, Falstaff's defeat is shown in terms of infertile invention. Tamed, he is invited home for dinner by Page, and his last words in the play humbly complete a rhyming couplet:

Page. What cannot be eschew'd must be embrac'd.
Fal. When night-dogs run, all sorts of deer are chas'd.
  (V. v. 224–5)

The compliant pentameter testifies to Falstaff's quiet submission to the confines of a narrower world.

While the grotesque in *The Merry Wives* lacks the wider dramatic function that it has in *Henry IV*, it nevertheless retains considerable local force of a pictorial kind, and also adds a new dimension to the images of Falstaff with which we are already familiar. Both the festive associations of the grotesque and its other, macabre relationship with disease and mutilation have been stripped from the Falstaff of *The Merry Wives*. Inarticulate in the sense that he can no longer use his wit to extricate himself from knotty situations, he is still a sufficiently verbal creature to be able to express his predicament in appropriately vivid terms. His body is rich in raw materials, and what is impressed upon us by himself and others is a sense of its various liquid components and their capacity for sudden change in texture and consistency. The grotesque connections of the Falstaffian body with food and disease situated Falstaff himself on the borders of the human world; as a compound of oil and water, he now approaches the world of things. To Mrs Ford he is 'this whale, with so many tuns of oil in his belly' (II. i. 55–6) and 'this unwholesome humidity, this gross wat'ry pumpion' (III. iii. 34). Whale and pumpkin, formless receptacles of oil and water, are themselves images from the edge of the animal and vegetable worlds, and Falstaff's own monologues on his experience in the buck-basket confirm the growing sense of the mere materiality of his existence:[69]

> I had been drown'd but that the shore was shelvy and shallow
> – a death that I abhor; for the water swells a man; and what
> a thing should I have been when I had been swell'd! I should
> have been a mountain of mummy. (III. v. 12–16)

And he continues the story in a similar vein to 'Brook':

> stopp'd in, like a strong distillation, with stinking clothes that

fretted in their own grease. Think of that – a man of my
kidney. Think of that – that am as subject to heat as butter;
a man of continual dissolution and thaw. It was a miracle to
scape suffocation. And in the height of this bath, when I was
more than half-stew'd in grease, like a Dutch dish, to be
thrown into the Thames, and cool'd, glowing hot, in that
surge, like a horse-shoe; think of that - hissing hot. Think of
that, Master Brook. (III. v. 98–108)

The extraordinarily rapid shifts in the imagery play with the grotesque theme of the non-humanness of the human body. A compound of volatile liquids, the body is a 'distillation', subject to
'dissolution and thaw'; stewed and softened it can be suddenly
rigidified like iron (the horseshoe is a neat development of the
image of the curved bilbo, quoted above). And Falstaff's transformation of physical sensation into purely material terms is ac-
companied by an awareness of bodily utilities which are quite alien
to the self. Commenting on the likely reaction of his friends at
court to his sufferings, he believes that 'they would melt me out of
my fat, drop by drop, and liquor fishermen's boots with me' (III.
v. 90–1). In yet another extension of the syndrome of images
centring on grease, Falstaff imagines himself as the raw material
for a domestic product, fit to be rendered into dubbing like the oil-
laden whale. This dimension of the grotesque is an apt expression
of Falstaff's essentially passive role in *The Merry Wives*. As he
becomes a helpless victim of the manifold transformations of the
flesh, Falstaff's self-awareness reaches the limits of the non-human;
in his total physical subjugation, he contemplates his body in the
remote terms of the purely material world.

   This aspect of the grotesque, however, does not immediately
illuminate the main theme of the plot of *The Merry Wives*, which
is Falstaff's attempted seduction of Mrs Ford. His sufferings are a
result of his sexual failure, but they make no explicit comment on
the play's treatment of sexuality, except insofar as they represent
society's punitive attitude towards trangressions of sexual convention. Of the two factors which determine Falstaff's dramatic role
in *The Merry Wives* – the narrow social range of the characters
and the inflexible structure of the plot – it is the first which can
help us to establish the tone of the play and its socio-sexual attitudes. In punishment, Falstaff's greasiness is an image of the remote

materiality of the body, but grease elsewhere carries the sexual connotations that it has in satirical comedy. Mrs Page calls him 'this greasy knight' (in the context, a sexual allusion) and as he awaits the rendezvous with Mrs Ford in Windsor Park, Falstaff uses the image of himself in heavily erotic terms: 'Send me a cool rut-time, Jove, or who can blame me to piss my tallow?' (V. v. 13–14), he gasps. But to the bourgeois society of Windsor sexual oils feed the fires of hell. Mrs Ford feels that 'the best way were to entertain him with hope, till the wicked fire of his lust have melted him in his own grease' (II. i. 58–60), and the infernal implications of that fire are made explicit by Falstaff in Windsor Park: 'I think the devil will not have me damn'd, lest the oil that's in me should set hell on fire' (V. v. 31–3). The number of scriptural and proverbial allusions in the play are vital in creating the kind of social atmosphere in which lechery can be treated both as an object of ridicule and as the road to damnation. Phrases such as 'the story of the Prodigal', 'a legion of angels', 'Cain-coloured beard', 'a Herod of Jewry', 'Goliath with a weaver's beam', 'as poor as Job', 'all Eve's daughters', 'the hundred Psalms' and 'as firm as faith'[70] epitomise the middle-class values, so noticeably absent from *Henry IV*, of common sense and piety. The religious undercurrent of the play, which helps to typify the social milieu of Windsor, is at the basis of the play's treatment of sexuality. Had Falstaff died in *The Merry Wives* he might not have been allowed to rest comfortably in 'Arthur's bosom'.

While the element of bourgeois piety in *The Merry Wives* remains an important factor in the oddly confined atmosphere of the play, the play nevertheless resists a convenient location in the development from sermon to satire during the 1590s. Scriptural allusion provokes none of the sensational grotesque typical of earlier, sermon-influenced prose and drama; nor does the play's concern with middle-class life admit it to the genre of satirical comedy (as opposed to citizen comedy), which requires the broader social range provided by an urban setting. If it is a festive comedy it is of a very different kind from *I Henry IV*, for Falstaff has become a ritual scapegoat rather than Carnival celebrant, and even then his role as 'scapegoat' is determined by the exigencies of the Italianate plot rather than by any overall ritualistic structure in the play.[71] Lacking a dramatic basis in sermon, satire or festive celebration, Falstaff's grotesque effusions have the air of being merely sporadic passages of *coloratura*: they are, indeed, his swan-song. By the end of the play, the recklessness of Elizabethan comic prose has surrendered to the cowed decency of the rhyming couplet, and such a shift from prose to verse informs us of the death of Falstaff as clearly as does the official obituary in *Henry V*.

Attempts to resuscitate Falstaff have variously failed. A consortium of Admiral's company hacks (Munday, Drayton, Wilson and Hathaway) tried to cash in on the success of the Falstaff plays by writing *Sir John Oldcastle* (1599). The play aimed to vindicate the name of Oldcastle by dissociating Sir John, Lord Cobham, the Protestant martyr, from Sir John, parson of Wrotham, who appears to be an imitation of Falstaff. But the echoes are certainly feeble:[72]

> I confesse I am a frayle man, flesh and bloud as other are: but set my imperfections aside, by this light ye have not a taller man, nor a truer subject to the Crowne and State, than sir John of Wrootham.

Two centuries later, James White made a rather less wooden effort to imitate Shakespearean comic prose in a mock forgery entitled *Original Letters Etc. of Sir John Falstaff* (1796). While his habit of beginning the letters 'Ha! Ha! Ha!' is scarcely a deft comic touch, White does occasionally rise to something approaching the Falstaffian. Here is part of a letter to 'Pistol' on the experience of being used as a grandstand at a royal procession:[73]

> Thou knowest I was trodden down like sugars for an export – yea, I was made a convenience – I was shap'd into a Promontory, which spectators of a subaltern height did flock to for a sight of passing Majesty – they did ascend and course o'er my belly like pismires, ants on a mole-hill, save that the compression was greater.

The grammatical formulae are right, but the Gulliverian experience is not. This is pleasing bizarrerie – fantasy rather than grotesque – and the play of wit is not linked closely to the sense of gross physical reality which the grotesque demands. White, however, is livelier than Robert Brough, whose *The Life of Sir John Falstaff* (1858) plumbs the depths of drab, Pickwickian jollity. ('Mr. Poins, against whom the culverin of Sir John's wrath, primed and loaded to the muzzle, was especially directed, had withdrawn himself prudently from the range of that fearful ordnance, and returned no answer.'[74]) Brough seems to realise that this ponderous, mock-heroic manner is not very funny; the fact that, when dealing with incidents which form part of *Henry IV*, he simply copies out passages from Shakespeare, speaks for itself. The most recent Falstaff appears in the pages of Robert Nye's *Falstaff* (1976). This character has nothing of Brough's Victorian pomposity, but Nye does not really reproduce the Falstaffian tone: the arch, elbow-nudging jokes and raucous puns are more often reminiscent of a Blackpool comedian than of an Elizabethan wit and debauchee. Despite the powers of survival which Shakespeare grants him, Falstaff could not outlive the sixteenth century.

The reasons for Falstaff's being a peculiarly Elizabethan (or rather sixteenth-century) creation should, however, be clear. The plays which he dominates are the culmination of Shakespeare's experiments with comic prose during the 1590s; the 1590s were, in this respect, dominated by Nashe, and Nashe is primarily responsible for developing a low comic style, suffused with grotesque imagery, which could serve as a model for a dramatist far more accomplished than Nashe himself. The Falstaff plays do, in fact, absorb the inchoate mixture of Nashe's literary material – sermon, satirical journalism and festive comedy. At the same time, the stylistic antecedents remain clear: Nashe's rhetoric of vituperation, stimulated in turn by Aretinian base comparisons and the comic violence of Marprelate and anti-Marprelate invective, is of central importance to our understanding of the novelty of the Falstaff plays and their place in 'the Shakespearean moment'. But their novelty, which lies chiefly in their elaboration of the grotesque from comic sub-plot to historical main plot, depends as much upon traditional as on topical elements. The devices of satirical journalism are grafted on to the residue of festive or folk imagery whose origins are impossible to trace far beyond its fifteenth- and sixteenth-century records in verse, *fabliaux*, the popular print and folk drama. Nor is it merely such a combination of the traditional and the topical which determines the Elizabethan-ness of the Falstaffian grotesque. The more important factor is the disappearance during the seventeenth century of what I have described, perhaps clumsily, as 'fat-wittedness'; it is, in the end, another way of talking about the dissociation of sensibility.[75] For during that century an increasingly forensic use of imagery destroyed a sense of the independent, internal life of words which Elizabethan writers exploit, and a move to compartmentalise experience destroyed the possibilities of linguistic and imagistic ramification from which literary grotesque derives. The result of this was a gradual decline in the writer's sense of language as a physical medium: the world of the body gave way to the world of the mind.

· 7 ·

Jonsonian grotesque:
Every Man Out of his Humour and *Bartholomew Fair*

•

1   LENTEN STUFF

To approach Jonsonian grotesque through a discussion of *Every
Man Out* (1599) and *Bartholomew Fair* (1614) might seem gratuitous. The two plays not only belong to quite separate periods
of Jonson's career, but the first is now regarded as virtually un-
stageable, if not unreadable, while the other is increasingly considered to be Jonson's finest achievement. Moreover, the plays were
designed to entertain different kinds of audience: *Every Man Out*,
though first performed by the Chamberlain's Men, was dedicated
to the young sophisticates at the Inns of Court; *Bartholomew Fair*
– acted at the Hope, which doubled as a bear-baiting pit – was
clearly aimed at a less exclusive range of theatre-goers. But perhaps
the most obvious dissimilarity between the two lies in their respective comic forms. Jonson himself described the earlier play, along
with *Cynthia's Revels* (1600) and *Poetaster* (1601), as 'comicall
satyre',[1] and the emphasis is on the satire. A series of narrowly
delineated social types expose themselves to our ridicule, and that
of the play's self-appointed moralists, in a number of loosely connected *vignettes*. The 'action' is carried along by an undercurrent
of ruthless contempt. *Bartholomew Fair*, on the other hand, is
nothing if not spirited, and while it is perhaps misleading to describe it as a 'festive comedy',[2] saturnalian elements do largely
determine the comic form of the play. It would seem, then, that
the two works represent those polarities of satire and saturnalia
between which the grotesque, in formal terms, is constantly
moving.

   The apparent dissonance begins to disappear, however, if we
consider the question of dramatic structure, for in this respect
Every Man Out and *Bartholomew Fair* resemble each other to a

131

far greater extent than they resemble any other of Jonson's plays
– so much so, I think, that the first can be seen as a prototype for
the second. Leaving aside, for the moment, Cordatus' description
of *Every Man Out* as *Vetus Comoedia* (and hence its Aristophanic
kinship with *Bartholomew Fair*), one is left with a strong impression that by composing *Every Man Out* in the way he did Jonson
was trying to do something which had not been attempted in
drama before, and that that something was what he achieved in
Bartholomew Fair. What distinguishes these plays from other Jonsonian drama is the looseness and multiplicity of plot; the aim is
not to produce the structural clarity of *Volpone* or *The Alchemist*,
which depend upon the elaboration of a single motif, a single
strand of action, in which each character has a clearly designated
role, but to break up the integrity of the plot in order to reveal the
diffuseness and variety of actual social relationships. And it is in
this sense that these plays attempt a form of realism with which
Shakespeare was never concerned. (That is to say, they seek to
embody in their dramatic structures the realities of human intercourse in a certain kind of society.) In both cases we are presented
with groups of characters who are engaged in apparently separate
lines of action; within these groups individual characters remain
fundamentally isolated; the groups themselves intermingle but
never fully coalesce. What such a structure aims to reflect are the
endless social configurations of city life, and the way in which
desultory collisions between individuals are constantly destroying
and reshaping fixed social patterns. This kind of volatility, typical
of early seventeenth-century comedy, as we have seen, is a direct
result of the growing awareness among writers of the city as literary
material, and the novelty of *Every Man Out* lies in Jonson's attempt
to create a dramatic structure which could properly accommodate
the subject matter of satirical journalism. Where he fails is in not
providing the coherence which the diffracted plot resists by developing a central theme through a unifying dramatic image; this he
triumphantly achieves in *Bartholomew Fair*.

Despite its ultimate failure as a play, *Every Man Out* occupies
an important position in the literary developments of the late
1590s, and I want to begin by sketching the literary *ambience* of
the play and the circumstances of its composition. The years 1596–
9 were a time in which the interests of Nashe, Shakespeare and
Jonson were in close conjunction, and this is partly due to the

hostility of William Brooke, Lord Cobham, the Lord Chamberlain from 1596 to 1597. During his brief tenure of office Shakespeare's company lost the Lord Chamberlain's patronage, and in a letter to William Cotton we find Nashe complaining that the players had fallen on hard times. The trouble arose from the fact that the Cobhams, whose family name was also Oldcastle, had for a long time been the subject of literary attacks, and their consequent hostility towards writers only provoked further sallies.[3] Falstaff, as is well known, had originally been called Oldcastle, and the 'Mr Brook' of *The Merry Wives* was a further dig at the same family. In the summer of 1597 Jonson collaborated with Nashe on the notorious *The Isle of Dogs* (now lost), which landed Jonson in jail and forced Nashe to flee to Yarmouth. Though William Brooke had died in March his son Henry had succeeded to the titles and probably pressed for severe action to be taken against the players. Certainly it was he who became a chief satirical target for Nashe and Jonson, and in 1598 both *Lenten Stuffe* and *Every Man In his Humour* ridiculed the family in their elaborately punning references to 'cobs' (i.e. herrings), and the noble pedigree of that fish. But it was not simply an interest in needling the Cobhams which drew the three writers together. At the same time Jonson was learning artistically from Shakespeare. The discovery of Bobadilla, the braggart soldier, waking from his drunken slumbers in the third scene of *Every Man In* is obviously modelled on the first appearance of Falstaff, while Thorello in the same play is an equally clear imitation of Ford in *The Merry Wives*. It was perhaps in recognition of this tribute that Shakespeare, as tradition has it,[4] ensured that *Every Man In* was performed by the Chamberlain's Men and took a leading role himself. But in the summer of 1599, when the bishops issued their ban on verse satire and satirical pamphlets (Nashe and Harvey won special mention), Jonson saw his opportunity of exploiting on stage the vogue for satire in a novel and far less Shakespearean manner. *Every Man Out* is a theatrical version of the same literary material which the bishops had just outlawed.[5]

Jonson began his career, then, in association with the two writers most closely concerned with the development of the low style in pamphlet satire and drama, and, of course, with the grotesque mode in comic prose. The language of the detractors in *Every Man Out* is unmistakably of this genre: 'be humorous, looke with a good starch't face, and ruffle your brow like a new boot' (I. ii. 57–

9); 'he looks like a mustie bottle, new wickerd, his head's the corke' (I. ii. 200–1); 'I think thou dost varnish thy face with the fat on't, it lookes so like a glew-pot' (V. v. 43–4). The fascination with face-wrinkling and grimacing which is a persistent feature of the play is also a characteristically Nasheian trick, and it is exactly this kind of attention to the detail of physical surfaces which is the great strength of Jonson's early prose. It is his ability to render in terse, metaphorical language the textural qualities of the thing he is describing that constitutes much of his satirical power, and this he derives – in part, at least – from the developments in comic prose which I have been discussing. And while the minutiae of Jonson's debt to contemporary English writers have long been established,[6] it is also worth pointing out that his receptivity to new styles of comic prose may well be the result of a first-hand knowledge of Aretino's writing. We know that a source for *Epicoene* was his comedy *Il Marescalco*,[7] and Mario Praz has argued most convincingly that the character of Volpone is based on Aretino himself.[8] When we discover too that Jonson actually owned a copy of the *Ragionamenti* [9] it becomes clear that his interest in the Italian satirist was genuine and that he is as likely as Nashe to have been acquainted with the work itself. Many of the stylistic similarities between Aretino and Nashe form the basis of an equally compelling comparison between Aretino and Jonson. When Praz writes:[10]

> is it really necessary to quote passages from the *Ragionamenti* to demonstrate that the author of *Volpone*, more than any other writer of his time, has come close to the picturesque eloquence, to the art of making the language ferment and seethe like the very corruption it describes, to the spellbound contemplation of the spectacle of human turpitude, which were proper to the Scourge of Princes?

he is pointing to that strange quality of style which combines tactility, density and volatility which is the essence of the satirical grotesque. Praz had not, perhaps, read Nashe; it is a quality of style which, in their respective accounts of the turbulent depravities of the urban scene (superbly characterised by Mitis in *Every Man Out* as 'the warping condition of this greene, and soggy multitude', III. viii. 72–3), the three writers share.

Jonson, however, had not learned much from Aretino as a

dramatist at the time of writing *Every Man Out*. While it is true that Carlo Buffone's instruction of Sogliardo in the more doubtful arts of being a courtier is closely paralleled by Andrea's instruction of Maco in *La Cortigiana*,[11] the plot structure of *Every Man Out* bears no relation to the plots of Aretinian comedy. This is because the dominant influence on the play is that of non-dramatic satire: Nashe's *Pierce Penilesse*, Lodge's *Wits Miserie*, the Theophrastan character (Casaubon's edition of Theophrastus was published in 1592), and the verse satire of Hall, Guilpin and Marston are Jonson's primary models. The fragmented and tabulatory nature of this kind of material determines the atomised structure of *Every Man Out*, and the essential stasis of the play is a result of the intractability of the source material. The comment on Mitis in the preliminary character sketches ('a person of no action, and therefore we have reason to affoord him no Character') is scarcely vindicated by the drama that follows, unless 'action' can be taken to mean the isolated posturings of fairground freaks. The play is built less upon action than display, and the characters are juxtaposed, rather than related, in the sense that they fail entirely to modify each other's behaviour. Fungoso, the young spendthrift up from the country, may be anxious to emulate the sartorial extravagances of Fastidious Briske, but this obsession – as with the obsessions of the other characters – is exaggerated beyond any desire to win social acceptance into a private monomania. Moreover, the serial quality of non-dramatic satire with its vivid but disconnected sketches is reproduced in *Every Man Out* by the play's insistence on the fragmentary nature of urban social relations; the hiatuses between character descriptions in, say, *Pierce Penilesse* are turned by Jonson into the spaces between people which the city creates, and the impossibilities of relation in pamphlet satire become failures of social communication in 'comicall satyre'.

If such disintegration was bound to make for artistic incoherence, Jonson did at least attempt to control his material in a moralistic way; here again the influence of pamphlet satire is powerful. The secularisation of that kind of writing produced uncertainties in the role of the author: was he a priest, a clown, or something else? Jonson's own uneasiness in creating this hybrid prose-pamphlet-drama is reflected in the number of surrogate personae which he needs in order to satisfy himself that the viciousness of his characters is being suitably chastised. The choral duo, Mitis

and Cordatus, are stuffy, academic commentators on the play itself;
Asper, the 'Presenter', is an independent moralist who mutates in
the play proper to Macilente, a character motivated by envy rather
than righteous indignation; finally, there is Carlo Buffone, a 'Pub-
like, scurrilous, and prophane Jester' (*Characters*, l.27), who provides the Nasheian entertainment condemned by Jonson's more
rigorous selves. By separating the various roles of the satirical
journalist, and placing them in a hierarchical relationship, Jonson
reassures himself of the dignity of his enterprise while indulging
his taste, and that of his audience, for the comic grotesque.

This fragmentation of personae in *Every Man Out* is matched
by a stylistic fragmentation not simply in the sense that different
characters speak in a different manner, but in the sense that the
grotesque language of detraction is itself more clipped, more asyn-
detic, than the language of Nashe and Shakespeare[12] (it is, perhaps,
closer to the livelier parts of Lodge's *Wits Miserie*):

> hee lookes like a shield of brawne, at *Shrovetide*, out of date,
> and readie to take his leave: or a drie poule of ling upon
> *Easter-eve*, that hath furnisht the table, all *Lent*, as he has
> done the citie this last vacation. (IV. iv. 109–13)
> S'lud, hee lookes like an image carved out of boxe, full of
> knots: his face is (for all the world) like a *dutch* purse, with
> the mouth downeward; his beard the tassels: and hee walkes
> (let me see) as melancholy as one o' the Masters side in the
> *Counter*. (V. vi. 33–7)

These staccato utterances, while clearly in the manner of Nashe,
have an air of constriction about them which is unlike the precipitate style of his pamphlets. Partly it is a matter of the intrusive
punctuation, which Jonson laboured over;[13] it is also possible that
the splutter of descriptive afterthoughts which is a recurrent, stylistic feature of the play, e.g. 'A swine without a head, without braine,
wit, any thing indeed, ramping to gentilitie' (III. iv. 64–6), is a
result of Jonson's study of Florio. Florio's Italian dictionary, *A
Worlde of Wordes* (1598), provided Jonson with the material for
his preliminary sketches of the characters in the play, as Herford
and Simpson point out.[14] The multiplication of synonyms, which
is Florio's basic lexicographical principle, is the basis for these
descriptions, and seems to have influenced the style of caricature
in the play as a whole. But having said that, one is also left with

the feeling that the moralist in Jonson was determined to check the
dangerous proliferation of words which comic prose enjoys. Terms
are multiplied, but syntactically disconnected, and the dominant
tendency of the play towards separation and fragmentation looks
like the moralist's attempt to quell the effusiveness and the sense
of interrelatedness upon which the grotesque depends. Consequently, while Macilente can produce the same sort of derisory thrusts
as Carlo Buffone, Jonson allows him to speak at length only when
regulated by the formal metres of blank verse. And it is by their
tendencies to speak in either prose or verse that Jonson tries to
establish the relative moral authority of his satirical personae.

The problem is that Jonson was trying to create a drama from
the material of prose satire which could also incorporate the tone
of ruthless, moral indignation characteristic of verse satire. Although Jonson despised Marston's bizarre style, the tone of *Every
Man Out* is not dissimilar from *The Scourge of Villanie*. Asper's
furious declamations demonstrate this quite clearly:

> Ile strip the ragged follies of the time,
> Naked, as at their birth . . .
>   and with a whip of steele,
> Print wounding lashes in their yron ribs. (*Induction*,
> ll. 17–20)

Compare the final couplet of the proemium to *The Scourge*:[15]

> Quake guzzell dogs, that live on putred slime,
> Skud from the lashes of my yerking rime.

The language is more comically frenzied than Jonson's but the tone
is essentially the same.

Both Jonson and Marston are scourgers, and both are also Cir-
cean writers: the spectacles they create are of a grotesque world
peopled by monsters who must be whipped and purged. But in the
case of *Every Man Out* this leads to a certain ambivalence. Carlo
Buffone is condemned in the character sketches for his incessant
bestilisation of humanity – 'that (more swift than *Circe*) with
absurd *simile's* will transforme any person into deformity' – and
yet this tendency is implicit throughout the whole play. Carlo
comments on Sogliardo's initiation in the rites of tobacco smoking:

there wee might see SOGLIARDO sit in a chaire, holding his

snowt up like a sow under an apple-tree, while th' other
open'd his nostrils with a poking-sticke, to give the smoke a
more free deliverie. (IV. iii. 93–6)

But when Sogliardo plans to go to a tavern to mix with the 'most
choise gallants', Carlo points out that 'when any stranger comes
in among'st 'hem, they all stand up and stare at him, as he were
some unknowne beast, brought out of *Affrick* . . .' (III. vi. 176–9).
Bestialisation in *Every Man Out* is ubiquitous. Carlo simply articulates more vividly than anyone else in the play the view that
the depravities of urban society turn people into monsters, and
that in their blindness to their own monstrosity they can only see
the beast in others. Despite Jonson's insistence that Carlo is not
his spokesman, it is Carlo's vision of humanity that the play
endorses.

The grotesque, then, in *Every Man Out*, has a narrowly satirical
purpose; it operates at the furthest remove from the saturnalian
grotesque of Rabelais or of *I Henry IV*. In fact, the play seems
actually to invert festive values. The conception of Carlo Buffone
is potentially Falstaffian; he 'hath an extraordinary gift in pleasing
his palat, and will swill up more sacke at a sitting, then would
make all the Guard a posset' (*Characters*, ll. 30–2). And he rejoices
in the more unctuous pleasures of the flesh: 'Let a man sweate
once a weeke in a hot-house, and be well rub'd, and froted, with
a good plumpe juicie wench, and sweet linnen: hee shall ne're ha'
the poxe' (IV. iii. 74–6), he advises Puntarvolo. To entertain the
company at the Mitre he orders a loin of pork; Macilente is disgusted: 'Porke? heart, what dost thou with such a greasie dish', to
which Carlo replies, 'O, it's the only nourishing meat in the
world.'[16] Indeed, at the end of his celebration of the pleasures of
pork Carlo's enthusiasm launches a Rabelaisian outburst[17] which
is unique in the play: 'S'light, fed with it, the whorson strummell-
patcht, goggle-ey'd Grumbledories, would ha' *Gigantomachiz'd*'
(V. v. 42f.). Macilente is the perfect antagonist; he rejects the roast
pig which is to be the central symbol of *Bartholomew Fair*, and to
Carlo he is 'that lean bald-rib MACILENTE', 'a drie crust', a
'pummise' (V. iv. 24–7) and 'a lanke raw-bon'd anatomie'
(IV. iv. 25). At the centre of *Every Man Out*, if the play could be
said to have a centre, is a battle between the fat and the lean, but
the protagonists are cast in unusual roles. Carlo is an anti-Falstaff.

The values of the play demand that his wit be treated as mere scurrility and his gluttony as revolting, physical excess. His very name, Buffone, draws attention to the reprehensibly parasitic aspect of the festive celebrant which in *I Henry IV* is an endless source of comedy; he is closer to the Italian *buffone* or Greek *parasitos*, who would earn free meals by abusing the guests at a dinner party, than he is to the Carnival Lord.[18] It is Macilente's opinion that 'the worst use a man can put his wit to, of thousands, [is] to prostitute it at every taverne and ordinarie' (I. ii. 191–3) which epitomises the social values of this play and casts an envious shadow over the bohemian world of the Boar's Head at Eastcheap. The tavern in *Every Man Out* is not the Boar's Head, but the Mitre, and it is at the Mitre that the battle between the fat and the lean is lost. The meal which Carlo has ordered for the company goes uneaten, the banquet uncelebrated; the arrival of the constable and officers to arrest Fastidious Briske destroys the possibility of festive reconciliation, and the last scene of the play takes place in the Counter prison. Meanwhile, Carlo too has been silenced: his lips are physically sealed by Puntarvolo, enraged by Carlo's mockery of his much loved and lately departed dog.[19] The action is symbolic. In the anti-festive world of *Every Man Out* the orifice which is the source of grotesque verbal humour and the receptacle of meat and wine must literally be dammed up. Although Carlo's derogation of humanity coincides with Jonson's own moral vision in the play, he ensures that Carlo himself is seen to be as bestial as those he condemns. And although Jonson carefully dissociates Asper, the most authoritative of his satirical personae, from the malicious envy of Macilente, it is Macilente whose Lenten spirit broods over *Every Man Out*. He has the last words in the play, and he uses them to summon up his anti-type:

> I will not . . . begge a *Plaudite*, for gods sake; but if you (out of the bountie of your good liking) will bestow it; why, you may (in time) make leane MACILENTE as fat, as Sir JOHN FAL-STAFFE. (V. xi. 82–7)

The allusion polarises both the characters and the plays.

Every Man Out and *I Henry IV* fulfil the two opposed conceptions of sixteenth-century grotesque which, at the beginning of the book, I associated with Schneegans and Bakhtin. Schneegans saw the grotesque primarily as a negative, satirical mode, while to

Bakhtin the grotesque was a celebration of the physical, 'a banquet for all the world'.[20] To the extent that both critics used Rabelais as their yardstick, Bakhtin's approach is the more convincing, but given the complex relationships between sermon, satire and saturnalia with which sixteenth-century grotesque operates, one-sided theories of this kind must remain of limited critical application. This is so because they fail to take account of the different values which Renaissance writers place upon language, and it is in this respect that Bakhtin's enthusiasm for the positive, even life-enhancing, qualities of the grotesque would be inappropriate when considering Jonson. We have seen how the grotesque thrives upon rhapsody, upon prolixity, and this, of course, is the hall-mark of Nashe's style. But while Jonson had clearly learned a good deal from Nashe's comic prose when composing *Every Man Out*, the values which the two writers assign to language are entirely different. Nashe is an explorer, valuing multiplicity and plenitude. Jonson, however, is constantly aware of the moral weakness implied by verbal proliferation and its association with other, more physical forms of incontinence: 'Wheresoever, manners, and fashions are corrupted, language is. It imitates the publicke riot. The excesse of Feasts, and apparell, are the notes of a sick State; and the wantonnesse of language, of a sick mind',[21] as he puts it in *Discoveries*. To Jonson's Lenten temperament, garrulity, like other forms of excess, is evidence of a perverted sensibility, and he uses the expansive, stylistic procedures of the comic grotesque to reveal the stupidity or viciousness of his characters. As a dramatist he is aware of the stylistic vitality of the grotesque, but as a moralist he is determined to expose its dangerous irregularities. Consequently, it would be wrong to see Jonsonian grotesque as part of a Rabelaisian tradition defined by Bakhtin's criteria of linguistic exuberance and physical communality. For although much of Jonson's comic prose has its roots in such a tradition, as well as in the satirical journalism which derives from Aretino, his moral earnestness pulls him in an opposite direction. He stands at the end of a period of immense linguistic and stylistic innovation, and his conservative instincts would undoubtedly have led him to sympathise with the pleas of eighteenth-century writers for purity and firmness of diction, for 'correctness', the qualities most alien to the Elizabethan grotesque.

2   THE FATNESS OF THE FAIR

In view of Jonson's deep mistrust of festivity and prolixity, the achievement of *Bartholomew Fair* is all the more remarkable. Nowhere in his drama is didactic intention less obtrusive, and yet nowhere does a moral statement about human nature emerge so coherently from the rambling, literary structures of the grotesque.

First performed eleven years after the death of Elizabeth, *Bartholomew Fair* is the apotheosis of the Elizabethan grotesque. The scrivener's remark in the induction that 'the language some where savours of *Smithfield*, the Booth, and the Pig-broath' (Induction, ll. 150–1) is something of an understatement. It is a triumphant integration not only of comic language and comic spectacle, but also of diverse theatrical forms: elements from Aristophanic comedy, the medieval allegorical drama, and contemporary satire are fused in a central dramatic image which encapsulates the seething, physical activity of the grotesque. In the Fair Jonson discovered an image which the wildly exploratory writing of Nashe was incapable of formulating, but which nevertheless epitomises his total achievement; it is the urban palimpsest of the Rabelaisian tripe-feast, and in staging the play at the Hope theatre Jonson 'observ'd a speciall Decorum, the place being as durty as *Smithfield*, and as stinking every whit' (Induction, ll. 158–60). (The Hope was used for bear-baiting two days a week, a fact which lends further significance to the name or Ursula – often abbreviated in the play to 'Urs' or 'Ursla' – and identifies her closely with the place itself.) The Fair is also the solution to the problem he set himself in *Every Man Out*: how to structure dramatically the spectacle of the varied and disorderly relationships which the city breeds; in fact, how to put the city on stage. In *Every Man Out* he allowed Cordatus to explain what he was trying to do:

> is it not an object of more state, to behold the *Scene* full, and reliev'd with varietie of speakers to the end, then to see a vast emptie stage, and the actors come in (one by one) as if they were dropt downe with a feather, into the eye of the spectators? (II. iii. 297–301)

But the programme resulted in a mixture of diffuseness and inertia. This was due partly to Jonson's construction of an elaborate defence-system of surrogate personae, who saturated the meagre plot

in commentary and annotation, and partly to the absence of any
unifying themes and images. In this attempt to create the sense of
crowdedness and variety which typifies the city, Jonson sacrificed
dramatic coherence to incidental colour, using Carlo Buffone to
encrust the action with a patina of 'adulterate similes'. The reason
that no such disjunction between language and action exists in
Bartholomew Fair is because the central image of the Fair is the
informing, structural principle of the play as a whole.

An image of this kind could not be constructed merely by filling
the stage with a 'varietie of speakers'. But neither would the highly
formal stagecraft of *Volpone* and *The Alchemist* serve to suggest
the ungovernable muddle of city life. Instead, Jonson returned to
a medieval tradition of staging to emblematise the contemporary,
satirical vision of the city as a panorama of vice.[22] While the text
of the play is packed with references to the topography of Elizabethan London – Cheapside, Moorfields, Picthatch, Cow-lane,
Puddle-wharf – and to its fashions and temptations, the theatrical
edifice of the Fair turns the specific and the ephemeral into permanent symbols of human appetite. Ursula's pig-booth and the
puppet-theatre, 'the tents of the wicked' in the eyes of Zeal-of-the
land Busy, are the focal points of the action; they also correspond
to the mansions or *sedes* of the mystery plays, described by Glynne
Wickham as 'symbols for the identification of place'.[23] But perhaps
the best analogy is with the fifteenth-century morality, *The Castle
of Perseverance*: the play was staged within a circular *platea* on
which certain mansions acted as the fixed, symbolic locations of
the world, the flesh and the devil, which the peripatetic *Humanum
Genus* encounters in his journey through life.[24] At the Hope *Bartholomew Fair* would have been performed on a trestle stage within
a circular arena, and the symbolic locations on stage have a similar
function to those of *The Castle*.[25] Indeed, Knockem points out the
pig-booth to Quarlous with the words, 'this is old *Ursla's* mansion,
how like you her bower?' (II. v. 39–40). Ursula's mansion is the
magnetic centre of the Fair, to which nearly all the characters are
at some point attracted. Acting as a tavern, a brothel, a public
lavatory and a bank for stolen goods, the pig-booth is also the
seedy metropolis in microcosm. But through its correspondence
with the *sedes* of medieval drama its function in the play is not
merely to provide a theatrical equation for contemporary urban
squalor. R. B. Parker has argued persuasively that the booth was

situated stage left, in the position of hell-mouth,[26] and the smoky fire which burns within certainly bears out this contention. Ursula's complaints to Mooncalf that 'Hell's a kind of cold cellar to't' (II. ii. 44), and 'must you be drawing the ayre of pacification . . . while I am tormented, within, i' the fire' (II. v. 61–3) and her pained attack on Quarlous and Winwife, 'Curse of hell, that ever I saw these Feinds' (II. v. 161) are utterances also redolent of the inferno. So the Fair and its mansions compose a theatrical image which is both realistic and symbolic: the linguistic detail of the play establishes the Fair as a satirical image of contemporary London, while its staging, much of which is implicit in the text, transforms that image into a symbol of the temptations to which all human flesh is prone.

Such a mixture of the realistic and the symbolic is partly accommodated by the Aristophanic structure of the play. This has been explored in some detail by J. M. Potter, who has this to say:[27]

> A single episode is related not to the other episodes but to a central theme or conflict which is expressed in the agon and the resolution of the play. Thus the structure is not A leads to B leads to C leads to Y, but A, B, and C lead to Y.

This is true of *Every Man Out*, too: just as the various lines of action in *Bartholomew Fair* lead to the denouement at the puppet theatre, so in the earlier play the separate strands of the plot converge in the ruined banquet at the Mitre. But Jonson's understanding of *Vetus Comoedia* in *Every Man Out* was limited by the Renaissance association of that genre with Roman satire,[28] and this partly accounts for the harsh, anti-festive tone of the play. *Bartholomew Fair* is more genuinely Aristophanic in that its topical satire mingles freely with symbolic and saturnalian elements, and it is precisely this balance which determines the play's quite different moral vision. In these terms the ritual feast and sacrifice of the symbolic roast pig is necessarily ambivalent; so too are the denizens of the Fair, who are both the cony-catchers of Elizabethan pamphlet notoriety and the somewhat tarnished deities of Ancient Greece.[29] Despite the infernal odours of the pig-booth, the idols of the Fair have their own validity, and neither the satirical detractions of Quarlous nor the Puritan fulminations of Busy are morally endorsed by the play itself. Further, the balance between satire and saturnalia is carefully preserved in the language of *Bartholomew*

Fair. When Ursula accuses Knockem of malicious gossip: 'You are one of those horsleaches, that gave out I was dead, in Turne-bull streete, of a surfet of botle ale, and tripes', he counters, 'No 'twas better meat, *Urs*: cowes udders, cowes udders!' (II. iii. 13–17). In Rabelais's rural France tripe is a festive food: in seventeenth-century London it has degenerated into an image of urban squalor – part of the satirist's language of abuse. But with the improbable 'cowes udders' Knockem restores to Ursula the connotations of plumpness and succulence which befit her role as festive miscreant, while failing to retract the satirical imputation of prostitution. (Turnbull Street was famous for its brothels.) The exchange epitomises the way in which the realistic and the symbolic, the satirical and the saturnalian, co-exist in the play.

Bartholomew Fair has attracted a considerable amount of critical attention, and two prominent themes have emerged from this. The one is concerned with fertility and infertility, the other with the notion of licence.[30] But to argue for the centrality of either of these themes would be misguided. The first three acts develop the former, while the focus of act four is clearly on the latter; moreover, to divorce the two means divorcing the linguistic and imagistic texture of the play from its moral concerns. I hope to avoid that pitfall in what I aim to do in the remainder of this chapter; that is, to show how the Jonsonian grotesque of *Bartholomew Fair* reaches a moral tatement about human nature (and, perhaps, about male and female nature) which is dissimilar both from Shakespeare's drama of the body in *Henry IV* and from Jonson's own previous visions of humanity.

The first act of *Bartholomew Fair* takes place in Littlewit's London home and, outside the symbolic context of the Fair, the dominant note of the act is one of realistic, satirical comedy. With the exception of Justice Overdo all the visitors to the fair are introduced, proposals for the expedition are launched, and a clear demarcation is thus established between the characters who come to the Fair from without and those who are its permanent inhabitants. Of the visitors the obvious candidate for the role of satirical commentator in Quarlous – wit, cynic and man-about-town. His name, in fact, suggests that he is contentious and quarrelsome, and the long diatribe against his companion Winwife's predilection for rich widows is a cascade of disgusted abuse:

> There cannot be an ancient *Tripe* or *Trillibub* i' the Towne,
> but thou art straight nosing it, and 'tis a fine occupation
> thou'lt confine thy selfe to, when thou ha'st got one; scrub-
> bing a piece of *Buffe*, as if thou hadst the perpetuity of
> *Pannyer-alley* to stinke in; or perhaps, worse, currying a
> carkasse, that thou hast bound thy selfe to alive . . . A sweet
> course for a man to waste the brand of life for, to be still
> raking himselfe a fortune in an old womans embers; we shall
> h'a thee, after thou hast beene but a moneth marryed to one
> of 'hem, looke like the *quartane ague*, and the black *Jaundise*
> met in a face, and walke as if thou had'st borrow'd legges of
> a *Spinner*, and voyce of a *Cricket*. (I. iii. 63–83)

The tone of fascinated, physical revulsion is reminiscent of Nashe
in his most castigating manner, though the theme of the debase-
ment of sex by avarice is perhaps more typical of Roman satire.[31]
Quarlous's vision of the female body as rotten offal, rank as a
tannery, verges on the hysterical; indeed, it is difficult to believe
that he is actually talking about sex, for the harshness of the tone
is matched by a series of literally abrasive images – of tanning,
scraping and grating – which reduce copulation to an industrial
process. The ostensible subject of his harangue is infertility, but the
obliterating disgust of Quarlous's indictment of infertile sex demolishes his credentials as a satirical commentator to whom we
should seriously attend. The sheer length of the speech (forty-six
lines in all) gives it an air of irrelevance, of unreality, and it is of
course delivered outside the world of the Fair, which is to test all
such histrionic moral attitudes.

For Quarlous has yet to confront Ursula, the fecund centre both
of the Fair and of the play; her booth and its temptations act as
both lodestone and moral touchstone for the characters who visit
it. 'This is the very *wombe*, and *bedde* of enormitie! grosse, as her
selfe!' (II. ii. 106–7) comments the shocked Adam Overdo, but this
description of the pig-booth as a breeding-ground of fleshy vice is
entirely apt. Ursula may be one of Quarlous's old 'trillibubs' – the
suggestion is of obesity – but she is scarcely the desiccated, sterile
creature of his perverted imagination. Her body, like Falstaff's, is
composed of volatile organic matter:

> I am all fire, and fat, *Nightingale*, I shall e'en melt away to
> the first woman, a ribbe againe, I am afraid. I doe water the

ground in knots, as I goe, like a great Garden-pot you may
follow me by the S.S. I make. (II. ii. 50–4) A poore vex'd
thing I am, I feele my selfe dropping already, as fast as I can:
two stone a sewet aday is my proportion. (II. ii. 79–81)

Again, like Falstaff, her body has fertile properties; Falstaff's sweat
'lards the lean earth', while Ursula's waters it like a gardener's can.
But the symbolic associations of this commerce between body and
earth are more explicit in Jonson's creation. As Eve, 'the first
woman', Ursula is representative of common, female humanity,
and as the pig-woman she is identified with Demeter, goddess of
fertility. In *The Golden Bough* Frazer writes:[32]

> Passing next to the corn-goddess Demeter, and remembering
> that in European folk-lore the pig is a common embodiment
> of the corn-spirit, we may now ask whether the pig, which
> was so closely associated with Demeter, may not have been
> originally the goddess herself in animal form?

Ursula herself is similarly inseparable from the pigs which are her
trade, and her body undergoes the same processes of dissolution.
She is 'all fire and fat', slowly melting in the heat, and she is
'mother o' the Pigs' and 'some walking Sow of Tallow' (II. v. 75,
78–9). A further comment of Frazer's is relevant here: 'at the
Thesmophoria the women appear to have eaten swine's flesh. The
meal, if I am right, must have been a solemn sacrament or com-
munion, the worshippers partaking of the body of the god.'[33] The
closeness of the identification is not, I think, fortuitous. By divesting
Ursula of personality, which Falstaff clearly has, Jonson enables
her to accrete mythic and symbolic qualities[34] so that, despite her
relative lack of interest as a 'character', her booth becomes a focal
point for the various strands of action in the play.

The first visitors to Ursula's 'mansion' are Winwife and Quarlous, who greet her with amused repulsion, and, in keeping with
the play's balancing of satire and saturnalia, the conflict between
the fat and the lean that follows is conducted in explicitly sexual
terms. Ursula begins somewhat sentimentally:

I, I, Gamesters, mocke a plaine plumpe soft wench o' the
Suburbs, doe, because she's juicy and wholesome: you must
ha' your thinne pinch'd ware, pent up i' the compasse of a

dogge-collar, (or 'twill not do) that lookes like a long lac'd
Conger. . . . (II. v. 83–7)

But the gamesters relentlessly heap on the obscenity:

> *Quar.* Yes, hee that would venture for't, I assure him, might
> sinke into her, and be drown'd a weeke, ere any friend hee
> had, could find where he were.
> *Win.* And then he would be a fort'night weighing up againe.
> *Quar.* 'Twere like falling into a whole *Shire* of butter: they
> had need be a teeme of *Dutchmen*, should draw him out.
> (II. v. 95–101)

Roused to fury, now, Ursula rallies to curse them with the very
image of emaciated womanhood for which Quarlous had earlier
expressed such revulsion (compare Aretino's description of the
Mother of Discipline quoted in chapter 2):

> Hang 'hem, rotten, roguy Cheaters, I hope to see 'hem plagu'd
> one day (pox'd they are already, I am sure) with leane play-
> house poultry, that has the boany rumpe, sticking out like
> the Ace of Spades, or the point of a Partizan, that every rib
> of 'hem is like the tooth of a Saw: and will so grate 'hem
> with their hips, & shoulders, as (take 'hem altogether) they
> were as good lye with a hurdle. (II. v. 104–10)

And the battle now becomes physically violent. Armed at the beginning of the encounter with a firebrand, Ursula goes back into
her booth to reinforce herself with a scalding pan, and in the
ensuing skirmish she is burned by the oil. 'Curse of hell, that ever
I saw these Feinds', she moans; Quarlous and Winwife make a
speedy departure, and the Fair people run for suitable
medicaments.

The scene is worth quoting in detail because it epitomises the
confrontations in the play as a whole. In Ursula, 'the fatnesse of
the *Fayre*' (II. ii. 118), different images of woman conjoin, and the
conflict between the fat and the lean becomes a conflict between
female and male. She is associated with Eve and Demeter, but she
is also the grotesque embodiment of femaleness; she compares her
own voluminous hips with Mooncalf's 'Grasse-hoppers thighes',
while the 'quagmire' of her womb, which Quarlous derides, typifies
the reaction of an appalled male to the disturbing obscurities of

female sexuality. At the same time Ursula fulfils the traditional notion of female nature as being chaotic and discordant, and the pig-booth takes on the appearance of hell's kitchen as she wields her firebrand and scalding pan against the 'Feinds', Quarlous and Winwife. Indeed, this image of Ursula has been effectively linked with the *Discordia* figure of the emblem books.[35] The portrait of Ursula is densely composed, and it is ultimately based on a view of female nature which was current from Plato down to the sixteenth century. This view derives from the belief that woman, by contrast with the more rational male, was subservient to the behaviour of her autonomous, animal womb.[36] Rabelais comments in the *Tiers Livre*:[37]

> Certes Platon ne sçait en quel ranc il les doibve colloquer, ou des animaus raisonnables, ou des bestes brutes. Car Nature leurs a dedans le corps posé en lieu secret et intenstin un animal, un membre, lequel n'est ès hommes, onquel quelques-foys sont engendrées certaines humeurs salles . . . par la poincture et frétillement douloureux desquelles (car ce membre est tout nerveux et de vif sentement) tout le corps est en elles esbranlé, tout les sens raviz, toutes affections intérinées, tout pensemens confonduz.
> [Certainly Plato does not know which category to put them in, that of rational animals or brute beasts. For Nature has placed inside their bodies in a secret, inward place an animal, a member, which men do not have, in which at certain times are engendered certain salt humours . . . by whose pricking and painful quivering (for this member is all made of nerve and lively feeling) their whole body is disturbed, their senses ravished, all their emotions upset and thoughts confused.]

But while Ursula, pig-woman and termagant, with her huge womb and insatiable physical needs, is a pattern of ungovernable female nature, the vital question to ask of her role in *Bartholomew Fair* is whether or not she is merely the object of the misogynistic satire which was popular enough at the time. To explain why she is not takes us to the central themes of the play.

Quarlous is caught between his rejection of both the fat and the lean, between his contempt for Ursula's lubricity and his contempt for the sterility of Winwife's ageing widows. But Winwife, too, assumes an air of detachment; when offered the wares of the Fair, he sneers: 'That these people should be so ignorant to thinke us chapmen for 'hem! doe wee looke as if we would buy Ginger-bread? or Hobby-horses?' And to this Quarlous retorts, in a rare moment of judiciousness, 'Why, they know no better ware then they have, nor better customers then come. And our very being here makes us fit to be demanded, as well as others' (II. v. 13–18). Quarlous's observation is suitably self-chastening, for it is he who in the final scene of the play agrees to marry Dame Purecraft, the object of his earlier scorn. The two points are crucial. Quarlous and Winwife, Adam Overdo and Zeal-of-the-land Busy, variously attempt to dissociate themselves from the 'enormities' of the Fair and pretend that they are not 'of the Fair'. They ostentatiously deny in themselves the instinctive desires which the Fair stimulates. But the play's symbolism, built upon the medieval staging of *platea* and mansions, and upon the central figure of Ursula, works against these claims of immunity. The visitors claim to experience the Fair as something external to themselves, but it is not. The Fair is the summation of the lusts and appetites which they have come to gratify or condemn, and the populace of the Fair – as in the allegorical drama of the previous age – are static and depersonal-ised because they represent the mass of ineradicable human in-stincts which human beings must confront. Through her the Fair is imbued with the spirit of female disorderliness, but Jonson is not attempting to polarise male and female natures; by allegorising the Fair as the chaotic, inner world of instinct and appetite, he grants to the traditional, derogatory image of woman a universally human validity. Men in *Bartholomew Fair* must come to terms with the female in each of them.

The dual theme of female appetite and male hypocrisy is ex-tremely common in Jacobean satirical comedy, but its moral di-mensions in *Bartholomew Fair* are possibly unique. While scarcely an optimistic play, it nevertheless lacks the pervasive cynicism of Middleton's drama. *A Chaste Maid in Cheapside*, for instance, performed the year before *Bartholomew Fair* by the same company, Princess Elizabeth's Men, seems to have been suggestive to Jonson. The two plays share many features – the concern with fertility and infertility, images of dryness and wetness and of physical processes in general, anti-Puritan satire, the proximity of Smithfield, and so on[38] – but *A Chaste Maid* is far less morally certain, especially in its treatment of male and female appetite. The christening feast for

Mrs Allwit's illegitimate baby, at which a crowd of gossips con-
sume large quantities of wine and sweetmeats, might be described
as the grotesque centre-piece of the play, and it is this scene in
particular that generates the 'mood of soiled saturnalia' discussed
by R. B. Parker.[39] The males remain at a critical distance from the
feasting, and when Tim Yellowhammer, just down from Cambridge with his tutor, is embraced by one of the ladies, he pouts:

> O this is horrible,
> She wets as she kisses! [Aside] – Your handkercher, sweet tutor,
> To wipe them off as fast as they come on. (III. ii. 182–6)

This male distaste for female liquidity is expressed again at the end
of the scene, when Allwit and Davy examine the detritus of the
party:

> *Allwit.* . . . How hot they've made the room with their thick
>   bums! Dost not feel it, Davy?
> *Davy.* Monstrous strong, sir.
> *Allwit.* What's here under the stools?
> *Davy.* Nothing but wet, sir;
>   Some wine spilt here belike.
> *Allwit.* Is't no worse, think'st thou? (III. ii. 182–6)

But this derogatory view of female physicality is not effectively
counterbalanced, as it is in *Bartholomew Fair*, by the insistence
that a susceptibility to fleshly excess is a universal human weakness.
While it is true that Tim's adventure with the Welsh gentlewoman
exposes his earlier fastidiousness as hypocrisy, the morally more
repellent male figures of Yellowhammer and Allwit remain quite
unscathed by the events of the play. Far from being included in its
orgy of physical indulgence, they exploit the appetites of others for
their own material ends and leave the stage both satisfied and
unpunished. Middleton's images of physical disgust focus on the
female, while he allows the physical detachment of the more genuinely sinful males to preserve them from the penalties they deserve.
(The fate of Sir Walter Whorehound is the exception here, of
course.) And this disjunction between physical and moral revulsion
must consequently baffle attempts to find any coherent moral attitude towards the vices that Middleton so luridly depicts.

   Jonson's moral standpoint, by contrast, is based upon a less
ambivalent view of physical excess. *Bartholomew Fair* deliberately

removes the sins of the flesh from the realm of the demonic, and
forces those who would condemn such a weakness first to acknowledge it in themselves. The comic associations of Ursula's pig-booth
with hell are seized upon in all earnest by the Puritan fanatic, Zeal-
of-the-land Busy:

> But the fleshly woman, (which you call *Ursla*) is above all to
> be avoyded, having the marks upon her, of the three enemies
> of Man, the World, as being in the *Faire*; the Devill, as being
> in the fire; and the Flesh, as being her selfe. (III. vi. 33–7)

While Ursula undoubtedly bears the marks of the world and the
flesh, Busy's outrageous hypocrisy exempts her from the diabolical
aspersions. For Busy's own appetite impels him to partake of
Ursula's worldly sacrament, and in the company of two other
women, Win Littlewit and Dame Purecraft, he enters 'the tents of
the wicked' to eat roast pig. In doing so he embraces more fervently
than any of the other males the female principle of physical disorder, which he just as fervently condemns. But the exposure of
Busy's hypocrisy is not merely a matter of anti-Puritan satire: his
hysterical attacks upon the satanic character of the Fair caricature
the position of the established church towards human frailty, just
as Adam Overdo's hunting down of 'enormity' caricatures the
more unrealistically zealous applications of the law. In this respect
Bartholomew Fair resembles *Measure for Measure*, a play which
also uses the theatrical techniques of the allegorical drama. Isabella
and Angelo, frozen *exempla* of Church and law, find that their
unworldly principles cannot be sustained in the face of the comically subversive demands of human instinct. In these plays both
Jonson and Shakespeare are revealing the inadequacy of religious
and legal strictures to modify the instinctual drives of the human
flesh; both persuade the audience to withdraw their sympathies
from those whose fanaticism attempts to repress or exclude such
drives. If *The Merry Wives* is, formally, Shakespeare's most Jonsonian play, the moral vision of *Bartholomew Fair* makes this
Jonson's most Shakespearean play.

The role of Busy in *Bartholomew Fair* demonstrates a further
moral concern of Jonson's which is, however, rarely a dominant
theme in Shakespeare's plays. The dangers of verbosity, and the
idiocy which such verbal incontinence implies, is a Jonsonian theme
familiar to us from *Every Man Out*, but the greater structural and

moral complexity of *Bartholomew Fair* enables Jonson to deal with
the moral implications of garrulity in a rather more subtle manner.
The Puritan Busy battles against the excesses of the Fair with
words, and it is this which upsets the people of the Fair. Leatherhead calls officers to restrain him:

> *Lea.* Here he is, pray you lay hold on his zeale, wee cannot
> sell a whistle, for him, in tune. Stop his noyse, first!
> *Bus.* Thou canst not: 'tis a sanctified noise. I will make a loud
> and most strong noise till I have daunted the prophane
> enemy. (III. vi. 102–6)

And even when threatened with the physical punishment of the
stocks, the undaunted Busy continues to thunder: 'No, Minister of
darknesse, no, thou canst not rule my tongue, my tongue it is mine
own, and with it I will both knocke and mocke downe your
Bartholomew abhominations . . .'. Busy's stream of verbiage is
eventually checked by the confutation of the puppets, but from the
start his physical excesses have exploded the validity of what he
has to say. Busy is a caricature, and the incontinence of his speech
and the incontinence of his appetite grow to be synonymous, rather
than just hypocritically separate. Quarlous and Adam Overdo are
less obviously caricatures, but they are, with Busy, partners in
volubility. The three leading males claim various kinds of authority
for their harangues – social, legal, and religious, respectively – but
in each this authority is undermined. Their verbal torrents vaporise
into steam-clouds, gushingly defensive attempts to protect themselves from what Overdo calls 'enormity', and they do not grasp
that the world of the Fair is both innate and irresistible.

Throughout the play there is an ambiguous relationship between
the word and the flesh. On the one hand, Jonson's *dictum* in
Discoveries that garrulity is gluttony is fulfilled by Busy; on the
other hand, the play presents an explicit antagonism between
language and appetite. Verbal excess is used, vainly, as a means of
defence against physical excess, and Busy's attacks on the Fair, like
Quarlous and Winwife's encounter with Ursula, are a clash between the word and the flesh. The separation of the two is, ultimately, a sexual separation, for volubility in the play is revealed to
be a male characteristic, and excess of appetite (initially) a female
characteristic. Ursula is a far less cerebral figure than Falstaff, and
the grotesque of *Bartholomew Fair* does not emerge from a cel-

ebratory fusion of the word and the flesh. Ursula's colleagues clearly doubt her ability to cope with the verbal sallies of Quarlous and Winwife: 'Where's thy *Bartholomew* wit, now? *Urs*, thy Bar-tholomew-wit?' urges Knockem, and although she counters them boldly, he advises 'Peace, *Urs*, peace *Urs*, they'll kill the poore Whale, and make oyle of her. Pray thee goe in' (II. v. 102–3, 129–30). The conflict between the verbal and the physical is another facet of the central confrontations of the play, and in the end it can be expressed by the question of what is 'enormity'. Does 'enormity', or 'excess', or 'overdoing it' refer to physical indulg-ence, as Adam Overdo would insist, or does it refer to the verbal incontinence of those who, like himself, fulminate obsessively against the flesh? The predicament neatly contains both Jonson's well-known distaste for prolixity and his satirical duty to castigate vice. The paradox is surely intentional, for the play is concerned with the rehabilitation of the flesh in a fallen world. As in *Every Man Out*, the deluded characters are to be knocked out of their humours, but here the process is more gently reductive. In the last scene of *Bartholomew Fair* Adam Overdo assumes his most au-thoritative posture, as he prepares to unmask the vices inspired by the Fair, and, with Busy now deflated, his rhetorical extravaganza smacks a little of the Puritan orator:

> Now, to my enormities: looke upon mee, O *London*! and see mee, O *Smithfield*; The *example of Justice*, and *Mirror of Magistrates*: the true top of formality, and scourge of enorm-ity. Harken unto my *labours*, and but observe my *discoveries*; and compare *Hercules* with me, if thou dar'st, of old; or *Columbus*; *Magellan*; or our countrey man *Drake* of later times: Stand forth, you weedes of enormity, and spread. (V. vi. 33–40)

(Again, the ambiguity of 'my enormities' is deliberate.) What he reveals, of course, is his wife in a fit of vomiting. The stage direction reads, '*Mistresse* Overdoo *is sicke: and her husband is silenc'd*'; the voiding of food at last supersedes the voiding of words. What Adam Overdo must learn is what all the visitors to the Fair must learn: 'remember you are but Adam, Flesh, and blood! you have your frailty, forget your other name of Overdoo', says Quarlous.

Authority in *Bartholomew Fair* is, in fact, vested in the only character who belongs neither to the Fair itself, nor to its visitors.

Though quite unlike Jonson's typical 'authority figures', it is the madman, Troubleall, whose repeated admonition to all to 'Quit yee, and multiply yee' points to the equilibrium achieved in the final scene. Troubleall's authority is based less upon the traditional role of the wise fool as on the fact that, since the Fair itself is the antithesis of Reason, it is fitting that its spokesman should be a madman. And in his exaggerated respect for Justice Overdo's warrant the issue of legalism's failure to regulate instinct is caricatured. The notion underlying Troubleall's activities is that of licence – 'licence' meaning, conversely, the legal authority of a warrant (i.e. words) and 'unwarranted' physical indulgence – but his simple benediction, with its procreative message, transcends both these opposites. Troubleall does not appear in the play until act four, but this act he dominates. He has superseded Ursula, and his function is to bestow upon the anarchic and inarticulate world of the flesh a blessing of fertility. Behind the luxuriant surface of *Bartholomew Fair* is the dim outline of an image not of damnation, but of the Creation. Ursula's 'quagmire' is an image of primordial chaos, while Overdo and she are associated with both Adam and Eve, the word and the flesh. The resolution of the play involves the embrace of the one by the other, as the voluble reclaim their physicality. The only character who remains apart from the mundane is Troubleall, whose message, meaning 'Go forth and multiply',[40] suggests that in his madness he believes that he is God. There is consummate irony in the fact that, in *Every Man Out* and the other 'comicall satyres', when Jonson had knocked his characters out of their humours, the authority figure who remained was an image of Jonson himself.

The grotesque of *Bartholomew Fair*, then, emerges from a confluence of the forms of sermon, saturnalia and satire which, as I have argued throughout this book, determine the modes of expression of the Elizabethan grotesque. Each of these elements is vital to the structure of the play, but each is carefully held in check, and it is exactly this balancing of disparate forces that constitutes the peculiar tone of the play. Although it uses saturnalian motifs, *Bartholomew Fair* is not a festive comedy; its moral vision is sceptical in a way which admits the frailty of the flesh, which satirises those who would repress its urges, but which takes no positive delight in the celebration of the flesh. But neither is it a satirical comedy: on the one hand it lacks the bestialising and punitive violence of *Every Man Out* or, for that matter, *Volpone*, with its strongly purgatorial drive; on the other hand, the dramatic image of the Fair has a symbolic importance which goes beyond the topical urban satire we associate with that genre. Nor is it a luridly admonitory work; the demonic is evoked, but exorcised by comedy. Grotesque in *Bartholomew Fair* is, instead, both a human and a humane leveller, uniting its characters through their eventual apprehension of the gross physicality of the world and of their desires. The play works, if I may briefly recapitulate, in the following way. The grotesque image of the Fair not only provides a satirical definition of the city, but also acts as an external projection of the inner life of its visitors in the manner of the allegorical drama. This inner life is characterised as female riot and disorder, with Ursula as its comic embodiment; it is to Ursula that the visitors of the Fair are magnetically attracted. Male hypocrisy is tested against the comic principle of female disorder, and while the men attempt to resist the physical with a profusion of words, they learn that flesh and blood inevitably subvert the verbal authority of religious and legal prescription. Ultimately, the achievement of *Bartholomew Fair* lies in its creation of a rich and profoundly suggestive dramatic image – an image which itself epitomises the Elizabethan grotesque – where the language of comic prose is correlated by physical spectacle.

Conclusion

The Elizabethan grotesque is generated, in the first place, by the physicality of the language of comic prose, and the master of this peculiar literary mode is Nashe. I believe that Nashe's writing has been seriously underestimated, or ignored, partly because of its obliqueness to the major literary genres of the period, and partly because of its recklessly subversive quality, which deters criticism. To appreciate the sheer comic power of his work, as Dekker and Middleton, Shakespeare and Jonson, all did (and Harvey was compelled to), we must attend primarily to the life of the language itself. It is, above all, Nashe's capacity for embodiment, his ability to translate the sordid and the absurd, the ludicrous and frightening aspects of reality into a language of comparably physical character, which is the essence of his comic genius. In his capacity too, for extremely rapid assimilation of diverse material, the quality of his mind is similar to Shakespeare's, and among Elizabethans the sheer range of his vocabulary is second only to that of Shakespeare. Where Nashe failed completely was in accommodating his material to strong and abiding dramatic structures – for drama alone, I think, could have fulfilled his talents; but the restive quality of his imagination precluded that kind of achievement. He was, in many ways, a man on the brink: the popular basis of Rabelais's monstrous novel, i.e. folk-stories of the giants, would have seemed impossibly *gauche* and vulgar to him, while the drama that might have suited him, the satirical comedy of Jonson and Middleton, was not yet in existence, and he lacked the ability, or the openings, to create it himself. What he learned about writing from Aretino and the Marprelate fray was a sense of the ebullient, physical power of words, and this equipped him for the role of polemicist and satirical journalist. But what he achieved is of a greater importance than such functions normally permit. The verbal energy

156

of the pamphlets themselves still retain for us, as I hope I have now shown, their comic and disturbing impact. Their impact on his contemporaries was very considerable indeed. Whether the comic drama from *I Henry IV* to *Bartholomew Fair* would have been different without Nashe is impossible to assess, but it is a reasonable contention.

In another respect, however, it is precisely because the restiveness of Nashe's writing defies attempts to categorise it that his grotesque vision of the world is able to emerge so forcefully. When Montaigne compared the subjective and exploratory character of his essays to the grotesque composition on his wall, he was indicating their marginal quality, their diversity and strangeness, and elsewhere he describes his literary technique as an association of heterogeneous material. Nashe's writing shares this characteristic, and both writers are self-consciously observant not only of their tendency to digress, but also of their tendency to bring into conjunction images of a radically different kind. But Nashe is not a contemplative writer, and in his work this stylistic habit is coupled with a comic awareness of how these disparate objects of our perception collide, producing dizzying configurations of the incompatible: eyes and oysters; eviscerated stomachs and porridge pots; sweaty jumpers and tripes. He binds the domestic to the horrific, and one of his favourite analogies is between cooking and death. The basis of his grotesque vision is, ultimately, the relationship between the human body and the external world, and the body's capacity for metamorphosis. He was not, like Rabelais (or Lodge), a doctor, but his writing is rooted in a culture permeated at all levels by the language of the body. The enormous interest during the sixteenth century in medicine, surgery and nutrition may only have been of indirect importance to Nashe himself, but his taste for bizarre physical analogies was undoubtedly stimulated by the pre-scientific culture of which he was a part. In common with the writers of medical tracts he would have subscribed to Montaigne's belief, that 'Toutes choses se tiennent par quelque similitude', and this notion forms the stylistic basis of his writing. It is, then, not only the physicality of the language itself, but also the imaginative process of associating disparate aspects of the physical world, which constitutes the peculiarity of the Elizabethan grotesque.

The tone of the Elizabethan grotesque, however, is determined by rather different factors. Leaving aside the compilers of jest books, the only English prose writers prior to the 1590s who were prepared to confront the daily and disreputable aspects of life were religiously motivated.[1] The models available to a writer venturing into such territory were those of clown and preacher, and when Martin Marprelate and his subsequent opponents amalgamated these authorial roles in the religious controversy of 1588–90, they opened a new area of literary activity – satirical journalism. But for these pamphleteers the very fact that the authorial personae they adopted were of a hybrid nature meant that the tone of their writing remained uncertain, and this tonal instability is evident in the work of Nashe and his imitators. Satirical journalism, then, which is perhaps the best, though not the only, way in which we can characterise Nashe's writing, was the offspring of two quite distinct sub-literary traditions: the festive tradition of saturnalian clowning and the morally censorious tradition of the sermon. The convergence of these two modes, which produced a rather different literary form during the 1590s, was precipitated chiefly by the emergence in London of a group of aspirant *literati* and by their consequent awareness of the city itself as a potential literary subject. It is this uncertain combination of authorial roles which created in the early satirical journalism a suitable vehicle for the grotesque. Martin Marprelate, for instance, used the festive motif of the May-game for the purposes of topical satire in his ridicule of the priest, Glibbery of Halstead, in *Hay Any Worke for Cooper*, while his opponents seized upon the same device to provide a comic framework for their ferocious depictions of Martin's torture and death. Likewise, the purgatorial instincts behind Nashe's festive comedy, *Summers Last Will and Testament*, surface in the full-throated histrionics of *Christs Teares over Jerusalem*; yet the images of damnation evoked there are the product of the same fascination with the more lurid details of the London townscape which provided the satirical comedy of *Pierce Penilesse*. So the harnessing of the domestic and the demonic in images of the body which are alternately repulsive and celebratory, ludicrous and horrific, is matched by a constant shifting of tone from sheer hilarity, through satire, to strident moral outrage. And this procedure of disturbing the normal patterns of image and response in relation to the physical world is the very procedure from which the Elizabethan grotesque acquires its comically disturbing power as a mode of literary expression.

Nashe's followers in the line of Elizabethan pamphleteering share this power, though in a diminished form. The power is diminished in part simply because the enterprise was no longer quite so uncertain and exploratory, and its sermonising and saturnalian parenthood no longer so apparent; the disappearance of the demonic element, in particular, removes the sense of frenzy which is so characteristic of Nashe's writing. So we find in the Nasheian pieces of Lodge, Middleton and Dekker a less ambiguous concern with documenting the scabrous sides of urban life. Their deployment of grotesque imagery – with the exception, perhaps, of Middleton's *The Blacke Booke* – tends towards embellishment, whereas in Nashe the grotesque springs from the life of writing itself and is determined by the imaginative and stylistic processes of composition. Almost at the moment of its inception, then, satirical journalism sheds its associations with the literary factors conducive to the grotesque. Both Middleton and Dekker (Middleton more caustically; Dekker more compassionately) use the medium for social reportage; Middleton's foray into pamphleteering was brief, anyway, and for Dekker, who lived in London in some poverty for more than sixty years, the comic possibilities of urban squalor eventually wore thin. But the grotesque in comic prose evaporated for reasons other than the writers' establishment in their roles as social reporters. The stylistic tendency of seventeenth-century prose was towards clarity and brevity, whereas the grotesque depends upon ambivalence and prolixity.[2] The character writers, who might have sustained the grotesque mode in English prose, opted for the former and followed Theophrastus rather than *Pierce Penilesse*. In the section 'What is a Character' in the 'Overburian Characters' we are told that 'Character is also taken for an Egiptian Hierogliphicke, for an impresse, or shorte Embleme; in little comprehending much. . . . It is wits descant on any plaine song.'[3] The notions of *multum in parvo* and of wit as a mere embellishment on a firm substance of fact inevitably precluded the dynamism of the grotesque.

Nashe's legacy, however, was inherited by the dramatists – by Dekker, Middleton and others, but also, and more importantly, by Shakespeare and Jonson – and the grotesque in Elizabethan dramatic prose takes on a somewhat different character. For one thing, there was no place in the drama of the late 1590s, and onwards, for the sermonisers of earlier moralistic plays; Jonson had to satisfy his didactic urges by replacing these prophets of doom with a variety of satirical commentators whose moral authority was determined by the continence of their language. (Consequently, in *Every Man Out* the grotesque becomes a negative satirical force.) At the same time, though, the drama was able to employ the grotesque in festive motifs, notably the battles between Carnival and Lent, the fat and the lean, which are a profuse source of comic imagery in late sixteenth- and early seventeenth-century plays. The move towards satire is therefore challenged by, and held in balance with, the more traditional, saturnalian element in the theatre. Finally, the removal of the demonic from comic prose allowed sex to infiltrate the language of the grotesque, and sex too becomes a subject for both comedy and castigation, a battleground between the fat and the lean.

But there is little uniformity of tone among the major dramatists in the use of the grotesque in comic prose. Dekker was never really at ease with the brashness and acrimony of the new satirical comedy, and his best-known play, *The Shoemakers Holiday*, generally excludes the more disturbing aspects of the grotesque from its festive vision. *The Honest Whore*, which is perhaps his most successful play, is exceptional because the sentimentality implicit in the title is tested by a vigorous awareness of depravity and social flux in contemporary London. By contrast, it is on just such an awareness that Middleton's talent specifically depends. Lacking both the jollity and compassion of Dekker, and also the greater moral certainty of Shakespeare and Jonson, Middleton's comedies derive their power from a form of grotesque realism in which the chief focus of attention is the suppurating life of the city itself. None of his contemporaries is so exclusive in his use of festive motifs for the purposes of sexual satire.

Despite their pamphlet imitations of Nashe, as dramatists Dekker and Middleton remain mutually opposed. The reverse is true of Shakespeare and Jonson. The plays of theirs which reveal the influence of Nashe and the comic grotesque can, cautiously, be considered together — not, at any rate, in the polar terms in which their drama is usually described: indulgent Shakespeare and censorious Jonson. The two parts of *Henry IV* move from indulgence to purgation, from saturnalia to satire, while *The Merry Wives* is both a 'humours' play and one in which the action is based upon the Italian *lazzi* that Jonson loved. Jonson, less coherently and over a longer period of time, moved in the opposite direction, and the furiously purgative play, *Every Man Out*, was eventually re-modelled as the relatively indulgent *Bartholomew Fair*. Shake-speare is calmer, more fully in control. The pattern of *Henry IV* is the pattern of *Love's Labour's Lost* and of *Twelfth Night*: everyday knocks at the door of holiday. If the process of reawakening is harsher in *Henry IV* than in the comedies it is because that play is also concerned with the political health of the nation, as well as the physical health of its more aberrant members. But it would be an insensitive reader of the play who argued that Falstaff's ultimate fate impugned his obvious vitality. Despite Hal's sanctimonious claim to 'know you all' at the outset, the play cannot be read backwards. We must enjoy Falstaff before we can be rid of him, and in being rid of him it would be the merest hypocrisy to say that we did not enjoy him, because Falstaff is the embodiment of a world which has its own validity, however temporary, and that world is a vital part of our own humanity.

It is not a world for which Jonson had much instinctive sym-pathy. With the exception of *Every Man In*, his early comedy positively invited the moralistic applause which Shakespeare's com-edies consistently defy, and while the structure of *The Merry Wives* is Jonsonian in its use of Italianate motifs to knock Falstaff out of his 'humour', the tone of the play is considerably less rancorous than that of *Every Man Out*. Where Shakespeare and Jonson do conjoin is in their absorption, at the end of the 1590s, of Nashe's grotesque diction, and in their dramatic deployment of the new styles of comic prose which he largely fostered. But in *Every Man Out* festive abuse turns malign; indeed, the festive aspects of the grotesque are consciously inverted, and prolixity becomes a satir-ical vehicle for the exposure of the morally degenerate. It was not until he composed *Bartholomew Fair*, fifteen years later, that Jon-son was able to digest fully the literary influences which dominated the beginning of his career. This play is Jonson's masterpiece: it is a monument to his powers of assimilation, so often adversely compared with Shakespeare's ability in this respect. It combines Aristophanic and Italianate comic forms with the language of 1590s comic prose and the mythological detail of the Jacobean court masque, and it fuses these various elements in a coherent dramatic image – the Fair itself. Yet it is a play which retains a peculiarly Elizabethan quality. Jonson returned in *Bartholomew*

Fair to the subject matter of his earlier drama with a new feeling for the expansiveness and diversity of the raw, urban comedy which typifies the Elizabethan grotesque. As a result, *Bartholomew Fair* reaches depths of moral sanity which Jonson had never previously explored. In the last analysis, however, and despite the moderation of its judgments, the play remains quite distinct from Shakespeare's comedies. In Shakespeare, notably in the two parts of *Henry IV*, the grotesque is subsumed into a dialectical process of physical indulgence and physical purgation, while in Jonson the grotesque has a more clearly reductive function: violently destructive in *Every Man Out*; more indulgently levelling in *Bartholomew Fair*. And while Shakespearean grotesque describes a dramatic movement in terms of a physical process, Jonsonian grotesque works in a more static way to create a series of comic spectacles.

The paradox of Jonson's achievement in *Bartholomew Fair* is that the play both absorbs and defies the stylistic values of the Elizabethan grotesque, and, as such, it is a valediction to an era of reckless linguistic exploration. In the course of the seventeenth century a massive shift in attitudes towards literary style eventually debarred the kind of writing which has been the subject of this study. The trend towards tauter and sparer literary styles, modelled on Seneca, which had begun early in the century, was sustained by the great scientific achievements of the middle decades and by the consequent feeling among Restoration writers and academics that literary language might conform to the intellectual values of science and mathematics.[4] Montaigne's doctrine of association, for instance, is curtly disposed of by John Eachard in *Grounds and Occasions of the Contempt of the Clergy* (1670): 'He that has got a set of Similitudes, calculated according to the old Philosophy, and Ptolemy's System of the World, must burn his Commonplace Book, and go a gleaning for new ones.'[5] But the main objection was to the instability, and the apparent insubstantiality, of figurative language. Unaware of the powerful consonance between word and thing, between language and the body, which the pre-scientific Elizabethan culture had created, the Oxford don Samuel Parker wrote as follows:[6]

> Now to Discourse of the Natures of Things in Metaphors
> and Allegories is nothing else but to sport and trifle with
> empty words, because these Schems do not express the Na-

tures of Things, but only their Similitudes and Resemblances, for Metaphors are only words, which properly signifying one thing, are apply'd to signifie another by reason of some Resemblance between them. When therefore any thing is express'd by a Metaphor or Allegory, the thing it self is not expressed, but only some similitude observ'd or made by Fancy.

This elaborate assertion, wholly typical of the literary values of the period, unconsciously withers the achievements of Nashe, Shakespeare and Jonson and their experiments with the grotesque in comic prose; it would also demolish the peculiar strengths of the writing of the entire Renaissance period.

We cannot, however, finally abandon this subject without mention of its supreme anomaly. Sir Thomas Urquhart, born in Cromarty in 1611, published his translation of *Gargantua and Pantagruel* in 1653, and it is the last of the great English Renaissance translations. As a literal rendering of Rabelais, Urquhart's work is not very accurate, but his ability to mesh the most outlandishly academic vocabulary with the rudest colloquialism is perfectly adapted to the style of the original. Similarly, his facility in spawning multiple synonyms, which outdo Rabelais's own mammoth lists, and his skill in coining vituperative epithets give the translation a dynamically inventive power which a more faithful rendering could hardly have achieved. A brief quotation cannot do justice to the stylistic scope of Urquhart's Rabelais, but the episode in which the cake-bakers of Lerne castigate the Shepherds as 'Slapsauce fellows, slabberdegullion druggels ... scurvie sneaksbies ... blockish grutnols, doddipol joltheads, jobbernol goosecaps ... slutch calf-lollies, grouthead gnat-snappers ... codshead loobies ... Turdie gut, shitten shepherds' (*Gargantua*, ch. XXV) gives some impression of his talent for execration! The year before the appearance of *Gargantua and Pantagruel* Urquhart had published a work called *The Jewel*, which contained his plans for a universal language. The preface begins, simply enough, with the statement that 'Words are the signes of things ...', but the proposals themselves would have made John Eachard or Samuel Parker blench. They include the following:[7]

Fourthly, By vertue of adjectitious syllabicals annexible to nouns and verbs, there will arise of several words, what compound, what derivative, belonging in this language to one noune or to one verb alone, a greater number then doth pertaine to all the parts of speech in the most copious language in the world besides. . . .

Nineteenthly, Every word of this language, declinable or indeclinable, hath at least ten several synonymas. . . .

Three and twentiethly, Every word in this language signifieth as well backward as forward; and however you invert the letters, still shall you fall upon significant words: whereby a wonderful facility is obtained in making of anagrams. . . .

Nine and thirtiethly, Every word in this language is significative of a number because, as words may be increased by addition of letters and syllables, so of numbers is there a progress *in infinitum*.

In groping for a system which might equate language and number, Urquhart actually inverts the linguistic prescriptions of Restoration writers who sought a mathematical relationship between words and things in order to restore discipline to literary discourse. His enterprise is curiously poised, and not in merely chronological terms, between the sixteenth and eighteenth centuries, between the figurative abundance of the Elizabethan and the scientism of the Augustans.

Urquhart is the last exponent of a grotesque mode of comic prose which flourished in the late Elizabethan period. And while it is true that Swift and Sterne, for instance, belong to a Rabelaisian tradition, the entirely different cultural conditions of the eighteenth century could not have reproduced either the distinct verbal quality or the tone of Elizabethan comic prose. In the Romantic period, and after, the grotesque underwent a radical change: as the mind turned in upon itself, the rich, physical world of Nashe, Shakespeare and Jonson was replaced by the supernatural territory of nightmare and Gothic fantasy, where horror mingles not with comedy but with beauty, and in the twentieth century the fear of the demonic has in turn given way to a nauseating sense of the absurd. Consequently, the grotesque has shifted from being a supremely physical mode of artistic expression, through a period of supernaturalism, to a strikingly metaphysical role. In his book on the later development of the grotesque Wolfgang Kayser concluded with a tripartite definition: 'The grotesque is the estranged world. . . . The grotesque is a play with the absurd' and, finally, it is 'an attempt to invoke and subdue the demonic aspects of the world'.[8] I have no intention, in my own conclusion, of attempting to refute such a definition. What I would refute is the notion that a concept of the grotesque which is valid for twentieth-century literature can also be valid for sixteenth-century literature. The Elizabethan grotesque is the result of an identifiable and unrepeatable phase in the development of English culture.

Notes

Archiv   Archiv für das Studium der Neuren Sprachen und Literaturen
EC   Essays in Criticism
EHR   Economic History Review
ELH   English Literary History
ELN   English Language Notes
HLQ   Huntingdon Library Quarterly
JWCI   Journal of the Warburg and Courtauld Institutes
MLN   Modern Language Notes
MLR   Modern Language Review
MP   Modern Philology
N & Q   Notes and Queries
PBSA   Papers of the Bibliographical Society of America
PMLA   Publications of the Modern Language Association of America
PQ   Philological Quarterly
Ren D   Renaissance Drama
RES   Review of English Studies
SAB   Shakespeare Association Bulletin
SEL   Studies in English Literature, 1500–1900
SP   Studies in Philology
TLS   Times Literary Supplement
UTQ   University of Toronto Quarterly

1 LITERARY GROTESQUE: A SIXTEENTH-CENTURY BACKGROUND

1 For a brief, general introduction, with a literary bias, to the social
and economic background, see L. G. Salingar, 'The Social Setting', in
The Age of Shakespeare, ed. Boris Ford (Harmondsworth, revised
1956) and Brian Gibbons, *Jacobean City Comedy* (1968), 32–49; on
education see Joan Simon, *Education and Society in Tudor England*
(Cambridge, 1966); on inflation see R. B. Outhwaite, *Inflation in
Tudor and Early Stuart England* (London, 1969); on plague see F. P.
Wilson, *The Plague in Shakespeare's London* (Oxford, 1927).
2 Skelton was known to the Elizabethans not so much as a poet but a

clown, a perpetrator of 'merry jests'; see Maurice Pollet, *John Skelton: Poet of Tudor England*, trans. John Warrington (London, 1971), chapter ten, 'Legend and Reputation'. Pollet writes that by 1580 'Skelton had suddenly grown old, outmoded. He disappeared from the poetic scene. No one dreamed of republishing him' (p. 167).

3 The authors are usually considered to have been Job Throkmorton and John Penry; see William Pierce, *An Historical Introduction to the Marprelate Tracts* (London, 1908).

4 *A Defence of the Government Established in the Church of England* (1587).

5 See J. L. Lievsay, *The Englishman's Italian Books: 1550–1700* (Philadelphia, Penn., 1969).

6 See Philip Thomson, *The Grotesque* (London, 1972).

7 See Heinrich Schneegans, *Geschichte der grotesken Satire* (Strasburg, 1894).

8 *Ibid.*, p. 33 ('jene frivole, ohne irgend welchen Grund das Erhabene in den Staub ziehende Geistesrichtung').

9 *Ibid.*, p. 39 ('die bis zur Unmöglichkeit, gesteigerte Karikatur des in der Wirklichkeit Nichtseinsollenden').

10 Mikhail Bakhtin, *Rabelais and his World*, trans. Hélène Iswolsky (Cambridge, Mass., 1968), p. 315.

11 A. B. Grosart, ed., *The Works of Gabriel Harvey, D.C.L.* (London, 1884), II, 229.

12 Giorgio Vasari, *Le Vite*, ed. Paola della Pergola *et al.* (Milan, 1962), I, 140–1.

13 Albert Thibaudet and Maurice Rat, eds, *Montaigne: oeuvres complètes* (Paris, 1962), p. 181.

14 For a fuller account of the origins of the term grotesque see Wolfgang Kayser, *The Grotesque in Art and Literature*, trans. Ulrich Weisstein (Bloomington, Indiana, 1963). Kayser does argue – unconvincingly, I think – that there are 'sinister' elements in the ornamental grotesque.

15 See the remarks of Carel van Mander in the *Schilderboek* (1604): 'he did much work in the manner of Jeroon van den Bosch and produced many spookish scenes and drolleries', quoted by F. Grossman, *Bruegel: The Paintings* (London, 1955), p. 7.

16 Vasari himself, however, found Bruegel's grotesque as merely frivolous as the Roman paintings: 'la qual carta gli fu disegnata da un pittore che gli fece intagliare i sette peccati mortali, con diverse forme di demoni, che furono cosa fantastica e da ridere ... e tante altre fantastiche e capricciose invenzioni che sarebbe cosa fastidiosa a volere di tutte ragionare' ['which picture was designed for him by a painter who had engraved for him the seven deadly sins, with various shapes of demons, which made a fantastic and comical sight ... and so many other fantastic and wanton inventions that it would be tiresome to recount them all'], della Pergola, *op. cit.*, V, 220–1. ('La qual carta' refers to Bruegel's *The Alchemist*.)

17 See M. Dorothy George, *English Political Caricature* (Oxford, 1959), I, 6–7; Benno Geiger, *I Dipinti ghiribizzosi di Giuseppe Arcimboldi* (Florence, 1954), fig. 25.

18 R. B. McKerrow, ed., *The Works of Thomas Nashe*, revised, F. P. Wilson (Oxford, 1958), I, 167.

19 A. B. Grosart, ed., *The Non-Dramatic Works of Thomas Dekker* (London, 1884), II, 120.

20 *The Winter's Tale*, IV. iv. 773–8. References to Shakespeare are to Peter Alexander's one volume edition, London, 1951.

21 E. W. Gosse, ed., *The Complete Works of Thomas Lodge* (Glasgow, 1883), II, 18.

22 McKerrow, *op. cit.*, II, 240.

23 G. R. Hibbard, *Thomas Nashe: A Critical Introduction* (London, 1962), p. 123.

24 Alice Walker and Gladys Willcock, eds, *The Arte of English Poesie* (Cambridge, 1936), p. 261.

25 James Spedding, R. L. Ellis and D. D. Heath, eds, *The Works of Francis Bacon* (London, 1857–74), VIII, 76.

26 Thomas Vicary, *The Anatomie of the Bodie of Man*, eds F. J. and P. Furnivall (1888), p. 79. The notion derives from Aristotle; see *Generation of Animals*, trans. A. Peck (Cambridge, Mass., 1943), I, 101–3, 109.

27 John Huarte, *The Examination of Mens Wits*, trans. R. C. (London, 1594), pp. 25–6.

28 Tomaso Garzoni, *The Hospitall of Incurable Fooles* (London, 1600), sig. B1^r.

29 McKerrow, *op. cit.*, I, 379.

30 This point would have been lost on A.-F. Le Double, author of *Rabelais: anatomiste et physiologiste* (Paris, 1899). The comparisons of parts of the body with food, household objects, etc. in Rabelais's anatomisation of Quaresmeprenant are claimed to be literally accurate; many rather notional diagrams are provided as evidence.

31 Cf. Geiger, *op. cit.*, fig. 19 ('Faccia corrosa di uomo: paesaggio fantastico').

32 Grosart, *The Non-Dramatic Works of Thomas Dekker*, II, 212.

33 *Ibid.*, II, 214.

34 Cf., especially, the development of this motif from 'The Temptation of St Anthony' (dated 1556) to the design for 'Invidia' (dated 1557).

35 E. H. Gombrich, *Art and Illusion: A Study in the Psychology of Pictorial Representation* (London, 1960), p. 89.

36 Robert Hughes, *Heaven and Hell in Western Art* (London, 1968), p. 227.

37 McKerrow, *op. cit.*, II, 84. Brueghel's depiction of the seething monstrosities of sin in 'The Fall of the Rebel Angels' (dated 1562) is a close illustration of this idea.

38 W. B. D. D. Turnbull, ed., *The Anatomie of Abuses* (London, 1836), p. 226.

39 See Kayser, *op. cit.*, p. 185.

40 Jacques Boulenger and Lucien Scheler, eds, *Rabelais: oeuvres complètes* (Paris, 1955), pp. 22–3.
41 See Natalie Zemon Davis, *Society and Culture in Early Modern France* (1975), especially chapter four ('The Reasons of Misrule').
42 John Taylor, *Jack a Lent, His Beginning and Entertainment* (London, 1620), sig. B2ᵛ. Taylor says that he wrote the work in 1617 (sig. B3ʳ).
43 These have been well documented by C. L. Barber in *Shakespeare's Festive Comedy* (Princeton, N.J., 1959); see also Ian Donaldson, *The World Upside-Down* (Oxford, 1970).
44 The continental situation provoked this sort of alarm. M. A. Shaaber in *Some Forerunners of the Newspaper in England 1476–1622* (Philadelphia, Penn., 1929) lists thirty-eight newsbooks concerning France and the Netherlands, chiefly of a sensational kind, in 1590 alone; see pp. 170–1. And it is surely no coincidence that Shakespeare's history plays, dealing with the disease of civil war, appear during this decade.
45 See, for example, Adam Hill, *The Crie of England* (London, 1593); Thomas Dekker, *Newes from Graves-end* (London, 1604); William Warde, *Gods arrowes* (London, 1607). A favourite instance of God's destruction of the wicked city was Jerusalem: see John Stockwood, *A very fruitfull and necessarye sermon of the moste lamentable destruction of Jerusalem* (1584), one of the sources for Nashe's *Christs Teares*.
46 See, for instance, 'Simon Smel-knave', *The Fearefull and Lamentable Effects of Two Dangerous Comets* [1591], and 'Adam Fouleweather', *A Wonderfull, Strange and Miraculous, Astrologicall Prognostication* [1591]. The second is printed by McKerrow as a dubious work of Nashe.
47 A. B. Grosart, ed., *The Life and Complete Works in Prose and Verse of Robert Greene, M.A.* (London, 1881–6), XII, 165.

2 THE LOW STYLE IN ELIZABETHAN COMIC PROSE

1 See, for example, *Hamlet*, III. iv. 48; R. B. McKerrow, ed., *The Works of Thomas Nashe*, revised F. P. Wilson (Oxford, 1958), III, 176, I, 215 and II, 251; Estienne Tabourot, *Les Bigarrures du Seigneur des Accords* (1583); Albert Thibaudet and Maurice Rat, eds, *Montaigne: oeuvres complètes* (Paris, 1962), pp. 973 and 941. See also Barbara C. Bowen, 'What does Montaigne mean by "marqueterie"?', *SP*, LXVII (1970), 147–55.
2 See Walter J. Ong, S.J., 'Oral Residue in Tudor Prose Style', *Rhetoric, Romance and Technology* (Ithaca, New York, 1971), especially pp. 33–4.
3 Thibaudet and Rat, *op. cit.*, p. 620. (I.e. 'without beginning, middle or end'.)
4 *Ibid.*, p. 736.

5   *Ibid.*, p. 48.
6   *Ibid.*, p. 34.
7   *Ibid.*, p. 1047. (It is not really possible to keep the pun on 'similitude' in English.)
8   McKerrow, *op. cit.*, I, 377–8. The influence of this work on Shakespeare's treatment of the themes of sleep and guilt in *Macbeth* has been most convincingly demonstrated by Ann Pasternak Slater in 'Macbeth and the Terrors of the Night', *EC*, XXVIII (1978), 112–28.
9   Recent scholars have endorsed Sykes's argument that *The Blacke Booke* and *Father Hubburd's Tales* are Middleton's work. See H. Dugdale Sykes, 'Thomas Middleton's Early Non-Dramatic Work', *N & Q*, CXLVIII (1925), 435–8.
10 The *blason* is also a source of parody in its proper, heraldic sense. Cf. Henry Chettle, *Kind-Hartes Dreame* (1592), ed. G. B. Harrison (1923), p. 61 ('his standard, being three Rats and a paire of shackells, drawn in a white field, cheuernd with Newgate chaine, (in memorie of his long communitie therewith) and loftily borne on a broome staffe'). Mock coats of arms were a popular ingredient of Elizabethan comic literature; other examples of a more or less grotesque nature can be found in *The Arundel-Harington Manuscript of Tudor Poetry*, ed. Ruth Hughey (Columbus, Ohio, 1960), I, 231 ('The Coppie of a Libell. Written against Bashe'); McKerrow, *op. cit.*, II, 271–2, and C. H. Herford and Percy Simpson, eds, *Ben Jonson* (Oxford, 1925–52), III, 504 (all references to Jonson are to this edition).
11 W. A. Ringler, ed., *The Poems of Sir Philip Sidney* (Oxford, 1962), p. 12.
12 Jacques Boulenger and Lucien Scheler, eds, *Rabelais: oeuvres complètes* (Paris, 1955), p. 622.
13 A. H. Bullen, ed., *The Works of Thomas Middleton* (London, 1896), VIII, 42–3.
14 Cf. B. Geiger, *I Dipinti ghiribizzosi di Giuseppe Arcimboldi* (Florence, 1954), figs 42 ('Il Cantiniere') and 43 ('Il Cuoco').
15 Eliot's part in the literary relationships and influences of the 1590s is of some interest. He was, apparently, a friend of *both* Nashe and Harvey; see Clifford Chalmers Huffman, 'Gabriel Harvey on John Florio and John Eliot', *N & Q*, CCXVIII (1975), 300–2. He was also the source of Shakespeare's French dialogue, at least in *Henry V*; see J. W. Lever, 'Shakespeare's French Fruits', *Shakespeare Survey* VI (1953), 79–90. Finally, he had read Rabelais, from whom he borrowed a considerable amount in compiling *Ortho-Epia Gallica*.
16 John Eliot, *Ortho-Epia Gallica* (London, 1593), A3^v.
17 *Ibid.*, B2^v–B3^r.
18 See T. L. Summersgill, 'The Influence of the Marprelate Controversy upon the Style of Nashe', *SP*, XLVIII (1951), 145–60, for example.
19 J. B. Leishman, ed., *The Three Parnassus Plays* (London, 1949): *The Returne from Parnassus* (second part), I. ii. 249–51.
20 McKerrow, *op. cit.*, I, 282.

21 A. B. Grosart, ed., *The Works of Gabriel Harvey, D.C.L.* (London, 1884), I. 214.

22 McKerrow, *op. cit.*, I, 267.

23 Grosart, *op. cit.*, II, 76.

24 Erasmus, *Opera omnia* (Leyden, 1704), V, 1010.

25 Louise B. Osborn, ed., *The Life, Letters and Writings of John Hoskyns* (New Haven, Conn., 1937), pp. 122–3. Hoskyns's example may refer to Nashe; see McKerrow, *op. cit.*, I, 219.

26 See *I Henry IV*, II. iv. 246–7: 'When thou hast tired thyself in base comparisons hear me speak but this', and I. ii. 77–9: 'Thou hast the most unsavoury similes, and are indeed the most comparative rascalliest sweet young prince.'

27 See G. K. Hunter, *John Lyly: The Humanist as Courtier* (London, 1962), chapter 2.

28 R. W. Bond, ed., *The Complete Works of John Lyly* (Oxford, 1892), III, 133.

29 McKerrow, *op. cit.*, I, 160. The publication of Casaubon's Theophrastus in the same year as *Pierce Penilesse* greatly influenced the development of the satirical character sketch. See B. Boyce, *The Theophrastan Character in England to 1642* (Cambridge, Mass., 1947).

30 Boulenger and Scheler, *op. cit.*, p. 533.

31 In a letter to the *TLS* (4 May 1962) A. J. Kirkman listed twenty-four of Nashe's coinages in current use. We would not now think of any of these as 'grotesque', but the list is evidence of Nashe's remarkable facility of invention.

32 McKerrow, *op. cit.*, III, 11.

33 *Ibid.*, III, 207 (*Oxford English Dictionary*: Mulliegrums . . . 'A grotesque, arbitrary form').

34 *Ibid.*, I, 192.

35 *Ibid.*, II, 183. The passage is from the preface to the 2nd edn (1594).

36 In the preface to *Lenten Stuffe* (1599) he orders the reader to 'renounce eating of greene beefe and garlike till Martlemas, if it be not the next stile to *The strife of Love in a Dreame* . . .' (this was the English title of the *Hypnerotomachia*), McKerrow, *op. cit.*, III, 149.

37 Leo Spitzer, 'Le prétendu réalisme de Rabelais', *MP*, XXXVII (1939), 142. ('Le comique grotesque est précisément cette horreur qui se dégage du vide qui a été, il y a un instant encore, du solide' . . . 'le terrain vague de l'inexistant' . . . 'neutralise encore le sentiment de l'horreur du néant que provoque tout nélogisme.')

38 McKerrow, *op. cit.*, 115.

39 *Ibid.*, III, 41.

40 *Ibid.*, III, 186.

41 *Ibid.*, V. 129.

42 See O. J. Campbell, 'The Relationship of *Epicoene* to Aretino's *Il Marescalco*', *PMLA*, XLVI (1931), 752–62.

43 See E. Meyer, *Machiavelli and the Elizabethan Drama* (Weimar, 1897); cited by Campbell, *op. cit.*, p. 759.

44 See David McPherson, 'Aretino and the Harvey-Nashe Quarrel',

PMLA, LXXXIV (1969), 1551–8.

45 McKerrow, *op. cit.*, III, 152.

46 E. W. Gosse, ed., *The Complete Works of Thomas Lodge* (Glasgow, 1883), IV, 63.

47 See Harry Sellers, 'Italian Books Printed in England before 1640', *The Library*, V (1924), 105–28.

48 See A. B. Grosart, ed., *The Life and Complete Works in Prose and Verse of Robert Greene, M.A.* (London, 1881–6), II, 345 and Anthony Munday, *The English Romayne Life*, ed. G. B. Harrison (London, 1925).

49 Apart from Florio's *First Fruites* (1576) and *Second Fruites* (1591) there appeared works such as William Thomas' *Principall Rules of the Italian Grammar* (1550), Scipio Lentulus' *Italicae grammatices institutio*, trans H. G. (1575), and Claudius Holyband's *The Pretie Historie of Arnalt and Lucenda* (1575), reissued in 1597 as *The Italian Schoole-maister*. See also Frances Yates, 'Italian Teachers in Elizabethan England', *JWCI*, I (1937), 103–16.

50 See Alice Harmon, 'How Great was Shakespeare's Debt to Montaigne?', *PMLA*, LVII (1942), 988–1008.

51 McKerrow, *op. cit.*, III, 123.

52 See McKerrow, *op. cit.*, I, 259–60.

53 G. B. de Sanctis, ed. *Pietro Aretino: Tutte le commedie* (Milan, 1968), p. 119.

54 *Ibid.*, p. 212.

55 G. Aquilecchia, ed., *Pietro Aretino: Sei giornate* (Bari, 1969), p. 19.

56 McKerrow, *op. cit.*, II, 247.

57 *Ibid.*, II, 213.

58 *Ibid.*, III, 93.

59 Aquilecchia, *op. cit.*, pp. 36–7.

60 McKerrow, *op. cit.*, III, 129.

61 *Ibid.*, I, 163.

62 *Ibid.*, I, 167.

63 Aquilecchia, *op. cit.*, p. 78.

64 McKerrow, *op. cit.*, III, 147.

65 Thibaudet and Rat, *op. cit.*, p. 295.

66 Grosart, *The Works of Gabriel Harvey, D.C.L.*, I, 201.

67 *Ibid.*, I, 218.

68 *Ibid.*, II, 45.

69 Aquilecchia, *op. cit.*, p. 18.

70 McKerrow, *op. cit.*, II, 303.

71 Aquilecchia, *op. cit.*, p. 243.

72 McKerrow, *op. cit.*, I, 345.

73 Aquilecchia, *op. cit.*, p. 49.

74 *Ibid.*, pp. 90–1.

75 McKerrow, *op. cit.*, III, 198–9.

76 De Sanctis, *op. cit.*, pp. 60–1. *Sconcacarsi* is a portmanteau word formed from *sconciarsi*, the disparaging opposite of *acconciarsi*, to dress or adorn oneself, and *cacare*.

77 McKerrow, *op. cit.*, I, 181.
78 *Ibid.*, III, 191.
79 *Ibid.*, I, 370.
80 De Sanctis, *op. cit.*, p. 181.
81 Aquilecchia, *op. cit.*, p. 28.
82 McKerrow, *op. cit.*, II, 291.
83 *Ibid.*, II, 127.
84 *Ibid.*, I, 275.
85 De Sanctis, *op. cit.*, p. 79 and McKerrow, *op. cit.*, II, 183.
86 De Sanctis, *op. cit.*, p. 79.
87 Aquilecchia, *op. cit.*, p. 83.
88 Mario Tonello, 'Lingua e polemica teatrale nella *Cortigiana* di Pietro Aretino' in *Lingua e strutture del teatro Italiano del Rinascimento*, ed. G. Folena (Padua, 1970), p. 245 ('È comune ad ogni livello, nell' Aretino, questo concretizzare, questo portare ogni fatto, ogni situazione nell' ambito delle facoltà sensoriali').
89 Pietro Aretino, *La Terza et ultima parte de ragionamenti* (1589), sig. A5^v. (There is a pun on *copia* in the rhetorical sense, and probably on *corna*.)
90 Aquilecchia, *op. cit.*, p. 257.
91 *Ibid.*, pp. 127–8.
92 McKerrow, *op. cit.*, III, 219.
93 *Ibid.*, III, 154.
94 *Ibid.*, III, 41.
95 *Ibid.*, III, 134.
96 *Ibid.*, I, 306.
97 *Ibid.*, III, 121.

3 COMEDY AND VIOLENCE IN ELIZABETHAN PAMPHLET LITERATURE

1 See Huntingdon Brown, *Rabelais in English Literature* (Cambridge, Mass., 1933). An elaborate attempt has been made to show that Nashe was influenced by Rabelais by Werner von Koppenfels in 'Thomas Nashe und Rabelais', *Archiv*, CCVII (1970), 277–91. However, the parallels he draws are not very convincing, as they are nearly all quite common motifs of sixteenth-century comic literature. Most of these examples are taken from *Gargantua*; an English version of the folk-tale, based on Girault's *Les grandes et inestimables Cronicques du . . . Gargantua*, was in existence by 1592 (see Brown, *op. cit.*, pp. 31–2), and it is possible that Nashe had seen that.
2 Essex is said to have presented a copy of the *Epistle* to Queen Elizabeth. See William Pierce, *An Historical Introduction to the Marprelate Tracts* (1908), p. 159, n. 3.
3 William Pierce, ed., *The Marprelate Tracts: 1588, 1589* (1911), p. 17.
4 *Ibid.*, pp. 17, 230, 221.

5 James Spedding, R. L. Ellis and D. D. Heath, eds, *The Works of Francis Bacon*, VIII, 76–7.

6 Jacques Boulenger and Lucien Scheler, eds, *Rabelais: oeuvres complètes* (Paris, 1955), p. 106.

7 R. B. McKerrow, ed., *The Works of Thomas Nashe*, revised F. P. Wilson (Oxford, 1958), I, 59. Several anti-Marprelate tracts are included by McKerrow in his edition of Nashe, but he came to doubt their authorship by the time the edition was complete. However, there is convincing argument for Nashe's authorship of *An Almond for a Parrat* by D. J. McGinn in 'Nashe's Share in the Marprelate Controversy', *PMLA*, LIX (1944), 952–84.

8 McKerrow, *op. cit.*, I, 83.

9 From *Pappe with an Hatchet* (London, 1589), probably by Lyly; R. W. Bond, ed., *The Complete Works of John Lyly* (Oxford, 1892), III, 404.

10 V. A. Kolve, *The Play Called Corpus Christi* (Stanford, Calif., 1966), pp. 180–200.

11 McKerrow, *op. cit.*, I, 135.

12 Boulenger and Scheler, *op. cit.*, p. 86.

13 Philip Thomson, *The Grotesque* (London, 1972), p. 42.

14 Arnold Davenport, ed., *The Poems of John Marston* (Liverpool, 1961), p. 97.

15 McKerrow, *op. cit.*, I, 177–8.

16 *Ibid.*, III, 87.

17 *Ibid.*, I, 322.

18 *Ibid.*, I, 306.

19 *Ibid.*, I, 361.

20 *Ibid.*, I, 373.

21 Boulenger and Scheler, *op. cit.*, p. 227.

22 McKerrow, *op. cit.*, III, 34.

23 *Ibid.*, III, 35.

24 *Ibid.*, III, 180–1.

25 Davenport, *op. cit.*, p. 143.

26 See C. G. Harlow, 'Nashe's Visit to the Isle of Wight and his Publications of 1592–4', *RES*, n.s. XIV (1963), 225–42.

27 McKerrow, *op. cit.*, II, 327.

28 *Ibid.*, II, 320.

29 Boulenger and Scheler, *op. cit.*, p. 574.

30 McKerrow, *op. cit.*, II, 168–9.

31 *Ibid.*, I, 356–7.

32 *Ibid.*, I, 349.

33 L. B. Jennings, *The Ludicrous Demon* (Berkeley, Calif., 1963), p. 17.

34 McKerrow, *op. cit.*, II, 231.

35 *Ibid.*, III, ll, 260–5.

36 Boulenger and Scheler, *op. cit.*, chapter IX.

37 McKerrow, *op. cit.*, II, 69.

38 *Ibid.*, II, 58–9.

39 *Ibid.*, II, 172.
40 *Ibid.*, II, 84.
41 Geoffrey Keynes, ed., *The Works of Sir Thomas Browne* (London, 1964), I, 24.
42 William Bullein, *A Dialogue against the Fever Pestilence*, eds Mark W. and A. H. Bullen (London, 1888), p. 73.
43 See F. P. Wilson, *The Plague in Shakespeare's London* (Oxford, 1927) for this and other information about the plague.
44 F. P. Wilson, ed., *The Plague Pamphlets of Thomas Dekker* (Oxford, 1925), p. 3.
45 *Ibid.*, p. 61.
46 *Ibid.*, p. 34.
47 *Ibid.*, p. 26.
48 *Ibid.*, p. 55.
49 *Ibid.*, p. 52.

4 NASHE AND THE BEGINNING OF SATIRICAL JOURNALISM

1 See, for example, 'Great excesse in bootehose'; W. B. D. D. Turnbull, ed., *The Anatomie of Abuses* (London, 1836), pp. 52–3.
2 I.e., *The examination of usurie, in two sermons* and *The first sermon of Noahs drunkenness.*
3 See Robert Robinson, *A most wonderfull and true report . . .* (1586), described in W. C. Hazlitt, *Hand-Book to the Popular, Poetical and Dramatic Literature of Great Britain* (1867), p. 335, but now lost (?).
4 William Jones, *A wonder woorth the reading . . .* (1617), quoted by M. A. Shaaber, *Some Forerunners of the Newspaper in England 1476–1622* (Philadelphia, Penn., 1929), p. 155.
5 Derived from Donatus's discussion of satire in *De Tragoedia et Comoedia*; see, also, A. B. Kernan, *The Cankered Muse* (New Haven, Conn., 1959), pp. 54–8.
6 Marshall McLuhan, *The Gutenberg Galaxy* (Toronto, 1965), pp. 195–6.
7 R. B. McKerrow, ed., *The Works of Thomas Nashe*, revised F. P. Wilson (Oxford, 1958), I, 190.
8 *Ibid.*, II, 155.
9 *Ibid.*, I, 355.
10 *Ibid.*, I, 282.
11 John Stockwood, *A very fruitfull and necessarye sermon of the moste lamentable destruction of Jerusalem* (London, 1584), sigs C2ᵛ–C3ʳ.
12 McKerrow, *op. cit.*, II, 71.
13 *Ibid.*, II, 327.
14 *Ibid.*, III, 226.
15 I omit the anonymous *The Returne of the Knight of the Poste from Hell* (London, 1606) from the list because, although explicitly a continuation of *Pierce Penilesse*, the author's warning to the reader to 'imagine me of a more solid and dull composition' (sig. A3ᵛ) is

only too apt. He makes no attempt to learn from Nashe's style.

16 Of course, *The Wonderfull Yeare* is not 'secularised' in the sense that it ascribes the plague to causes other than divine retribution. But in that sense neither is *A Journal of the Plague Year*, written in 1721; cf. 'I look'd upon this dismal Time to be a particular Season of Divine Vengeance'; Daniel Defoe, *A Journal of the Plague Year*, ed. Louis Lanza (London, 1969), p. 68.

17 This must to some extent be due to official discouragement. A ban on handling religious matters in the theatre was in force throughout Elizabeth's reign, but became stricter after the Marprelate controversy. See Glynne Wickham, 'Stage Censorship: Biblical Drama in Transition' in *English Drama to 1710*, ed. C. Ricks (London, 1971), III, pp. 52–4.

18 H. Harvey Wood, ed., *The Plays of John Marston* (London, 1934–9), III, 179.

19 The popularity of this kind of literature was enduring. Rowlands continued to plagiarise Greene more than ten years after his death. See J. L. Lievsay, 'Newgate Penitents: Further Aspects of Elizabethan Pamphlet Sensationalism', *HLQ*, VII (1944), 47–69.

20 Excluding Greene's *A Quip for an Upstart Courtier*. The Nasheian elements in this work were probably supplied by Nashe himself. See D. J. McGinn, 'A Quip from Tom Nashe' in *Studies in the English Renaissance Drama*, ed. J. W. Bennett *et al.* (New York, 1959), pp. 172–88. McGinn also argues that this was the 'Comedie' which Greene refers to as having been written in collaboration with Nashe.

21 E. W. Gosse, ed., *The Complete Works of Thomas Lodge* (Glasgow, 1883), IV, 40–2.

22 This is part of the sub-title of the German edition of Lycosthenes's work; see Rudolph Wittkower, 'Marvels of the East: A Study in the History of Monsters', *JWCI*, V (1942), 185.

23 Gosse, *op. cit.*, IV, 35.

24 *Ibid.*, IV, 25.

25 *Ibid.*, IV, 8–9.

26 *Ibid.*, IV, 27–8.

27 *Ibid.*, IV, 79.

28 A. H. Bullen, ed., *The Works of Thomas Middleton* (London, 1886), VIII, 13.

29 *Ibid.*, VIII, 14.

30 Charles Dickens, *Martin Chuzzlewit*, ed. G. Russell (London, 1951), p. 353.

31 Bullen, *op. cit.*, VIII, 14.

32 *Ibid.*, VIII, 15. 'Grease' has sexual connotations in Elizabethan literature, cf. 'Let's consult together against this greasy knight' (*The Merry Wives of Windor*, II. i. 95–6); images of grease, fat, tallow etc. form grotesque links in the play between Falstaff's obesity and his lust. Middleton's Naud, too, is 'glory-fat'.

33 David Holmes has conjectured that Middleton composed three plays before 1604: *Blurt, Master-Constable* (1601–2), *The Phoenix*

(1602), and *The Family of Love* (1602); see D. M. Holmes *The Art of Thomas Middleton* (Oxford, 1970), Appendix A.
34 Bullen, *op. cit.*, VIII, 26.
35 *Ibid.*, VIII, 22.
36 *Ibid.*, VIII, 32.
37 David Rouland, trans., *The Pleasaunt Historie of Lazarillo de Tormes*, ed. J. E. V. Crofts (Oxford, 1924), p. 49. The similar relationship of Lazarillo and Pilcher in *Blurt, Master Constable* ('As long as thou dogst a Spaniard, thou'lt ne'er be fatter . . .', I. ii. 200–1) is further evidence that Middleton knew this work.
38 *Ibid.*, VIII, 70.
39 *Ibid.*, VIII, 71.
40 *Ibid.*, VIII, 95.
41 A. B. Grosart, ed., *The Non-Dramatic Works of Thomas Dekker* (1884), II, 135–6.
42 *Ibid.*, II, 70.

5 THE GROTESQUE AND SATIRICAL COMEDY

1 See entries in Henslowe's diary 1592–7 tabulated in *The Revels History of Drama in English*, III, eds Clifford Leech and T. W. Craik (1975), pp. 60–83.
2 A letter from the Privy Council to Richard Topcliffe and others describes it as 'a lewd play that was played in one of the playhouses on the Bankside, containing very seditious and slanderous matter, we caused some of the players to be apprehended and committed to prison, whereof one of them was not only an actor but a maker of part of the said play', quoted by E. K. Chambers in *The Elizabethan Stage* (Oxford, reprinted 1951), IV, 323.
3 The young gallant in the first of *Father Hubburd's Tales* ends up like this after gambling away his patrimony: 'within few days practice he was grown as absolute in cheating, and exquisite in pandarism, that he outstripped all Greene's books *Of the Art of Cony-catching*; and where before he maintained his drab, he made his drab now maintain him'; A. H. Bullen, ed., *The Works of Thomas Middleton* (London, 1886), VIII, 84–5.
4 E. Arber, ed., *Transcript of the Registers of the Company of Stationers of London, 1554–1640* (London, 1875–94), III, 677.
5 *Ibid.*, III, 678.
6 The dates of Marston's early plays are a subject of some controversy. I am convinced by the argument that *Histrio-mastix* was performed at one of the Inns of Court in the winter of 1598–9, and was not a revision of a play from Paul's boys' old repertoire; see Philip J. Finkelpearl, 'John Marston's *Histrio-mastix* as an Inns of Court Play: A Hypothesis', *HLQ*, XXIX (1966), 223–34. It is also likely that *Jack Drum's Entertainment* was acted in the Spring of 1600 and followed by *Antonio and Mellida* in the autumn; see A.

Caputi, *John Marston, Satirist* (Ithaca, N.Y., 1961), pp. 259–61 and Philip J. Finkelpearl, *John Marston of the Middle Temple* (Cambridge, Mass., 1969), pp. 268–71.

7 H. Harvey Wood, ed., *The Plays of John Marston* (Edinburgh, 1934–9), III, 190.

8 Cf. R. B. McKerrow, ed., *The Works of Thomas Nashe*, revised F. P. Wilson (Oxford, 1958), I, 207–8 and Harvey Wood, *op. cit.*, III, 207.

9 Alfred Harbage, *Shakespeare and the Rival Traditions* (New York, 1952).

10 Brian Gibbons, *Jacobean City Comedy* (London, 1968), pp. 27–8.

11 Though only those wealthy enough to afford the very high admission prices at the private theatres could exercise a 'preference'; see Harbage, *op. cit.*, pp. 45–7 for a discussion of the relative charges.

12 A. B. Grosart, ed., *The Complete Works of Thomas Nashe* (London, 1881–5), I, 175. The passage occurs in *Martins Months Minde* (1589), excluded from the canon by McKerrow.

13 See H. N. Hillebrand, *The Child Actors* (Urbana, Ill., 1926), pp. 143–50.

14 Harbage, *op. cit.*, p. 70.

15 James Spedding, R. L. Ellis and D. D. Heath, eds, *The Works of Francis Bacon* (1857–74), VIII, 76.

16 Quoted by Harbage, *op. cit.*, p. 79.

17 References to Dekker are to Fredson Bowers, ed., *The Dramatic Works of Thomas Dekker* (Cambridge, 1953–61).

18 Reprinted in *Drama and Society in the Age of Jonson* (London, 1937), pp. 305–6.

19 McKerrow, *op. cit.*, V, 141.

20 See J. B. Leishman, ed., *The Three Parnassus Plays* (London, 1949), pp. 24–33 (all references are to this edition). The possibility of Owen Gwyn's authorship of the second part of *The Return* is discussed by Marjorie L. Reyburn and Sidney Thomas in 'A Note on Owen Gwyn and *The Returne from Parnassus*, Part II', *PMLA*, LXXVI (1961), 298–300.

21 Quoted by Edward Hutton in *Pietro Aretino: The Scourge of Princes* (London, 1922), pp. xiii–xiv.

22 The detail of the 'night-capps' seems to be a reminiscence of the usurer in *Pierce Penilesse*, who wore 'a garnish of night-caps' (McKerrow, *op. cit.*, I, 163).

23 Shakespeare is regarded merely as the author of *Venus and Adonis* and *The Rape of Lucrece*, yet Ingenioso's comment, 'you that are a plagie stuffed cloake-bagge of all iniquitie' (*The Return*, part two, 1656–7), suggests an acquaintance with *I Henry IV*; cf. 'that stuffed cloak-bag of guts' (II. iv. 438–9).

24 This is quite the reverse of M. C. Bradbrook's assertion that 'Marston ... acknowledged as his original Pietro Aretino, with whom the writer of the Parnassus plays compared him'; *The Growth and Structure of Elizabethan Comedy* (London, 1955), p. 105.

25 Cf. Sylvester's translation of Du Bartas: 'The foamy slime, itselfe
transformeth oft / To green half-Tadpoles, playing there aloft, /
Half-made, half-unmade; round about the Flood, / Half-dead, half-
living; half a frog, half-mud', *The Complete Works of Joshua
Sylvester*, ed. A. B. Grosart (London, 1880), I, 32.
26 W. Greg, ed., *Wily Beguiled* (Oxford, 1912), p. vii.
27 See Baldwin Maxwell, '*Wily Beguiled*', *SP*, XIX (1922), 206–37.
28 The links of body imagery in Elizabethan satire with Celtic
'incantational satire', rat-rhyming and other kinds of spell are
discussed by M. C. Randolph in an excellent article, 'The Medical
Concept in English Renaissance Satiric Theory: Its Possible
Relationships and Implications', *SP*, XXXVIII (1941), 125–57.
29 Cf. Carlo Buffone on Puntarvolo in *Every Man Out*, IV. v. 109–13.
30 Harvey's alternate attacks on Nashe in *Foure Letters* (London,
1592) for Aretinizing and Tarletonizing imply a similar association
between the satirical journalist and the old-fashioned clown.
31 Harvey Wood, *op. cit.*, I, 52.
32 McKerrow, *op. cit.*, III, 190.
33 Firke is thinking of the lower portion of a pig's face, including the
nose, cheeks and mouth. This cut seems to have disappeared from
English butchers', but in a *triperia* in Naples I have seen a truly
grotesque window display of *muso*, which is exactly that part of the
animal.
34 See 'Oliver Oat-meale', *A Quest of Enquirie* (London, 1595) in
which a woman of this trade is abused by her husband: 'Saist thou
me so, thou Tripe, thou hated scorne? /Goe swill thy sowse-tubs,
loathed pudding wife' (sig. A4ᵛ); 'Your friends cast in your teeth
your marriage with the Tripe wife, what a beastly filthy slut she hath
beene, and still is' (sig. B1ʳ).
35 See John Brand, *Observations of the Popular Antiquities of Great
Britain*, revised H. Ellis (London, 1895), I, 89–90.
36 See Peter Ure, 'Patient Madman and Honest Whore: the Middleton-
Dekker Oxymoron' reprinted in *Elizabethan and Jacobean Drama:
Critical Essays by Peter Ure*, ed. J. C. Maxwell (London, 1974).
37 Cf. *1 Honest Whore*, II. i. 16–17 and *2 Honest Whore*, V. ii. 368–9;
1 Honest Whore, II. i. 55–6 and *2 Honest Whore*, V. ii. 104–5;
1 Honest Whore, II. i. 131–2 is also ominous.
38 Detailed studies of the Dekker and Middleton canons include P. B.
Murray, 'The Collaboration of Dekker and Webster in *Northward
Ho* and *Westward Ho*', *PBSA*, LVI (1962), 482–7 and D. J. Lake,
The Canon of Thomas Middleton's Plays (London, 1975). Both
reach their conclusions from a statistical analysis of minute internal
evidence: styles of contraction, expletive etc. It seems to me
debatable whether one regards this as proof. Lake's conclusion that
Blurt, Master Constable is by Dekker ignores the fact that the sexual
attitudes in the play are the reverse of those expressed by Dekker in
all his other work. I am more convinced by D. M. Holmes's
arguments in *The Art of Thomas Middleton* (Oxford, 1970) and

consequently discuss the play as part of the Middleton canon as he does.

39 It has been edited from Bibliothèque Nationale MS. fr. 837 by Grégoire Lozinski in *Bibliothèque de l'école des hautes études: sciences historiques et philologiques*, CCLXII (Paris, 1933).

40 Thomas Paynell, trans., *Regimen sanitatis Salerni* (4th edn, London, 1541), sig. E3ᵛ; Thomas Elyot, *The Castle of Health* (2nd edn, London, 1541), p. 23; Thomas Cogan, *The Haven of Health* (London, 1584), pp. 146–7.

41 *Ibid.*, p. 139: 'And that flesh might be more plentifull and better cheape, two days in the weeke, that is Friday and Saturday, are specially appointed to fish, and now of late yeres by the providence of our prudent princesse *Elizabeth*, the Wednesday also is in a maner restrained to the same order . . .'.

42 Cf., for instance, Boccaccio, *Decameron* (fifth tale: second day) where a similar fate overtakes Andreuccio of Perugia while staying in Naples.

43 Holmes, *op. cit.*, p. 10.

44 See R. B. Parker, ed., *A Chaste Maid in Cheapside* (London, 1969), pp. xlvii–lix.

45 R. B. Parker, *op. cit.*, p. lix. But why Parker should cite this work in particular is mysterious. It is a Jungian analysis based entirely on post-Renaissance literature, and its conclusions have very little to do with what Parker himself says about Middleton.

46 R. B. Parker, 'Middleton's Experiments with Comedy and Judgement', in *Jacobean Theatre*, eds J. R. Brown and B. Harris (London, 1960), 179–99.

6 SHAKESPEAREAN GROTESQUE: THE FALSTAFF PLAYS

1 The Dametas scenes in the *Arcadia* are, perhaps, an exception, but here again the rhetorical patina makes the comedy somewhat mannered. Very occasionally Lyly writes in a way which prefigures Nashe's prose style; see, for instance, *Midas*, III. ii. 37–44 and *Mother Bombie*, III. iv. 96–108.

2 See Ifor Evans, *The Language of Shakespeare's Plays* (2nd edn, 1959); Caroline Spurgeon, *Shakespeare's Imagery and What It Tells Us* (Cambridge, 1935); W. H. Clemen, *The Development of Shakespeare's Imagery* (London, 1951).

3 Milton Crane, *Shakespeare's Prose* (Chicago, Ill., 1951), p. 99.

4 William Pierce, ed., *The Marprelate Tracts: 1588, 1589* (1911), pp. 362–3.

5 R. B. McKerrow, ed., *The Works of Thomas Nashe*, revised F. P. Wilson (Oxford, 1958), I, 267.

6 *Ibid.*, I, 319.

7 L. M. Buell, 'A Prose Period in Shakespeare's Career?', *MLN*, LVI (1941), 119.

8 McKerrow, *op. cit.*, V, 194–5. McKerrow explains that this is a reference to the Chamberlain's Men.

9 So writes the pseudonymous author (Richard Lichfield) of *The Trimming of Thomas Nashe*; see *The Works of Gabriel Harvey*, *D.C.L.*, ed. A. B. Grosart (London, 1884), III, 31.

10 J. Dover Wilson, ed., *The First Part of the History of Henry IV* (Cambridge, 1946), p. 191.

11 J. Dover Wilson, ed., *Love's Labour's Lost* (2nd edn, Cambridge, 1962), p. xxx.

12 See Peter Alexander, *Shakespeare's 'Henry IV' and 'Richard III'* (Cambridge, 1929); Andrew S. Cairncross, ed., *King Henry VI*, part one (1960); Emrys Jones, *The Origins of Shakespeare* (Oxford, 1977).

13 This kind of performance may be based upon a festive motif not mentioned by C. L. Barber, i.e. the mock mayor ceremony; see A. R. Wright, *British Calendar Customs*, ed. T. E. Lones (London, 1936–40), III, 29–30, 'At Oswaldkirk . . . A mock lord mayor and lady mayoress, dressed as comically as possible, are elected. . . . In his proclamation, the mock mayor declares what reductions he intends to make in the prices of tea, coffee, tobacco and snuff', and 158, 'At East-the-Water, Bideford . . . the mayor and his lady, a man in female attire, are carried to all the inns in the town, where they are freely treated with drink, in return for which they make mock speeches to the assembled crowd, that is, as long as they can do so'.

14 McKerrow, *op. cit.*, II, 208.

15 D. G. Allan, 'The Rising in the West 1628–31', *EHR*, 2nd series, V (1952–3), 76.

16 John Stow, *The Annales or Generall Chronicle of England . . . unto the ende of this present yeare 1614*, continued by E. Howes (London, 1615), p. 889.

17 'Yet are these nothing in comparison of his auncient burlibond adjunctes' (*An Almond for a Parrat*), McKerrow, *op. cit.*, III, 347; 'the Danes . . . stand so much upon their unweldy burlibond souldiery', *ibid.*, I, 177; 'these beggarly contemners of wit are huge burlybond Butchers like *Ajax*', *ibid.*, II, 220. Chines of beef are also Nasheian: 'Noblemen he would liken to . . . guilded chines of beefe', *ibid.*, I, 190; 'lies as big as one of the Guardes chynes of beefe, who can abide?', *ibid.*, I, 269. The quotations are from *An Almond for a Parrat*; *Pierce Penilesse*; *The Unfortunate Traveller*; *Pierce Penilesse*; *Strange Newes*.

18 The image of the head as a house recalls the pictures of Arcimboldi and Brueghel (see chapter 2) and looks forward to Bardolph: 'A calls me e'en now, my lord, through a red lattice, and I could discern no part of his face from the window', which is the page's comment on Bardolph's fiery features (*2 Henry IV*, II. ii. 76–8).

19 See especially Frances Yates, *A Study of 'Love's Labour's Lost'* (London, 1934) and Richard David, ed., *Love's Labour's Lost* (5th edn, London, 1956), pp. xxxvii–li. In the light of David's discussion

of allusions to the Nashe-Harvey quarrel the possibility that Shakespeare is imitating Lyly, who also used the penthouse image, seems less likely.

20 McKerrow, *op. cit.*, I, 285 (*Strange Newes*).
21 Crane, *op. cit.*, p. 79
22 McKerrow, *op. cit.*, II, 232.
23 It has been shown that the plays in which flytings are most prominent are *Love's Labour's Lost*, *The Taming of the Shrew*, the two parts of *Henry IV* and *The Merry Wives of Windsor*; see Margaret Galway, 'Flyting in Shakespeare's Comedies', *SAB*, X (1935), 183–91.
24 McKerrow, *op. cit.*, II, 210.
25 Grosart, *op. cit.*, I, 168–9.
26 *Ibid.*, III, 26.
27 McKerrow, *op. cit.*, III, 247, 290, 233.
28 James L. Sanderson in ' "Buff Jerkin": A Note to *I Henry IV*', *ELN*, IV (1966–7), 92–5 reveals a pun on the female sexual organ.
29 McKerrow, *op. cit.*, I, 283.
30 See Vickers, *op. cit.*, p. 96. His account of the scene is very similar to Leo Kirschbaum's in 'The Demotion of Falstaff', *PQ*, XLI (1962), 58–60.
31 McKerrow, *op. cit.*, III, 35. Dover Wilson compares 'the most omnipotent villain' (I. ii. 106–7), 'the incomprehensible lies' (I. ii. 178–9) and 'gorbellied Knaves' (II. ii. 87) in the appendix to his edition of *I Henry IV*.
32 McKerrow, *op. cit.*, III, 93. Commenting on Falstaff's 'O, you shall see him laugh till his face be like a wet cloak ill laid up' (*2 Henry IV*, V. i. 81–2) A. R. Humphreys suggests that 'Face-wrinkling seems to have prompted Shakespeare's wit; cf. *Tw.N.*, III, ii. 74–5 – "He does smile his face into more lines than is in the new map with the augmentation of the Indies" ', A. R. Humphreys, ed., *The Second Part of King Henry IV* (London, 1966), p. 161 n. Nashe's description of Harvey suggests that it was rather he who prompted Shakespeare's interest in face-wrinkling; cf. also 'our faces . . . are most deformedlye welked and crumpled', McKerrow, *op. cit.*, I, 370 (*The Terrors of the Night*). Details of this sort illustrate just how pervasive Nashe's influence on Shakespeare is in this period.
33 For continental versions see the following: 'La Description du merveilleux conflict . . . faicte entre . . . caresme et charnaige' (c. 1530) reprinted in A. de Montaiglon and J. de Rothschild, eds, *Recueil de poésies Françoises des XVe et XVIe siècles* (Paris, 1855–78), X, 110–27 (the introduction cites a number of other French and Italian versions); Grégoire Lozinski, ed., 'La Bataille de caresme et de charnage', *Bibliothèque de l'école des hautes études: science historiques et philologiques*, CCLXII (Paris, 1933); *El Contrasto del carnovale & de la quaresima* (Florence, 1525) and *Il Gran contrasto e la sanguinosa guerra di carnevale a madonna quaresima* (Florence, 1628). See also Claude Gaignebet, *Le Carnaval* (Paris, 1974).

34 Lozinski, *op. cit.*, p. 34; Montaiglon, *op. cit.*, X, 117.

35 Boulenger and Scheler, *op. cit.*, p. 642.

36 John Huarte, *The Examination of Mens Wits*, trans. R.C. (London, 1594), p. 26.

37 McKerrow, *op. cit.*, I, 269 (*Strange Newes*).

38 See also J. Dover Wilson, *The Fortunes of Falstaff* (Cambridge, 1943), pp. 27–31.

39 McKerrow, *op. cit.*, II, 228.

40 *Ibid.*, I, 373.

41 Taylor, *op. cit.*, sig. B2ʳ.

42 See C. L. Barber, *Shakespeare's Festive Comedy* (Princeton, N.J., 1959), pp. 77–81.

43 See Keith Thomas, 'The Place of Laughter in Tudor and Stuart England', *TLS* (21 January 1977), pp. 77–81.

44 Laurent Joubert, *Traité du ris* (2nd edn, Paris, 1579), p. 326.

45 Wolfgang Kayser, *The Grotesque in Art and Literature*, trans. Ulrich Weisstein (Bloomington, Ind., 1963), p. 21.

46 Cf. McKerrow, *op. cit.*, III, 17, 'if thou wilt have the Doctour for an Anatomie . . . I am the man will deliver him to thee to be scotcht and carbonadoed' (*Have With You*).

47 Cf. McKerrow, *op. cit.*, I, 200, 'wee make our greedie paunches powdring tubs of beefe' (*Pierce Penilesse*).

48 McKerrow, *op. cit.*, II, 180 (*Christs Teares*). Manningtree in Essex was well-known for its Carnival festivities and morality play performances; see, for instance, Nashe's 'The Choice of Valentines'.

49 *Ibid.*, II, 225–6.

50 Dover Wilson, *op. cit.*, p. 158.

51 McKerrow, *op. cit.*, III, 62–3. But there is another parallel in Spenser's account of the birth of Orgoglio in *The Faerie Queene* I, vii, 9, discussed by S. K. Heninger Jr in 'The Orgoglio Episode in *The Faerie Queene*', *ELH*, XXVI (1959), 171–87.

52 A. R. Humphreys, ed., *The First Part of King Henry IV* (London, 1960), pp. 88–9.

53 Hotspur's comment on poetry (''Tis like the forced gait of a shuffling nag', III. i. 135) also has a Nasheian ring; cf. Nashe on Harvey's verses which 'run hobling like a Brewers Cart upon the stones', McKerrow, *op. cit.*, I, 275 (*Strange Newes*).

54 Much of this material, however, which sixteenth-century writers put to satirical use is to be found in Pliny, *Natural History*, VII, ii.

55 Crane, *op. cit.*, p. 83.

56 Vickers, *op. cit.*, p. 111.

57 George Eliot, *Middlemarch*, ed. W. J. Harvey (London, 1965), p. 179.

58 Hal's reference to Falstaff as 'Martlemas' (II. ii. 98) is the only explicit allusion to his festive role in part two, and even so the festive associations are doubtful; 'martlemas beefe (so commonly called) or over-salted beefe is not laudable', William Vaughan, *Directions for Health* (London, 1617), p. 49.

59 See J. A. Barish, *Ben Jonson and the Language of Prose Comedy* (Cambridge, Mass., 1967), chapter 2.

60 Cf., for example, Donne, 'Love's War'; D. S. Bland, ed., *Gesta Grayorum* (Liverpool, 1968), pp. 65–7; Jean Le Maire de Belges, *Le Triumphe de dame vérolle* (Lyon, 1539), *passim*. See also Humphreys, *op. cit.*, p. 66, and M. A. Shaaber, ed., *A New Variorum Edition of Shakespeare: The Second Part of Henry the Fourth* (London, 1940), pp. 169–70.

61 Shaaber, *op. cit.*, p. 168.

62 *Ibid.*, p. 145.

63 Barber, *op. cit.*, p. 217.

64 See Madelaine Doran, 'Imagery in *Richard II* and *Henry IV*', MLR, XXXVII (1942), 113–22.

65 The dating is based on the conclusions of William Green in *Shakespeare's 'Merry Wives of Windsor'* (Princeton, N.J., 1962), chapter 2.

66 A. C. Bradley, 'The Rejection of Falstaff', *Oxford Lectures on Poetry* (London, 1909), p. 247.

67 The most probable source is 'The Tale of the Two Lovers of Pisa' from *Tarltons Newes out of Purgatory*; see Geoffrey Bullough, *Narrative and Dramatic Sources of Shakespeare*, II (London, 1968).

68 The subject is discussed by Sallie Sewell in 'The Relationship between *The Merry Wives* and Jonson's *Every Man in his Humour*', *SAB*, XVI (1941), 175–89.

69 For 'mummy' H. J. Oliver, ed., *The Merry Wives of Windsor* (London, 1971) suggests ' "a pulpy substance or mass" (*Oxford English Dictionary*, SB.[1] l.c.)'.

70 The list is taken from Oliver, *op. cit.*, p. lxxvii.

71 J. A. Bryant in 'Falstaff and the Renewal of Windsor', *PMLA*, LXXXIX (1974), 296–301 finds such a structure, but his failure to acknowledge Italian source material for the plot of *The Merry Wives* considerably weakens his argument.

72 J. William Hebel, ed., *The Works of Michael Drayton* (Oxford, revised 1961), I, 439.

73 White, *op. cit.*, p. 33.

74 Brough, *op. cit.*, p. 60.

75 See especially L. C. Knights, 'Bacon and the Seventeenth-Century Dissociation of Sensibility' in *Explorations* (London, 1946).

7 JONSONIAN GROTESQUE: *EVERY MAN OUT OF HIS HUMOUR AND BARTHOLOMEW FAIR*

1 For a discussion of 'comicall satyre' as a genre see O. J. Campbell, *Comicall Satyre and Shakespeare's 'Troilus and Cressida'* (San Marino, Calif., 1938).

2 As does Ian Donaldson; see *The World Upside-Down* (Oxford, 1970), p. 51.

3 For a detailed account of the anti-Cobham satire see Alice B. Scoufos, 'Nashe, Jonson and the Oldcastle Problem', *MP*, LXV (1968), 307–24.

4 See Nicholas Rowe, *Some Account of the Life of Mr. William Shakespeare* (London, 1709), pp. xii–xiii.

5 *Every Man Out* was first performed in the late autumn of 1599 at the recently built Globe theatre; see C. H. Herford and P. and E. Simpson, eds, *Ben Jonson* (Oxford, 1925–52), IX, 185–6.

6 See C. R. Baskervill, *English Elements in Jonson's Early Comedy* (Austin, Texas, 1911); Baskervill's references to Nashe are ubiquitous, and he adds: 'The influence of Nashe is especially conspicuous. To my mind, he set the tone for English satire', p. 149.

7 See O. J. Campbell, 'The Relationship of *Epicoene* to Aretino's *Il Marescalco*', *PMLA*, XLVI (1931), 752–62.

8 See Mario Praz, *The Flaming Heart* (Gloucester, Mass., 1958), pp. 182–5.

9 The volume includes *La Prima parte de ragionamenti di M. Pietro Aretino, La Seconda parte* . . . and Annibale Caro's *Commento di Ser Agresto da Ficarvolo sopra la prima ficata del padre Siceo. Con la diceria de nasi.* The volume is dated 1584, but may, in fact, have been published by Windet in 1593. The copy is in the Bodleian library, Oxford; shelfmark, Douce A. 642. This is a significant omission from McPherson's catalogue of Jonson's library; see David McPherson, 'Ben Jonson's Library and Marginalia: An Annotated Catalogue', *SP*, LXXI (1974), X, 1–106.

10 Praz, *op. cit.*, p. 182.

11 Though the ultimate non-dramatic source is probably Erasmus's 'Ementita nobilitas' in *The Colloquies.*

12 See J. A. Barish, *Ben Jonson and the Language of Prose Comedy* (Cambridge, Mass., 1967), especially pp. 45–61.

13 Jonson considerably revised his punctuation for the 1616 folio, consistently adding more stops; see Herford and Simpson, *op. cit.*, I, 361. On the punctuation of *Every Man Out*, *ibid.*, III, 414–15 and IX, 48–51.

14 *Ibid.*, IX, 413–16.

15 Arnold Davenport, ed., *The Poems of John Marston* (Liverpool, 1961), p. 102.

16 Galen is the chief authority for the nutritious value of pork claimed by most sixteenth-century dietaries, but some writers agreed with Macilente. Thomas Cogan contends that 'young pigs commonly called rosting pigs, though they be commonly eaten, & accounted light meate, yet they are not verie wholsome, by reason of their overmuch moysture, & they breede in our bodies much superfluous humors, wherefore they neede good wine aswel as brawne, the one because it is over hard & grosse, the other because it is over moyst & slimy', *The Haven of Health* (London, 1584), p. 118.

17 Jonson's debt to Rabelais is discussed by Huntingdon Brown in *Rabelais in English Literature* (Cambridge, Mass., 1933), pp. 81–94;

he compares Carlo Buffone's speech in praise of debt *(Every Man Out*, I. i) with Panurge's similar eulogy *(Tiers Livre*, chs. iii–iv).

18 See Enid Welsford, *The Fool: His Social and Literary History* (London 1935), chapter 1, 'The Professional Buffoon'. Welsford comments that 'On the whole, the Italian buffoon of the fourteenth century seems to occupy a somewhat less degraded position than the Greek and Roman parasite . . .', p. 12, but his role is clearly not that of the Lord of Misrule. Nevertheless she identifies Carlo Buffone with Falstaff.

19 In Aubrey's jottings on Ralegh the incident is identified as the punishment actually meted out by Ralegh to a man called Charles Chester; see Herford and Simpson, *op. cit.*, IX, 405. This is the same character who is described by Nashe in *Pierce Penilesse*, where he is disguised as 'Charles the Fryer'; see R. B. McKerrow, ed., *The Works of Thomas Nashe*, revised F. P. Wilson (Oxford, 1958), I, 190.

20 Mikhail Bakhtin, *Rabelais and his World*, trans. Hélène Iswolsky (Cambridge, Mass., 1968), p. 302.

21 Herford and Simpson, *op. cit.*, VIII, 593.

22 For a full discussion of this aspect of the play's staging see Eugene M. Waith, 'The Staging of *Bartholomew Fair*', *SEL*, II (1962), 181–95.

23 Glynne Wickham, *Early English Stages: 1300 to 1600* (London, 1959–72), I, 159.

24 See Richard Southern, *The Medieval Theatre in the Round* (revised 1975).

25 See Wickham, *op. cit.*, II (2), 71–8.

26 See R. B. Parker, 'The Themes and Staging of *Bartholomew Fair*', *UTQ*, XXXIX (1970), 293–309.

27 John M. Potter, 'Old Comedy in *Bartholomew Fair*', *Criticism*, X (1968), 294.

28 See Campbell, *Comicall Satyre*, pp. 4–8.

29 See C. G. Thayer, *Ben Jonson: Studies in the Plays* (Norman, Oklahoma, 1963). Thayer identifies Ursula with Demeter, Knockem with Poseidon, and Leatherhead with Dionysus, and compares the play with Aristophanes' *Thesmophoriazusae*, set at the women's festival of Demeter. I would add that the scene in which Littlewit's puppets lift their dress to reveal their sexlessness echoes the exposure of Mnesilochus by the women at the Thesmophoria.

30 See, on the one hand, Potter, *op. cit.*, and Thayer, *op. cit.*; on the other hand, Ray L. Heffner, 'Unifying Symbols in the Comedy of Ben Jonson' in *English Stage Comedy*, ed. W. K. Wimsatt Jr (New York, 1954), pp. 74–97, and Donaldson, *op. cit.*, who acknowledges Emrys Jones as the source of the idea; see p. 51.

31 Herford and Simpson indicate borrowings from Martial and Juvenal in Quarlous's outburst; X, 181. Nashe uses the image of the living bound to the dead in *The Unfortunate Traveller*; see McKerrow, *op. cit.*, II, 231.

32 J. G. Frazer, *The Golden Bough: Spirits of the Corn and of the Wild*, II (London, 1912), p. 16.

33 *Ibid.*, pp. 19–20.

34 The tissue of mythological references in the composition of Ursula, and in the play as a whole, is a result of Jonson's work on court masques. The manuscript of *The Masque of Queens* (1609), for instance, which he presented to Prince Henry, contains elaborate marginal notes of a mythological and anthropological nature.

35 See Jackson I. Cope, 'Bartholomew Fair as Blasphemy', *Ren D*, VIII (1965), 127–52. Cope discusses emblem book depictions of *Discordia*, who carries a fire-brand, is lame in the legs, and who is surrounded by clouds (the 'vapours' of the pig-booth?). He also points out that in Valeriano's *I Ieroglifici* (Venice, 1625) the pig is discussed as a symbol of chaos. I notice, too, that in Cesare Ripa's *Iconologia* (1603) *Discordia* is introduced as 'Donna in forma di furia infernale', p. 104; cf. Winwife on Ursula: 'Mother o' the *Furies*, I thinke, by her firebrand' (II. v. 77).

36 On medieval and Renaissance medical views of women see Vern L. Bullough, 'Medieval Medical Views on Women', *Viator*, IV (1973), 485–501; M. A. Screech, *The Rabelaisian Marriage* (1958), pp. 87–91; Natalie Zemon Davis, *Society and Culture in Early Modern France* (1975), ch. 5, 'Women on Top'.

37 Rabelais, *Oeuvres complètes*, eds Jacques Boulenger and Lucien Scheler (Paris, 1955), pp. 467–8. This is a classic sixteenth-century description of hysteria; for a full account of the relations between female disorderliness, the wandering womb and hysteria see Ilza Veith, *Hysteria: The History of a Disease* (Chicago, Ill., 1965).

38 These themes have been discussed by Ruby Chatterji in 'Theme, Imagery and Unity in *A Chaste Maid in Cheapside*', *Ren D*, VIII (1965), 105–26 and R. B. Parker, ed., *A Chaste Maid in Cheapside* (London, 1969), pp. xlvii–lix, but neither notice their close similarity with the themes and images of *Barthlomew Fair*.

39 *Ibid.*, p. lix.

40 E. A. Horsman, ed., *Bartholomew Fair* (1960), thinks that Troubleall means 'God reward you and increase your family', p. 100. But he is surely thinking of God's command in Genesis; *Oxford English Dictionary* cites Florio's Montaigne (1603) for its earliest example of 'quit' meaning 'leave' or 'depart'.

CONCLUSION

1 Exception might be made here of the rogue pamphlets of John Awdeley (?), *The Fraternitie of Vacabondes* (1561) and Thomas Harman, *A Caveat or Warneing, for Commen Cursitors* (1566). Neither, however, have much eye for individual detail, and in view of their tendency to document types their pamphlets are of more sociological than literary interest. Harman's compilation of

underworld argot appears to have had little or no influence on writers outside the self-contained tradition of the cony-catching tract.

2 The stylistic transition has been well discussed by Morris Croll; see *Style, Rhetoric and Rhythm: Essays by Morris W. Croll*, eds J. M. Patrick and R. O. Evans (Princeton, N.J., 1966); see also George Williamson, *The Senecan Amble* (London, 1951).

3 W. J. Paylor, ed., *The Overburian Characters* (Oxford, 1936), p. 92.

4 See C. J. Horne, 'Literature and Science', in *From Dryden to Jonson*, ed. Boris Ford (Harmondsworth, revised, London, 1963) and John Carey, 'Seventeenth Century Prose', in *English Poetry and Prose: 1540–1674*, ed. Christopher Ricks (London, 1970); both discuss the importance of the Royal Society in determining literary style during the late seventeenth century.

5 Quoted by Joan Bennett in 'An Aspect of the Evolution of Seventeenth-Century Prose', *RES*, XVII (1941), 281–97.

6 Samuel Parker, *A Free and Impartial Censure of the Platonick Philosophie* (1666), p. 75.

7 *The Works of Sir Thomas Urquhart* (reprinted Edinburgh, 1834), pp. 200f.

8 Wolfgang Kayser, *The Grotesque in Art and Literature*, trans. Ulrich Weisstein (Bloomington, Indiana, 1963), pp. 184–8.

Select bibliography

The bibliography is divided into two sections: (1) Primary sources, i.e. material written before 1700 (2) Secondary sources, i.e. material written after 1700.

1 PRIMARY SOURCES

Anon., *El Contrasto del carnovale & de la quaresima*, Florence, 1525.

Anon., *Les Songes drolatiques de Pantagruel*, Paris, 1565.

Anon., *The Returne of the Knight of the Poste from Hell*, London, 1606.

Anon., *Vox Graculi, or Jack Dawes Prognostication*, London, 1623.

Anon., *Il Gran contrasto e la sanguinosa guerra di carnevale a madonna quaresima*, Florence, 1628

Anon., *Wily Beguiled*, ed. W. W. Greg, Malone Society Reprints, Oxford, 1912.

Anon., 'La Battaile de caresme et de charnage', ed. Grégoire Lozinski, *Bibliothèque de l'école des hautes études: sciences historiques et philologiques*, CCLXII, Paris, 1933.

Anon., *The Three Parnassus Plays*, ed. J. B. Leishman, Ivor Nicholson & Watson, London, 1949.

Anon., *Gesta Grayorum*, ed. D. S. Bland, Liverpool University Press, 1968.

Arber, Edward, ed., *Transcript of the Register of the Company of Stationers of London, 1554–1640*, 5 vols, London, 1875–94.

Aretino, Pietro, *La Prima parte de ragionamenti, La Seconda parte de ragionamenti*, London, 1584.

Aretino Pietro, *La Terza et ultima parte de ragionamenti*, London, 1589.

Aretino, Pietro, *Pietro Aretino: Tutte le comedie*, ed. G. B. de Sanctis, Mursia, Milan, 1968.

Aretino, Pietro, *Pietro Aretino: Sei giornate*, ed. Giovanni Aquilecchia, G. Laterza & Sons, Bari, 1969.

Aretino, Pietro, *Selected Letters*, trans. George Bull, Penguin, Harmondsworth, 1976.

Aristophanes, *The Thesmophoriazusae*, trans. Benjamin Bickley Rogers, Heinemann, London, 1924.

Aristotle, *Generation of Animals*, trans. A. L. Peck, Heinemann, London, 1943.

Bacon, Francis, *The Works of Francis Bacon*, eds James Spedding, R. L. Ellis and D. D. Heath, 14 vols, London, 1857–74.

Browne, Sir Thomas, *The Works of Thomas Browne*, ed. Geoffrey Keynes, 4 vols, Faber, London, 1964.

Bullein, William, *A Dialogue against the Fever Pestilence*, eds Mark W. and A. H. Bullen, London, 1888.

Bullough, Geoffrey, ed., *Narrative and Dramatic Sources of Shakespeare*, 8 vols, Routledge & Kegan Paul, London, 1957–75.

Chettle, Henry, *Kind-Hartes Dreame*, ed. G. B. Harrison, Bodley Head, London, 1923.

Chettle, Henry, *Piers Plainness*, ed. J. Winny, Cambridge University Press, 1957.

Clowes, William, *The Selected Writings of William Clowes*, ed. F. N. L. Poynter, Harvey & Blythe, London, 1948.

Cogan, Thomas, *The Haven of Health*, London, 1584.

Colonna, Francesco, *The Strife of Love in a Dream*, trans. R[obert] D[allington], London, 1592.

Cotgrave, Randle, *A Dictionaire of the French and English Tongues*, London, 1611.

Defoe, Daniel, *A Journal of the Plague Year*, ed. Louis Lanza, Oxford University Press, London, 1969.

Dekker, Thomas, *The Non-Dramatic Works of Thomas Dekker*, ed. A. B. Grosart, 4 vols, London, 1884.

Dekker, Thomas, *The Plague Pamphlets of Thomas Dekker*, ed. F. P. Wilson, Clarendon Press, Oxford, 1925.

Dekker, Thomas, *The Dramatic Works of Thomas Dekker*, ed. Fredson T. Bowers, 4 vols, Cambridge University Press, 1953–61.

della Porta, Giovanni Battista, *De Humana physiognomonia*, Hanover, 2nd edn, 1593.

Drayton, Michael, *The Works of Michael Drayton*, ed. J. William Hebel, 5 vols, Basil Blackwell, Oxford, revised, 1961.

Earle, John, *Microcosmography*, ed. Alfred S. West, Cambridge University Press, 1951.

Eccles, Mark, ed., *The Macro Plays*, Oxford University Press, London, 1969.

Eliot, John, *Ortho-Epia Gallica*, London, 1593.

Elyot, Thomas, *The Castle of Health*, London, 2nd edn, 1541.

Erasmus, Desiderius, *Opera omnia*, 10 vols, Leyden, 1704.

Florio, John, *A Worlde of Wordes*, London, 1598.

Florio, John, *Queen Anna's New World of Words*, London, 1611.

'Fouleweather, Adam', *A Wonderfull Strange and Miraculous, Astrologicall Prognostication*, London [1591].

Galen, *Opera omnia*, ed. C. G. Kühn, 19 vols, Lipsiae, 1821–30.

Garzoni, Tomaso, *The Hospitall of Incurable Fooles*, London, 1600.

Greene, Robert, *The Life and Complete Works in Prose and Verse of Robert Greene, M.A.*, ed. A. B. Grosart, 15 vols, London, 1881–6.

Guilpin, Everard, *Skialetheia*, ed. D. Allen Carroll, University of North Carolina Press, 1974.

Hall, Joseph, *The Collected Poems of Joseph Hall*, ed. Arnold Davenport, Liverpool University Press, 1949.

Happé, H. R., ed., *Tudor Interludes*, Penguin, Harmondsworth, 1972.

Harington, Sir John, *The Metamorphosis of Ajax*, ed. E. S. Donno, Routledge & Kegan Paul, London, 1962.

Harrison, William, *Harrison's Description of England in Shakespeare's Youth*, ed. F. J. Furnivall, 3 vols, London, 1877.

Harvey, Gabriel, *The Works of Gabriel Harvey, D.C.L.*, ed. A. B. Grosart, 3 vols, London, 1884.

Harvey, Gabriel, *Marginalia*, ed. G. C. Moore Smith, Shakespeare Head Press, Stratford-upon-Avon, 1913.

Hill, Adam, *The Crie of England*, London, 1593.

Hoskyns, John, *The Life, Letters and Writings of John Hoskyns*, ed. Louise Brown Osborn, Yale University Press, New Haven, Conn., 1937.

Huarte, John, *The Examination of Mens Wits*, trans. R.C., London, 1594.

Jones, William, *A wonder woorth the reading . . .*, London, 1617.

Jonson, Ben, *Ben Jonson*, eds C. H. Herford, P. and E. Simpson, 11 vols, Clarendon Press, Oxford, 1925–52.

Jonson, Ben, *Bartholomew Fair*, ed. E. A. Horsman, Methuen, London, 1960.

Joubert, Laurent, *Traité du ris*, Paris, 2nd edn., 1579.

Joubert, Laurent, *Première et seconde partie des erreurs populaires touchant la medicine*, Paris, 1587.

Judges, A. V., ed., *The Elizabethan Underworld*, George Routledge & Sons, London, 1930.

Lodge, Thomas, *The Complete Works of Thomas Lodge*, ed. E. W. Gosse, 4 vols, Glasgow, 1883.

Lycosthenes, Conrad, *De Prodigiorum ac ostentorum chronicon*, Basel, 1557.

Lyly, John, *The Complete Works of John Lyly*, ed. R. W. Bond, 3 vols, Oxford, 1892.

'Marprelate, Martin', *The Marprelate Tracts: 1588, 1589*, ed. William Pierce, James Clarke, London, 1911.

Marston, John, *The Plays of John Marston*, ed. H. Harvey Wood, 3 vols, Oliver & Boyd, Edinburgh, 1934–9.

Marston, John, *The Poems of John Marston*, ed. Arnold Davenport, Liverpool University Press, 1961.

Middleton, Thomas, *The Works of Thomas Middleton*, ed. A. H. Bullen, 8 vols, London, 1885–6.

Middleton, Thomas, *A Chaste Maid in Cheapside*, ed. R. B. Parker, Methuen, London, 1969.

Montaiglon, A. de and J. de Rothschild, eds, *Recueil de poésies Françoises des XVe et XVIe siècles*, 13 vols, Paris, 1855–78.

Montaigne, Michel de, *The Essays of Montaigne. Done into English by John Florio*, ed. George Saintsbury, 3 vols, London, 1892–3.

Montaigne, Michel de, *Oeuvres complètes*, eds Albert Thibaudet and Maurice Rat, Gallimard, Paris, 1962.

Munday, Anthony, *The English Romayne Life*, ed. G. B. Harrison, Bodley Head, London, 1925.

Nashe, Thomas, *The Complete Works of Thomas Nashe*, ed. A. B. Grosart, 6 vols, London, 1881–5.

Nashe, Thomas, *The Works of Thomas Nashe*, ed. R. B. McKerrow, revised F. P. Wilson, 5 vols, Basil Blackwell, Oxford, 1958.

Nashe, Thomas, *The Unfortunate Traveller and Other Works*, ed. J. B. Steane, Penguin, Harmondsworth, 1972.

'Oat-meale, Oliver', *A Quest of Enquirie*, London, 1595.

Parker, Samuel, *A Free and Impartial Censure of the Platonick Philosophie*, London, 1666.

Parsons, Robert, *A Booke of Christian exercise appertaining to resolution* . . ., London, 3rd edn., 1585.

Paylor, W. J., ed., *The Overburian Characters*, Basil Blackwell, Oxford, 1936.

Paynell, Thomas, trans., *Regimen sanitatis Salerni*, London, 4th edn., 1541.

Preston, Thomas, *Cambises*, reprinted in *Dodsley's Old English Plays*, ed. W. C. Hazlitt, vol. IV, London, 1874.

Puttenham, George, *The Arte of English Poesie*, eds Alice Walker and Gladys Willcock, Cambridge University Press, 1936.

Rabelais, François, *Gargantua and Pantagruel*, trans. Sir Thomas Urquhart and Peter Le Motteux, ed. W. E. Henley, 3 vols, 1900.

Rabelais, François, *Oeuvres complètes*, eds Jacques Boulenger and Lucien Scheler, Gallimard, Paris, 1955.

Ripa, Cesare, *Iconologia*, Rome 1603.

Roberts, Hugh, *The Day of Hearing*, Oxford, 1600.

Rouland, David, *The Pleasaunt Historie of Lazarillo de Tormes*, ed. J. E. V. Crofts, Basil Blackwell, Oxford, 1924.

Salgado, Gamini, ed., *Cony Catchers and Bawdy Baskets: An Anthology of Elizabethan Low Life*, Penguin, Harmondsworth, 1972.

Shakespeare, William, *The Complete Works of William Shakespeare*, ed. Peter Alexander, Collins, London, 1951.

Shakespeare, William, *The First Part of King Henry VI*, ed. Andrew S. Cairncross, Methuen, London, 1962.

Shakespeare, William, *The Second Part of King Henry VI*, ed. Andrew S. Cairncross, Methuen, London, 1957.

Shakespeare, William, *Love's Labour's Lost*, ed. Richard David, Methuen, London, 5th edn., 1956.

Shakespeare, William, *Love's Labour's Lost*, ed. J. Dover Wilson, Cambridge University Press, 2nd edn, 1962.

Shakespeare, William, *The Taming of the Shrew*, eds Sir Arthur Quiller-Couch and J. Dover Wilson, Cambridge University Press, 1928.

Shakespeare, William, *The First Part of the History of Henry IV*, ed. J. Dover Wilson, Cambridge University Press, 1946.

Shakespeare, William, *The First Part of King Henry IV*, ed. A. R. Humphreys, Methuen, London, 1960.

Shakespeare, William, *A New Variorum Edition of Shakespeare: The Second Part of Henry the Fourth*, ed. M. A. Shaaber, J. B. Lippincott, Philadelphia, Penn., 1940.

Shakespeare, William, *The Second Part of King Henry IV*, ed. A. R. Humphreys, Methuen, London, 1966.

Shakespeare, William, *The Merry Wives of Windsor*, ed. H. J. Oliver, Methuen, London, 1971.

Sidney, Sir Philip, *The Poems of Sir Philip Sidney*, ed. W. A. Ringler, Clarendon Press, Oxford, 1973.

Sidney, Sir Philip, *The Countess of Pembroke's Arcadia*, ed. Jean Robertson, Clarendon Press, Oxford, 1962.

'Smel-knave, Simon', *The Fearefull and Lamentable Effects of Two Dangerous Comets*, London, 1591.

Smith, Henry, *The examination of usurie, in two sermons*, London, 1591.

Smith, Henry, *The first sermon of Noahs drunkenness*, London, 1591.

Sprat, Thomas, *History of the Royal Society*, eds Jackson I. Cope and Harold Whitmore Jones, Routledge & Kegan Paul, London, 1959.

Stockwood, John, *A very fruitfull and necassarye sermon of the moste lamentable destruction of Jerusalem*, London, 1584.

Stow, John, *The Annales or Generall Chronicle of England . . . unto the ende of this presente yeare 1614*, continued by E. Howes, London, 1615.

Stubbes, Philip, *The Anatomie of Abuses*, ed. W. B. D. D. Turnbull, London, 1836.

Tarlton, Richard, *Tarlton's Jests, and News out of Purgatory*, ed. J. O. Halliwell, London, 1844.

Taylor, John, *Jack a Lent, His Beginning and Entertainment*, London, 1620.

Taylor, John, *All the Workes of John Taylor the Water Poet*, London, 1630.

Theophrastus, *Characters*, trans. J. M. Edmonds, Cambridge University Press, 1927.

Topsell, Edward, *The Historie of Four-footed Beasts*, London, 1607.

Urquhart, Sir Thomas, *The Works of Sir Thomas Urquhart*, reprinted, Edinburgh, 1834.

Urquhart, Sir Thomas, *The Admirable Urquhart*, ed. Richard Boston, Gordon Fraser, London, 1975.

Vasari, Giorgio, *Le Vite*, eds Paola della Pergola *et al.*, 9 vols, Club del Libro, Milan, 1962–6.

Vaughan, William, *Directions for Health*, London, 1617.

Vicary, Thomas, *The Anatomie of the Bodie of Man*, eds F. J. and P. Furnivall, London, 1888.

von Hutten, Ulrich, *et al.*, *On the Eve of the Reformation: 'Letters of Obscure Men'*, trans. F. G. Stokes, reprinted, Harper & Row, New York, 1964.

Warde, William, *Gods arrowes or two sermons, concerning the visitation of God by the pestilence*, London, 1607.

Young, S., ed., *Annals of the Barber-Surgeons*, London, 1890.

Zall, P. M., ed., *A Hundred Merry Tales and Other English Jest Books of the Fifteenth and Sixteenth Centuries*, University of Nebraska Press, 1963.

2 SECONDARY SOURCES

Alexander, Peter, *Shakespeare's 'Henry VI' and 'Richard III'*, Cambridge University Press, 1929.

Allan, D. G., 'The Rising in the West 1628–31', *EHR*, 2nd series, V (1952–3), 76–85.

Anselment, R. A., 'Rhetoric and the Dramatic Satire of Martin Marprelate', *SEL*, X (1970), 103–19.

Aydelotte, Frank, *Elizabethan Rogues and Vagabonds*, Clarendon Press, Oxford, 1913.

Bakhtin, Mikhail, *Rabelais and his World*, trans. Hélène Iswolsky, The M.I.T. Press, Cambridge, Mass., 1968.

Bamborough, J. B., *The Little World of Man*, Longmans, London, 1952.

✓ Barasch, Frances K., *The Grotesque: A Study in Meanings*, Mouton, The Hague, 1971.

Barber, C. L., *Shakespeare's Festive Comedy: A Study of Dramatic Form and its Relation to Social Custom*, Princeton University Press, 1959.

Barish, J. A., *Ben Jonson and the Language of Prose Comedy*, Harvard University Press, Cambridge, Mass., 1967.

Baskervill, C. R., *English Elements in Jonson's Early Comedy*, University of Texas Bulletin, 1911.

Bennett, H. S., *English Books and Readers 1558 to 1603*, Cambridge University Press, 1965.

Bennett, Joan, 'An Aspect of the Evolution of Seventeenth-Century Prose', *RES*, XVII (1941), 281–97.

Berryman, John, 'Thomas Nashe and the Unfortunate Traveller', in *The Freedom of the Poet*, Farrar, Straus & Giroux, New York, 1976.

Bethell, S. L., *Shakespeare and the Popular Dramatic Tradition*, P. S. King & Staples, London, 1944.

Bethell, S. L., 'The Comic Element in Shakespeare's Histories', *Anglia*, LXXI (1952), 82–101.

Boas, F. S., *University Drama in the Tudor Age*, Clarendon Press, Oxford, 1914.

Borinski, Ludwig, 'Shakespeare's Comic Prose', *Shakespeare Survey*, VIII (1955), 56–68.

Bowen, Barbara, 'Rabelais and the Comedy of the Spoken Word', *MLR*, LXIII (1968), 575–80.

Boyce, Benjamin, *The Theophrastan Character in England to 1642*, Harvard University Press, Cambridge, Mass., 1947.

Bradbrook, M. C., *The Growth and Structure of Elizabethan Comedy*, Chatto & Windus, London, 1955.

Bradley, A. C., 'The Rejection of Falstaff', in *Oxford Lectures on Poetry*, Macmillan, London, 1909.

Brand, John, *Observations of the Popular Antiquities of Great Britain*, revised, H. Ellis, London, 1895.

Brockbank, J. P., 'The Frame of Disorder – *Henry VI*', in *Early Shakespeare*, eds J. R. Brown and B. Harris, Edward Arnold, London, 1961.

Brough, Robert, *The Life of Sir John Falstaff*, London, 1858.

Brown, Arthur, 'Citizen Comedy and Domestic Drama', in *Jacobean Theatre*, eds J. R. Brown and B. Harris, Edward Arnold, London, 1960.

Brown, Huntingdon, *Rabelais in English Literature*, Harvard University Press, Cambridge, Mass., 1933.

Bryant, J. A., 'Falstaff and the Renewal of Windsor', *PMLA*, LXXXIX (1974), 296–301.

Buell, L. M., 'A Prose Period in Shakespeare's Career?', *MLN*, LVI (1941), 118–22.

Bullough, Vern L., 'Medieval Medical Views on Women', *Viator*, IV (1973), 485–501.

Campbell, O. J., 'The Relationship of *Epicoene* to Aretino's *Il Marescalco*', *PMLA*, XLVI (1931), 752–62.

Campbell, O. J., *Comicall Satyre and Shakespeare's 'Troilus and Cressida'*, Huntingdon Library Publications, San Marino, Calif., 1938.

Caputi, A., *John Marston, Satirist*, Cornell University Press, Ithaca, N.Y., 1961.

Carey, John, 'Sixteenth and Seventeenth Century Prose' in *English Poetry and Prose, 1540–1674*, ed. Christopher Ricks, Sphere Books, London, 1970.

Cawley, A. C., 'The "Grotesque" Feast in the Prima Pastorum', *Speculum*, XXX (1955), 213–17.

Chambers, E. K., *The Mediaeval Stage*, 2 vols, Clarendon Press, Oxford, 1903.

Chambers, E. K., *The Elizabethan Stage*, 4 vols, Clarendon Press, Oxford, 1923.

Chambers, E. K., *The English Folk-Play*, Clarendon Press, Oxford, 1933.

Chatterji, Ruby, 'Theme, Imagery and Unity in *A Chaste Maid in Cheapside*', *Ren D*, VIII (1965), 105–26.

Clark, Carol, *The Web of Metaphor: Studies in the Imagery of Montaigne's 'Essais'*, French Forum, Lexington, Ken., 1978.

Clayborough, Arthur, *The Grotesque in English Literature*, Clarendon Press, Oxford, 1965.

Clemen, W. H., *The Development of Shakespeare's Imagery*, Methuen, London, 1951.

Cleugh, James, *The Divine Aretino*, Anthony Blond, London, 1965.

Colman, E. A. M., *The Dramatic Use of Bawdy in Shakespeare*, Longmans, London, 1974.

Cope, Jackson I., '*Bartholomew Fair* as Blasphemy', *Ren D*, VIII (1965), 127–52.

Crane, Milton, *Shakespeare's Prose*, University of Chicago Press, 1951.

Crane, W. G., *Wit and Rhetoric in the Renaissance*, Columbia University Press, New York, 1937.

Croll, Morris W., *Style, Rhetoric and Rhythm: Essays by Morris W. Croll*, eds J. M. Patrick and R. O. Evans, Princeton University Press, 1966.

Croston, A. K., 'The Use of Imagery in *The Unfortunate Traveller*', *RES*, XXIV (1948), 90–101.

Davis, Natalie Zemon, *Society and Culture in Early Modern France*, Duckworth, London, 1975.

Davis, W. R., *Idea and Act in Elizabethan Fiction*, Princeton University Press, 1969.

Donaldson, Ian, *The World Upside-Down*, Clarendon Press, Oxford, 1970.

Doran, Madeleine, 'Imagery in *Richard II* and *Henry IV*', *MLR*, XXXVII (1942), 113–22.

Evans, Ifor, *The Language of Shakespeare's Plays*, Methuen, London, 2nd edn., 1959.

Farnham, Willard, *The Shakespearean Grotesque*, Clarendon Press, Oxford, 1971.

Ford, Boris, ed., *The Age of Shakespeare*, Penguin, Harmondsworth, revised 1956.

Frazer, J. G., *The Golden Bough: A Study in Magic and Religion*, 12 vols, Macmillan, London, 3rd edn., 1911–15.

Gaignebet, Claude, *Le Carnaval*, Payot, Paris, 1974.

Galway, Margaret, 'Flyting in Shakespeare's Comedies', *SAB*, X (1935), 183–91.

Geiger, Benno, *I Dipinti ghiribizzosi di Giuseppe Arcimboldi*, Vallecchi, Florence, 1954.

George, M. Dorothy, *English Political Caricature: A Study of Opinion and Propaganda*, 2 vols, Clarendon Press, Oxford, 1959.

Gibbons, Brian, *Jacobean City Comedy*, Hart Davies, London, 1968.

Gombrich, E. H., *Art and Illusion: A Study in the Psychology of Pictorial Representation*, Phaidon Press, London, 1960.

Green, William, *Shakespeare's 'Merry Wives of Windsor'*, Princeton University Press, 1962.

Grossman, F., *Bruegel: The Paintings*, Phaidon Press, London, 1955.

Guiraud, Pierre, *Les Gros mots*, Presses Universitaires de France, Paris, 1975.

Harbage, Alfred, *Shakespeare and the Rival Traditions*, Macmillan, New York, 1952.

Harbage, Alfred, *Annals of English Drama 975–1700*,
rev. S. Schoenbaum, Methuen, London, 1970.

Harlow, C. G., 'Nashe's Visit to the Isle of Wight and his Publications
of 1592–4', *RES*, new series XIV (1963), 225–42.

Harmon, Alice, 'How Great was Shakespeare's Debt to Montaigne?',
PMLA, LVII (1942), 988–1008.

Harris, Bernard, 'Men Like Satyrs', in *Elizabethan Poetry*, eds J. R.
Brown and B. Harris, Edward Arnold, London, 1960.

Harris, Bernard, 'Dissent and Satire', *Shakespeare Survey*, XVII (1964),
120–37.

Hazlitt, W. C., *Hand-Book to the Popular, Poetical and Dramatic
Literature of Great Britain*, London, 1867.

Heffner, Ray L., 'Unifying Symbols in the Comedy of Ben Jonson' in
English Stage Comedy: English Institute Essays, 1954, ed. W. K.
Wimsatt, Jr, Columbia University Press, New York, 1954.

Heninger Jr, S. K., 'The Orgoglio Episode in *The Faerie Queene*', *ELH*,
XXVI (1959), 171–87.

Heninger Jr, S. K., 'Tudor Literature of the Physical Sciences', *HLQ*,
XXXII (1968–9), 101–33, 249–70.

Herr, A. F., *The Elizabethan Sermon: A Survey and a Bibliography*,
University of Pennsylvania, Philadelphia, Penn., 1940.

Hibbard, G. R., *Thomas Nashe: A Critical Introduction*, Routledge &
Kegan Paul, London, 1962.

Hillebrand, H. N., *The Child Actors*, University of Illinois Studies in
Language and Literature, 1926.

Holden, W. P., *Anti-Puritan Satire: 1572–1642*, Yale University Press,
New Haven, Conn., 1954.

Holmes, D. M., *The Art of Thomas Middleton*, Clarendon Press,
Oxford, 1970.

Hoppe, H. R., 'John Wolfe, Printer and Publisher, 1579–1601', *The
Library*, 4th series, XIV (1933), 241–88.

Horne, C. J., 'Literature and Science' in *From Dryden to Johnson*, ed.
Boris Ford, Penguin, Harmondsworth, rev. 1963.

Huffman, Clifford Chalmers, 'Gabriel Harvey on John Florio and John
Eliot', *N & Q*, new series, XX (1975), 300–2.

Hughes, Robert, *Heaven and Hell in Western Art*, Weidenfeld &
Nicolson, London, 1968.

Hunter, G. K., *John Lyly: The Humanist as Courtier*, Routledge &
Kegan Paul, London, 1962.

Hutton, Edward, *Pietro Aretino: The Scourge of Princes*, Constable,
London, 1922.

Jennings, Lee Byron, *The Ludicrous Demon*, University of California
Press, 1963.

Jones, Emrys, *The Origins of Shakespeare*, Clarendon Press, Oxford,
1977.

Jones, Richard F., 'Science and English Prose Style in the Third Quarter
of the Seventeenth Century', *PMLA*, XLV (1930), 977–1009.

Kaiser, Walter, *Praisers of Folly: Erasmus, Rabelais, Shakespeare*, Gollancz, London, 1964.

Kaula, David, 'The Low Style in Nashe's *The Unfortunate Traveller*', *SEL*, VI (1966), 43–57.

Kayser, Wolfgang, *The Grotesque in Art and Literature*, trans. Ulrich Weisstein, Indiana University Press, 1963.

Kernan, A. B., *The Cankered Muse*, Yale University Press, New Haven, Conn., 1959.

Kirschbaum, Leo, 'The Demotion of Falstaff', *PQ*, XLI (1962), 58–60.

Knight, G. Wilson, 'King Lear and the Comedy of the Grotesque' in *The Wheel of Fire*, Methuen, London, revised, 1949.

Knights, L. C., 'Elizabethan Prose', *Scrutiny*, II (1934), 427–38.

Knights, L. C., *Drama and Society in the Age of Jonson*, Chatto & Windus, London, 1937.

Knights, L.C., 'Bacon and the Seventeenth-Century Dissociation of Sensibility', in *Explorations*, Chatto & Windus, London, 1946.

Kolve, V. A., *The Play Called Corpus Christi*, Stanford University Press, 1966.

Koppenfels, Werner von, 'Thomas Nashe und Rabelais', *Archiv*, CCVII (1970), 277–91.

Kunzle, David, *The Early Comic Strip*, University of California Press, 1973.

Kurtz, L. P., *The Dance of Death and the Macabre Spirit in European Literature*, Columbia University Press, New York, 1934.

Lake, D. J., *The Canon of Thomas Middleton's Plays*, Cambridge University Press, 1975.

Leach, Edmund, 'Animal Categories and Verbal Abuse', in *New Directions in the Study of Language*, ed. E. H. Lenneberg, Harvard University Press, Cambridge, Mass., 1964.

Le Double, A.-F., *Rabelais: anatomiste et physiologiste*, Paris, 1899.

Leech, Clifford, 'The Unity of *2 Henry IV*', *Shakespeare Survey*, VI (1953), 16–24.

Leech, Clifford and Craik, T. W., eds, *The Revels History of Drama in English*, III, Methuen, London, 1975.

Leggatt, Alexander, *Citizen Comedy in the Age of Shakespeare*, University of Toronto Press, 1973.

Leggatt, Alexander, 'Artistic Coherence in *The Unfortunate Traveller*', *SEL*, XIV (1974), 30–46.

Lever, J. W., 'Shakespeare's French Fruits', *Shakespeare Survey*, VI (1953), 79–90.

Levin, Richard, 'The Structure of *Bartholomew Fair*', *PMLA*, LXXX (1965), 172–9.

Lievsay, J. L., 'Newgate Penitents: Further Aspects of Elizabethan Pamplet Sensationalism', *HLQ*, VII (1944), 47–69.

Lievsay, J. L., *The Englishman's Italian Books: 1550–1700*, University of Pennsylvania Press, Philadelphia, Penn., 1969.

Lothian, J. M., 'Shakespeare's Knowledge of Aretino's Plays', *MLR*, XXV (1930), 415–24.

McGinn, D. J., 'Nashe's Share in the Marprelate Controversy', *PMLA*, LIX (1944), 952–84.

McGinn, D. J., 'A Quip from Tom Nashe' in *Studies in the English Renaissance Drama*, ed. J. W. Bennett *et al.*, New York University Press, 1959.

Mackerness, E. D., '*Christs Teares* and the Literature of Warning', *English Studies*, XXXIII (1952), 251–4.

McLuhan, Marshall, *The Gutenberg Galaxy*, University of Toronto Press, 1965.

McPherson, D. C., 'Aretino and the Harvey-Nashe Quarrel', *PMLA*, LXXXIV (1969), 1551–58.

McPherson, D. C., 'Ben Jonson's Library and Marginalia: An Annotated Catalogue', *SP*, LXX1 (1974), 1–106.

Maxwell, Baldwin, '*Wily Beguiled*', *SP*, XIX (1922), 206–37.

Meyer, Edward, *Machiavelli and the Elizabethan Drama*, Weimar, 1897.

Miller, E. H., *The Professional Writer in Elizabethan England*, Harvard University Press, Cambridge, Mass., 1959.

Munz, Ludwig, *Pieter Bruegel: The Drawings*, Phaidon Press, London, 1961.

Murray, P. B., 'The Collaborations of Dekker and Webster in *Northward Ho* and *Westward Ho*', *PBSA*, LVI (1962), 482–7.

Nye, Robert, *Falstaff*, Hamish Hamilton, London, 1976.

O'Malley, C. D., 'Tudor Medicine and Biology', *HLQ*, XXXII (1968–9), 1–27.

Ong, Walter J., *Rhetoric, Romance and Technology*, Cornell University Press, Ithaca, N.Y., 1971.

Outhwaite, R. B., *Inflation in Tudor and Early Stuart England*, Macmillan, London, 1969.

Owst, G. R., *Literature and Pulpit in Medieval England*, Basil Blackwell, Oxford, rev. 1961.

Parker, R. B., 'Middleton's Experiments with Comedy and Judgement', in *Jacobean Theatre*, eds J. R. Brown and B. Harris, Edward Arnold, London, 1960.

Parker, R. B., 'The Themes and Staging of *Bartholomew Fair*', *UTQ*, XXXIX (1970), 293–309.

Partridge, Eric, *Shakespeare's Bawdy*, Routledge & Kegan Paul, London, revised 1955.

Perkins, David, 'Issues and Motivations in the Nashe-Harvey Quarrel', *PQ*, XXXIX (1960), 224–33.

Peter, J., *Complaint and Satire in Early English Literature*, Clarendon Press, Oxford, 1956.

Pierce, William, *An Historical Introduction to the Marprelate Tracts*, Archibald Constable, London, 1908.

Pollet, Maurice, *John Skelton: Poet of Tudor England*, trans. John Warrington, Dent, London, 1971.

Potter, John M., 'Old Comedy in *Bartholomew Fair*', *Criticism*, X (1968), 290–9.

Poynter, F. N. L., 'Medicine and Public Health', *Shakespeare Survey*, XVII (1964), 152–66.

Praz, Mario, 'Shakespeare's Italy', *Shakespeare Survey*, VII (1954), 95–106.

Praz, Mario, *The Flaming Heart*, Peter Smith, Gloucester, Mass., 1958.

Raleigh, Sir Walter A., *The English Novel*, London, 2nd edn., 1896.

Randall, Lilian M. C., *Images in the Margins of Gothic Manuscripts*, University of California Press, 1966.

Randolph, M. C., 'The Medical Concept in English Renaissance Satiric Theory', *SP*, XXXVIII (1941), 125–57.

Reyburn, Marjorie L. and Sidney, Thomas, 'A Note on Owen Gwyn and *The Returne from Parnassus*, Part II', *PMLA*, LXXVI (1961), 298–300.

Roe, F. C., *Sir Thomas Urquhart and Rabelais*, Clarendon Press, Oxford, 1957.

Rowe, Nicholas, *Some Account of the Life of Mr. William Shakespeare*, London, 1709.

Salingar, L. G., *Shakespeare and the Traditions of Comedy*, Cambridge University Press, 1974.

Sanderson, James L., ' "Buff Jerkin": A Note to *I Henry IV*', *ELN*, IV (1966–7), 92–5.

Schlauch, M., *Antecedents of the English Novel, 1400–1600*, Oxford University Press, London, 1963.

Schneegans, Heinrich, *Geschichte der grotesken Satire*, Strasburg, 1894.

Scoufos, Alice L., 'Nashe, Jonson and the Oldcastle Problem', *MP*, LXV (1968), 307–24.

Screech, M. A., *The Rabelaisian Marriage*, Edward Arnold, London, 1958.

Sellers, H., 'Italian Books Printed in England before 1640', *The Library*, 4th series, V (1924), 105–28.

Sewell, Sallie, 'The Relationship between *The Merry Wives* and Jonson's *Every Man in his Humour*', *SAB*, XVI (1941), 175–89.

Shaaber, M. A., *Some Forerunners of the Newspaper in England 1476–1622*, University of Pennsylvania Press, Philadelphia, Penn., 1929.

Simon, Joan, *Education and Society in Tudor England*, Cambridge University Press, 1966.

Smith, A. W., 'Folklore Elements in Social Protest', *Folklore*, LXXVII (1967), 241–53.

Southern, Richard, *The Medieval Theatre in the Round*, Faber, London, revised, 1975.

Spitzer, Leo, 'Le prétendu réalisme de Rabelais', *MP*, XXXVII (1939), 139–50.

Spurgeon, Caroline, *Shakespeare's Imagery and What It Tells Us*, Cambridge University Press, 1935.

Stirling, Brents, 'Shakespeare's Mob Scenes: A Reinterpretation', *HLQ*, VIII (1945), 213–40.

Stone, Lawrence, *The Crisis of the Aristocracy, 1558–1641*, Clarendon Press, Oxford, 1965.

Strutt, Joseph, *The Sports and Pastimes of the People of England*, revised J. C. Cox, Methuen, London, 1903.

Summersgill, T. L., 'The Influence of the Marprelate Controversy upon the Style of Nashe', *SP*, XLVIII (1951), 145–60.

Sykes, H. Dugdale, 'Thomas Middleton's Early Non-Dramatic Work', *N & Q*, CXLVIII (1925), 435–8.

Tanner, Tony, 'Reason and the Grotesque: Pope's Dunciad', *Critical Quarterly*, VII (1965), 145–60.

Thayer, C. G., *Ben Jonson: Studies in the Plays*, University of Oklahoma Press, 1963.

Thomas, Keith, 'The Place of Laughter in Tudor and Stuart England', *TLS* (1977), pp. 77–81.

Thomson, Philip, *The Grotesque*, Methuen, London, 1972.

Tillyard, E. M. W., *The Elizabethan World Picture*, Chatto & Windus, London, 1943.

Tillyard, E. M. W., *Shakespeare's History Plays*, Chatto & Windus, London, 1944.

Tonello, Mario, 'Lingua e polemica teatrale nella *Cortigiana* di Pietro Aretino', in *Lingua e strutture del teatro Italiano del Rinascimento*, ed. G. Folena, Liviana Editrice, Padua, 1970.

Townsend, Freda L., *Apologie for Bartholomew Fayre: The Art of Jonson's Comedies*, M.L.A., New York, 1947.

Upham, A. H., *The French Influence in English Literature*, Columbia University Press, New York, 1908.

Ure, Peter, *Elizabethan and Jacobean Drama: Critical Essays by Peter Ure*, ed. J. C. Maxwell, Liverpool University Press, 1974.

Veith, Ilza, *Hysteria: The History of a Disease*, University of Chicago Press, 1965.

Vickers, Brian, *The Artistry of Shakespeare's Prose*, Methuen, London, 1968.

Vickers, Brian, *Francis Bacon and Renaissance Prose*, Cambridge University Press, 1968.

Waith, Eugene M., 'The Staging of *Bartholomew Fair*', *SEL*, II (1962), 181–95.

Weimann, Robert, *Shakespeare and the Popular Tradition in the Theater*, ed. and trans. Robert Schwarz, Johns Hopkins University Press, Baltimore, Mld., 1978.

Welsford, Enid, *The Fool: His Social and Literary History*, Faber, London, 1935.

White, James, *Original Letters Etc. of Sir John Falstaff*, London, 1796.

Wickham, Glynne, *Early English Stages: 1330 to 1660*, 3 vols, Routledge & Kegan Paul, London, 1959–79.

Wickham, Glynne, 'Stage Censorship: Biblical Drama in Transition', *English Drama to 1710*, ed. Christopher Ricks, Sphere Books, London, 1971.

Williamson, George, *The Senecan Amble*, Faber, London, 1951.

Wilson, F. P., *The Plague in Shakespeare's London*, Clarendon Press, Oxford, 1927.

Wilson, F. P., 'Some English Mock-Prognostications', *The Library*, 4th series, XIX (1939), 6–43.

Wilson, J. Dover, *The Fortunes of Falstaff*, Cambridge University Press, 1943.

Wilson, J. Dover, 'The Origins and Development of Shakespeare's *Henry IV*', *The Library*, 5th series, 1 (1945), 2–16.

Wilson, J. Dover, *Shakespeare's Happy Comedies*, Faber, London, 1962.

Wilson, J. Dover, 'The Marprelate Controversy' in *The Cambridge History of English Literature*, III, eds A. W. Ward and A. R. Waller, Cambridge University Press, reprinted, 1964.

Wittkower, Rudolph, 'Marvels of the East: A Study in the History of Monsters', *JWCI*, V (1942), 159–97.

Wright, A. R., *British Calendar Customs*, ed. T. E. Lones, 3 vols, Folklore Society, London, 1936–40.

Wright, L. B., *Middle Class Culture in Elizabethan England*, University of North Carolina Press, 1935.

Wright, Thomas, *A History of Caricature and Grotesque in Literature and Art*, London, 1865.

Yates, Frances, *A Study of 'Love's Labour's Lost'*, Cambridge University Press, 1934.

Yates, Frances, 'Italian Teachers in Elizabethan England', *JWCI*, I (1937), 103–16.

Index

abuse, styles of, 68–9
Allan, D. G., 94
anatomy, 20–1, 38–9, 62
Arcimboldi, Giuseppe, 9, 13, 20
Aretino, Pietro, 5, 70, 72, 101,
   104, 129, 140; and Jonson,
   134–5, 147, 185 n.; and Nashe,
   26–36
Aristophanes, 141, 143, 186 n.

Bacon, Francis, 11, 19, 22, 37–8,
   67
Bakhtin, Mikhail, 6–7, 9, 15–16,
   139–40
Barber, C. L., 93, 107
Barish, Jonas A., 116
'base comparison', 22–4, 30–1,
   101, 110, 129
Baskervill, C. R., 185 n.
Beaumont and Fletcher, 76
blason and contre-blason, 20,
   170 n.
Boccaccio, 180 n.
Bosch, Hieronymus, 9, 14, 108
Bradbrook, M. C., 178 n.
Bradley, A. C., 122
Bridges, John, 4, 37
Brough, Robert, 128–9
Browne, Sir Thomas, 46
Bruegel, Pieter (the elder), 9–10,
   13, 26, 82, 104, 108–10,
   167 n.
Buell, L. M., 91
buffone, 139, 186 n.
Bull (the hangman), 38, 57
Bullein, William, 46–7

burlesque, 6–7, 19–20, 32–3,
   98–9

Calvin, Jean, 9
Cambises, 89
Campbell, O. J., 27
caricature, 29–30, 56–8, 73, 86,
   116
Carnival, 16, 39, 109, 113, 114,
   127; and the battle with Lent
   (the fat and the lean), 16, 82–5,
   103–7, 115–17, 138–9, 147,
   160, 182 n.
Castle of Perseverance, The, 142
Chapman, George, 63, 64, 91
Chester, Charles ('the Fryer'), 51,
   186 n.
Chettle, Henry, 170 n.
child actors, 63, 65–7
Clayborough, Arthur, 85
Clemen, W. H., 90
Clowes, William, 12
clown, journalist as, 3–4, 51–3,
   158
Cobham, William Brooke, Lord,
   133
Cogan, Thomas, 83, 185 n.
coinage, verbal, 24–6, 34, 37, 96
commonplace books, 24, 28, 162
Corpus Christi drama, 38
costume, 40–3, 50, 59–61, 84
Cotton, William, 91
Crane, Milton, 90, 97, 113

Davies, Sir John, 71
Day, John, 79